BEGINNER'S
IRAQI ARABIC
WITH 2 AUDIO CDS

HIPPOCRENE BEGINNER'S SERIES

Arabic
Armenian
Assyrian
Basque
Bulgarian
Chinese
Czech
Dari
Dutch
Finnish
French
Gaelic
Greek
Hungarian
Irish
Italian
Japanese
Lithuanian
Maori
Norwegian
Persian
Polish
Romanian
Russian
Serbo-Croatian
Shona
Sicilian
Slovak
Spanish (Latin American)
Swedish
Turkish
Vietnamese
Welsh
Yoruba

HIPPOCRENE'S BEGINNER'S SERIES

BEGINNER'S IRAQI ARABIC
WITH 2 AUDIO CDS

AN INTRODUCTION TO THE SPOKEN LANGUAGE OF IRAQ

Nawal Nasrallah
&
Nadia Hassani

HIPPOCRENE BOOKS, INC.
New York

Typesetting and design: Susan Ahlquist, Perfect Setting, East Hampton, NY
Cover and disc label design: Cynthia Mallard, Cynergie Studio,
Raleigh, NC
Cover painting: "Dialog" by Khalid Al-Jadir; reprinted courtesy of
Dr. Saad Al-Jadir
Audio producers: Robert Stanley Martin, Nawal Nasrallah, Nadia Hassani
Audio recorded and mastered at: World Music Connections/AM Studios,
New York, NY.

For information, address:
HIPPOCRENE BOOKS, INC.
171 Madison Ave.
New York, NY 10016

www.hippocrenebooks.com

ISBN-13: 978-0-7818-1098-2
ISBN-10: 0-7818-1098-1

Printed in the United States of America.

CONTENTS

A NOTE ON THE COVER

The cover painting is titled *Dialog*. The artist, Khalid Al-Jadir (1924–1988), was born in Baghdad, where he graduated from the College of Law and the Institute of Fine Arts. He obtained his Ph.D. in Islamic Art History from the Sorbonne in Paris. During his life, he had several exhibitions in Iraq, Germany, Romania, Switzerland, Denmark, Morocco, and Saudi Arabia. The author of several books on art history, he taught history and art history at schools in Riyadh, Baghdad, and Rabat.

PREFACE

Beginner's Iraqi Arabic is an introduction to the spoken Iraqi dialect. This book is suitable both for classroom use and self-study. It is designed for people with no previous knowledge of the Arabic language, as well as for those who are familiar with Modern Standard Arabic.

The book is based on the Baghdadi dialect, providing the learner with the broadest possible basis for communication. *Beginner's Iraqi Arabic* uses Roman script to transliterate Iraqi Arabic, making the lessons and dialogues easy to follow. You can learn Iraqi Arabic without the need to learn the Arabic script.

Like other Arabic dialects, Iraqi Arabic coexists alongside Modern Standard Arabic (*fuS-Ha* in Arabic), the *lingua franca* of the Arab world. *fuS-Ha* is the formal Arabic. It is limited to written communications and formal speeches and other presentations. *fuS-Ha* is the language taught in schools; it is the Arabic used in media, literature, and formal settings, including religious occasions. Even the most personal letters are written in *fuS-Ha*. One often finds that a person who masters *fuS-Ha* is shown special respect by people with little or no education. Because Arabic dialects are confined to their local populations, Iraqi authors, like other Arab writers, prefer not to use colloquial language in their work.

Iraqi Arabic is rarely written. While its vocabulary and pronunciation differ from those of Modern Standard Arabic, it also utilizes sounds that do not occur in Modern Standard Arabic, such as *ch*, *g*, *p*, and *v*. Like other Arabic dialects, Iraqi Arabic simplifies grammatical rules. Colloquial Arabic is almost always the language of choice for entertainment programs on radio and television. The Baghdadi dialect, the language of Iraq's capital, is the dominant language of Iraqi media.

The linguistic diversity of Iraq reaches far back into history. The region, known as Mesopotamia in ancient times, was home to a number of civilizations that prospered over millennia. The world's first major civilization was established there by the Sumerians in the fifth millennium BC. The Sumerians were followed by the Babylonians and Assyrians, whose language, Akkadian, is the oldest known Semitic language. Over the centuries, other Semitic language families evolved from Akkadian, such as Aramaic, from which Hebrew and Arabic developed. With the decline of the Akkadians, the region was dominated by numerous foreign civilizations, including the Hittites, the Persian Empire, and the Macedonian Empire of Alexander the Great.

In the seventh century AD Muslim Arabs founded the Abbasid Caliphate in Iraq and made Baghdad its capital. Baghdad became the religious, political, and commercial center of the Islamic world. It was then that Arabic, through its central position as the language of the Qur'an, became the principal language of the region. Arabic persisted as the prevalent language of Iraq even after the Turkish-speaking Ottomans incorporated Iraq into the Ottoman Empire in 1638. After the defeat of the Ottomans in World War I and a brief transitory period as a British mandate, Iraq became an independent country in 1932, with Arabic as its official language.

In addition to Arabic-speaking Iraqi Muslims, Iraq today is home to several other ethnicities, including the Kurds, Turkmen, and Assyrians. It is also home to many different religious groups, including Christians, Mandaeans, and Yazidis. Each of these ethnic and religious groups has its own language or distinctive dialect. All of them have left their mark on the spoken language of Iraq, adding variety to its vocabulary and idioms. Many contemporary Iraqi words and phrases can be traced back to the country's ancient languages, or to the non-Arabic languages of neighboring Turkey and Iran.

* * *

The foundation of this book is a series of everyday dialogues that increase in complexity as the learner progresses. New vocabulary is always explained prior to each dialogue. Additional vocabulary related to the topic of the unit is also provided. The grammar, expressions, and cultural information contained in the dialogues are fully explained in their proper context. The grammar is presented in a progressive, step-by-step manner for easy mastery. Each unit is supplemented with exercises that test and reinforce the learner's knowledge, with an answer key provided at the end of the book. The two-way glossary contains more than 6,000 entries, providing a useful dictionary as well.

ABBREVIATIONS

adj	adjective
adv	adverb
aux	auxiliary
coll	collective noun (see Unit 7)
conj	conjunction
f	feminine
imp	imperative
interr	interrogative
intrans	intransitive verb
lit	literally
m	masculine
n	noun
pl	plural
prep	preposition
pron	pronoun
sg	singular
trans	transitive verb
v	verb

UNIT 1
LETTERS AND SOUNDS OF THE
IRAQI ARABIC DIALECT

I. Pronunciation

The majority of Iraqi Arabic sounds have equivalents in English. However, there are a number of sounds that you need to practice in order to pronounce them the way the natives do.

1. Consonants with exact equivalents in English

Letter	*Example*
b as in English **b**ut	**b**iskit (cookies)
ch as in English **ch**urch	**ch**aan (he was)
d as in English **d**oor	**d**erub (road)
dh as in English **th**at	**dh**ak (that)
f as in English **f**oot	**f**loos (money)
g as in English **g**et	**g**aal (he said)
h as in English **h**ot	**h**ind (India)
j as in English **j**ust	**j**undi (soldier)
k as in English **k**ite	**k**elime (word)
l as in English **l**et	**l**a (no)
m as in English **m**at	**m**udeer (director)
n as in English **n**o	**n**aam (he slept)
p as in English **p**ut	**p**erde (curtain)
s as in English **s**o	**s**edd (he closed)
sh as in English **sh**e	**sh**emis (sun)
t as in English **t**ea	**t**ik**t**ib (she writes)
th as in English **th**eory	**th**elij (ice)

v as in English **v**ery	**v**idyo (videotape)
w as in English **w**as	**w**eled (boy)
y as in English **y**es	**y**iktib (he writes)
z as in English **z**oo	**z**ibid (butter)

The *hamza* (') is a glottal stop before, after, or between vowels. For example: *'akal* (he ate); *su'aal* (question); *wafaa'* (girl's name). As the glottal stop before an initial vowel, such as the initial *a* in *akal*, comes naturally to speakers of most Western languages, it is only indicated between vowels and at the end of a word.

2. Consonants that have no exact equivalents in English

Letter/sound	*Example*
DH is a deep, emphatic *d*-sound comparable to the *d* in English **d**umb	**DH**ireb (he hit)
gh is a gargling *r*-sound as in Parisian French **r**oulette	**gh**aaz (gas)
H is a hissing *h*-sound with a strong, throttling expulsion of air	**H**aleeb (milk)
kh is similar to the *ch*-sound in the German pronunciation of Ba**ch**	**kh**amse (five)
q is a *k*-sound but pronounced deeper in the back of the throat	**q**atar (country)
r is similár to the slightly rolled Spanish *r*-sound	**r**isem (he drew)
S is a deep, emphatic *s*-sound similar to that in the English **s**uch	**S**aar (he became)
T is a deep, emphatic *t*-sound similar to that in the English **t**ongue	**T**abeeb (doctor)
3 is similar to an *a*-sound, but pronounced deeper in the back of the throat	**3**aseer (juice)

3. Vowels

Iraqi Arabic has short and long vowels. The proper pronunciation of long vowels and short vowels is crucial, as the vowel length is an integral part of the word and determines its meaning.

3.1 Short vowels

Letter	Example
a as in English wh**a**t	**mal3ab** (stadium)
e as in English f**e**d	**beled** (country)
i as in English s**i**t	**dires** (he studied)
o as in English p**o**t	**moz** (bananas)
u as in English p**u**t	**kursi** (chair)

3.2 Long vowels

Letters/sound	Example
aa as in English pec**a**n	**il-3iraaq** (Iraq)
ee as in English f**ee**d	**jeeb!** (bring!)
oo as in English s**oo**n	**bazzoon** (cat)

3.3 Vowel clusters (diphthongs)

Letters/sound	Example
ai as in English t**ie**	**chai** (tea)
aw as in English **ou**t	**jawhere** (precious stone)
ei as in English m**a**de	**fei** (shade)
ie as in English w**ei**rd	**biet** (house)
oi as in English b**oi**l	**boi** (waiter)

4. Vocalization

Unlike English, there are no silent vowels and consonants in Iraqi Arabic. All letters are vocalized, including the glottal stop:

binaa' (building)
medrese (school)

II. Word stress

To determine which syllable in a word is stressed, follow these basic rules:

1. Words with two short vowels

In multi-syllable words with two short vowels, usually the first syllable is stressed:

jundi (soldier)
dires (he studied)
weled (boy)

2. Words with a long and a short vowel

In multi-syllable words that have a long as well as a short vowel, the stress usually falls on the syllable with the long vowel:

naayim (he is asleep)   **salaam** (peace)
aakul (I eat)   **jideed** (new)
thaani (second)   **mufeed** (useful)

3. Words with doubled consonants

In multi-syllable words with doubled consonants, the stress usually falls on the syllable containing the double consonants:

muhimm (important)   **yitwennes** (he has fun)
mu3allim (teacher)   **Seideliyye** (pharmacy)

III. Syllable separation

Words are usually broken into syllables where clusters of different consonants occur:

mas·baH (swimming pool)   **kah·ra·baa'** (electricity)
med·re·se (school)   **q·maash** (fabric)
iH·ti·faal (celebration)   **th·nien** (two)
sh·we·yye (a little)   **yiDH·Hak** (he laughs)

IV. Drills

1.1 Following the pronunciation guidelines given above, read aloud these words, bringing out the different phonetic qualities in the sounds *th* and *dh*, and *DH*:

thaalith (third)	**dhak** (that)
muthelleth (triangle)	**dhure** (corn)
mithil (similar to)	**DHeher** (back)
thoom (garlic)	**biedH** (eggs)
dhaab (it melted)	**feyeDHaan** (flood)
ustaadh (professor)	**DHuhur** (noon)

1.2 Following the pronunciation guidelines given above, read aloud these words, bringing out the different phonetic qualities in the sounds *h* and *H*:

ahlan (welcome)	**Hosh** (house)
hawe (air)	**yHibb** (he likes)
hiyye (she)	**Haleeb** (milk)
mehed (cradle)	**maHalle** (district)

1.3 Following the pronunciation guidelines given above, read aloud these words, bringing out the different phonetic qualities in the sounds *k* and *kh*:

akal (he ate)	**khubuz** (bread)
kaafi (enough)	**akhbaar** (news)
kursi (chair)	**khokh** (peaches)
akessir (I break)	**mukhaabaraat** (secret service)

1.4 Following the pronunciation guidelines given above, read aloud these words, bringing out the different phonetic qualities in the sounds *s* and *S*:

sode (black [*f*])	**Soda** (soft drink)
masraH (theater)	**Soore** (picture)
seyyaare (car)	**fuSal** (he fired)
baisikil (bicycle)	**wuSel** (he reached)

1.5 Following the pronunciation guidelines given above, read aloud these words, bringing out the different phonetic qualities in the sounds *t* and *T*:

teen (figs)	**maTaar** (airport)
taayer (tire)	**shaTT** (river)
shurbet (she drank)	**baTal** (hero)
timmen (rice)	**Teyyaare** (airplane)

1.6 Following the pronunciation guidelines given above, read aloud these words, bringing out the different phonetic qualities in the sounds *g* and *gh*:

gallee (he told me)	**goom!** (get up!)
thigeel (heavy)	**Baghdaad** (Baghdad)
yigder (he can)	**ghaali** (expensive [*m*])
kaaghed (paper)	**zgheyyir** (small [*m*])

1.7 Following the pronunciation guidelines given above, read aloud these words, bringing out the different phonetic qualities in the sounds *k* and *q*:

kursi (chair)	**yiqre** (he reads)
mektebe (library)	**qaamoos** (dictionary)
kerkook (Kirkuk [*city in northern Iraq*])	**iqtiSaad** (economy)
kelime (word)	**beqere** (cow)

1.8 Following the pronunciation guidelines given above, read aloud these words, bringing out the different phonetic qualities in the sounds *o* and *aw*:

loz (almonds)	**jaw** (weather)
joz (walnuts)	**aw** (or)
milyon (million)	**thawre** (revolution)
fog (above)	**mawlood** (born)
moz (bananas)	

1.9 Following the pronunciation guidelines given above, read aloud these words, bringing out the different phonetic qualities in the sounds *ee* and *ie*:

jeeb! (bring!)	**binti** (my daughter)
reef (countryside)	**ziet** (oil)
beer (water well)	**ijiet** (I came)
bareed (mail)	**ligiet** (I found)

1.10 Following the pronunciation guidelines given above, read aloud these words, bringing out the different phonetic qualities in the sounds ' (*hamza*) and *3*:

si'al (he asked)	**fu'aad** (a boy's name)
faa'ide (benefit)	**asmaa'** (names)
Sa3ub (difficult [*m*])	**3inwaan** (address)
maa3oon (plate)	**3ineb** (grapes)

1.11 Following the syllable stress guidelines given above, stress the proper syllable in each of the following words:

hemmien (also)	**shoofi!** (look!)
safeer (ambassador)	**kutub** (books)
faadiye (a girl's name)	**3ateeg** (old, for objects)
naghme (tune)	**fihem** (he understood)
3areeDH (wide)	**khelli nrooH** (let's go)

1.12 Read aloud the following words keeping in mind that, unlike English, the final *-e* in each word is pronounced:

shorbe (soup)	**dabbaabe** (tank)
samre (brunette [*f*])	**seyyaare** (car)
medrese (school)	

UNIT 2
INTRODUCTIONS

I. Dialogues

Dialogue One

Vocabulary

marHabe	hello
aani	I am
tsherrafne	nice to meet you
ahlan wa sahlan	nice to meet you

Dialogue

Salim: **marHabe, aani saalim majeed.**
(Hello, I am Salim Majeed.)

Ahmed: **tsherrafne. aani aHmed rasheed.**
(Nice to meet you. I am Ahmed Rasheed.)

Salim: **ahlan wa sahlan.**
(Nice to meet you.)

Dialogue Two

Vocabulary

inte	you (*m sg*)
mmien	from where

min	from
shinoo	what
shughlek	your (*m sg*) profession
Tabeeb	doctor
mudarris	teacher
b-	in

Dialogue

Salim: **inte mmien?**
(Where are you from?)
m sg

Ahmed: **aani min bostin.**
(I am from Boston.)

Salim: **shinoo shughlek?**
(What do you do? [*lit.* What's your profession?])
m sg   *m sg*

Ahmed: **aani Tabeeb. w-inte?**
(I am a doctor. And you?)
m sg

Salim: **aani mudarris b-kerkook.**
(I am a teacher in Kirkuk.)

Dialogue Three

Vocabulary

HaDHirtek	you (*m sg formal*)
amreeke	United States
il-3iraaq	Iraq

Dialogue

Ahmed: **HaDHirtek mmien?**
            (Where are you from?)
            m sg
            formal

Andrew: **aani min amreeke. w-HaDHirtek?**
            (I am from the United States. And you?)
            m sg
            formal

Ahmed: **aani min il-3iraaq.**
            (I am from Iraq.)

Andrew: **tsherrafne.**
            (Nice to meet you.)

II. Notes on Vocabulary and Expressions

Different forms of greetings

The expression *marHabe* (hello) is a common greeting in Iraq. The usual response is *ahlan* (welcome). These two words are used regardless of whether one speaks to a man, woman, or group.

When someone introduces himself or herself, one can respond by saying *ahlan wa sahlan* (welcome) or *tsherrafne* (*lit.* the honor is ours). Both words are used in the sense of "nice to meet you." They do not change with the speaker or addressee and can be used interchangeably. However, *tsherrafne* can only be used in situations when someone is introduced for the first time.

The expression *ahlan wa sahlan* (you're welcome) can also be used when welcoming people to your home.

First names and family names in Iraqi Arabic

In Dialogue Two, Salim introduces himself as *saalim majeed.* In Iraq, the first name is the first name of the speaker, and the second name is usually his or her father's first name.

Another way of saying one's name, usually in a more formal setting, is: first name + father's name + family name (such as *il-baghdaadi*). So Salim would introduce himself as *saalim majeed il-baghdaadi.*

Likewise, women also use their first name, followed by their father's first name and the family name. For example: *ilhaam hashim ij-juboori.* Married women keep their maiden names.

In formal settings, a person may be introduced or referred to as *is-seyyid* (Mr.), *is-seyyide* (Mrs.), or *il-aanise* (Miss), always followed by the full name. For example:

is-seyyid saalim majeed il-baghdaadi
(Mr. Saalim Majeed il-Baghdaadi)

is-seyyide ilhaam hashim ij-juboori
(Mrs. Ilhaam Hashim ij-Juboori)

il-aanise ibtisaam aHmed il-baSri
(Miss Ibtisaam Ahmed il-Basri)

Different ways of addressing people

There are two ways of addressing people: the formal and the informal "you." Both have a masculine and a feminine form.

In Dialogue Two, Salim asks Ahmed where he is from by saying *inte mmien?* If he was speaking to a woman or a girl, he would say *inti mmien?* Another, more formal way of addressing people in formal situations is *HaDHirtek* for men and *HaDHirtich* for women.

In formal situations, the first name is used, preceded by *seyyid* for men and *sit* for women, regardless of whether they are married or unmarried:

seyyid ibraheem **sit aHlaam**

Doctors or people who have advanced academic degrees may be addressed as "doctor." Use *diktor* for men and *diktore* for women, respectively.

When addressing teachers and university professors, it is common to say *ustaadh* for men and *ustaadhe* or *sit* for women. These are also respectful ways of addressing people in formal situations.

Other, informal ways of addressing family and friends are:

3ieni (*lit.* my eye) **galbi** (*lit.* my heart)

These words are sometimes used by sales personnel as a casual way of addressing customers.

III. Useful Vocabulary

usturaalye	Australia
kenede	Canada
ingiltere	England
almaanye	Germany
il-yaabaan	Japan
roosye	Russia

muhandis (*m*)/**muhandise** (*f*)	engineer
muterjim (*m*)/**muterjime** (*f*)	interpreter
mudeer (*m*)/**mudeere** (*f*)	manager
mumarriDH (*m*)/**mumarriDHe** (*f*)	nurse
sikirtier (*m*)/**sikirtiere** (*f*)	secretary

ma3a s-salaame	good-bye

IV. Grammar

Personal pronouns

Unlike English, Iraqi Arabic has two forms of "you" in the singular form: masculine and feminine.

aani	I
inte	you (*m sg*)
inti	you (*f sg*)
huwwe	he
hiyye	she
iHne	we
intu	you (*pl*)
humme	they

Indefinite nouns

There is no indefinite article in Arabic: *biet* means "house" as well as "a house."

The equivalent of the verb "to be"

Unlike English, forming a sentence with "to be" in the present tense does not require a verb. For example, the English sentence "I am sick" requires pronoun (I) + verb (am) + adjective (sick). In Arabic, one simply adds the adjective to the noun or pronoun:

aani mareeDH	I am sick
Salim mareeDH	Salim is sick

However, the adjective changes according to the gender and the number of the subject.

aani mareeDH	I (*m*) am sick
aani mareeDH<u>e</u>	I (*f*) am sick

inte mareeDH	you (*m sg*) are sick
inti mareeDHe	you (*f sg*) are sick
huwwe mareeDH	he is sick
hiyye mareeDHe	she is sick
iHne mareeDHeen	we (*m*) are sick
iHne mareeDHaat	we (*f*) are sick
intu mareeDHeen	you (*m pl*) are sick
intu mareeDHaat	you (*f pl*) are sick
humme mareeDHeen	they are sick

The conjunction *wa* (and)

In Dialogue One, the conjunction *wa* occurs in the sentence *ahlan wa sahlan*.

The *wa* changes depending on whether it is followed by a word beginning with a vowel. In these cases the "a" is dropped and the "w" is assimilated into the following word, as in the line *aani Tabeeb. w-inte?* from Dialogue Two.

The interrogative pronoun *mmien* (from where)

The word *mmien* means "from where?" or "where from?":

inte mmien?	Where are you (*m sg*) from?
inti mmien?	Where are you (*f sg*) from?
huwwe mmien?	Where is he from?
hiyye mmien?	Where is she from?
intu mmien?	Where are you (*pl*) from?
humme mmien?	Where are they from?

Possessive pronouns

In Arabic, possessive pronouns are suffixes added to the end of nouns.

In Dialogue Two, Salim asks *shinoo shughlek?* (What is your profession?) In Iraqi "your profession" is just one word: the noun *shugh(u)l* + the suffix *-ek* (the male singular possessive pronoun).

The possessive suffixes change with the speaker.

qelem**i**	my pen
qelem**ek**	your (*m sg*) pen
qelem**ich**	your (*f sg*) pen
qelem**e**	his pen
qelem**he**	her pen
qelem**ne**	our pen
qelem**kum**	your (*pl*) pen
qelem**hum**	their pen

The definite article *il-* (the)

The definite article *il-* is attached to the word as a prefix, as in *il-ghurfe* (the room).

However, since it is hard to pronounce *il-* when it is followed by certain consonants, the *l* in *il-* is assimilated into the initial consonant of the following word. For example, when one says "the car" in Iraqi Arabic, one combines *il* and *seyyaare* (car) into *is-seyyaare*.

This rule applies to 14 letters:

ch	**ich-cherikh** (the wheel)
d	**id-derub** (the road)
dh	**idh-dheheb** (the gold)
DH	**iDH-DHeher** (the back)
j	**ij-janTe** (the bag)
n	**in-noor** (the light)
r	**ir-ra'ees** (the president)
S	**iS-Seideliyye** (the pharmacy)

s	is-seyyid (Mr.)
sh	ish-shemis (the sun)
T	iT-Tabeeb (the doctor)
t	it-telifon (the phone)
th	ith-thaani (the second)
z	iz-ziet (the oil)

The definite article is also used when referring to certain cities and countries, e.g.

il-3iraaq	Iraq
il-baSre	Basra
il-mooSil	Mosul
il-qaahire	Cairo
il-maghrib	Morocco
is-si3oodiyye	Saudi Arabia

V. Exercises

Note: New vocabulary is presented in the exercises. All new words are accompanied by English equivalents in parentheses.

2.1 Fill in the blanks with the appropriate personal pronouns.

Example: I am happy. (*m sg*) → *aani farHaan.*

1.	I am happy. (*f*)	_____ *farHaane.*
2.	We are happy. (*m*)	_____ *farHaneen.*
3.	He is happy.	_____ *farHaan.*
4.	You are happy. (*m sg*)	_____ *farHaan.*
5.	She is happy.	_____ *farHaane.*
6.	You are happy. (*f sg*)	_____ *farHaane.*
7.	You are happy. (*m pl*)	_____ *farHaneen.*
8.	They are happy. (*mf pl*)	_____ *farHaneen.*

2.2 Form a sentence that conveys the English verb "to be":

Example: (he) (from Basra) → *huwwe min il-baSre*

1. (she) (from England)
2. (we) (from Canada)
3. (you [*f sg*]) (from Germany)
4. (he) (manager)
5. (they) (from Russia)
6. (you [*m sg*]) (interpreter)
7. (I [*m*]) (sick)
8. (you [*pl*]) (from Japan)

2.3 Add the the correct possessive pronoun suffix to the following words.

Example: *qelem* (your [*f sg*]) → *qelemich*

1. *ktaab* (book)   (your [*pl*])
2. *biet*   (their)
3. *qaamoos*   (your [*f sg*])
4. *koob* (cup)   (my)
5. *beled*   (our)
6. *mudarris*   (her)
7. *weled*   (your [*m sg*])
8. *bareed*   (his)

2.4 Fill in the appropriate personal pronoun.

Example: min maSir (I) → *aani min maSir*

1. _____ *min maSir*   (you [*f sg*])
2. _____ *min franse*   (he)
3. _____ *min almaanye*   (we)
4. _____ *min lubnaan*   (you [*pl*]; *lubnaan* → Lebanon)
5. _____ *min turkiye*   (they; *turkiye* → Turkey)

6. _____ *min spaanye*   (I; *spaanye* → Spain)
7. _____ *min baghdaad*   (she)
8. _____ *min amreeke*   (you [*m sg*])

2.5 Add the definite article *il-* to the following words.

Examples: *khabar* → *il-khabar*
              shemis → *ish-shemis*

1. *naar*   (fire)
2. *kursi*
3. *chemche*   (ladle)
4. *sur3a*   (speed)
5. *weqit*   (time)
6. *Haraare*   (heat)
7. *liel*   (night)
8. *DHaruf*   (envelope)
9. *derub*
10. *qameeS*   (shirt)

UNIT 3
TALKING ABOUT YOURSELF

I. Dialogues

Dialogue One

Vocabulary

mitzawwij	married (*m sg*)
ee	yes
3indek	you (*m sg*) have
awlaad	children
3indi	I have
arba3 banaat	four girls
ma sha'allah!	Amazing!/Great!
la	no
ma	not

Dialogue

Ahmed: **inte mitzawwij?**
  (Are you married?)
    m sg

Salim: **ee, aani mitzawwij.**
  (Yes, I am married.)

Ahmed: **3indek awlaad?**
  (Do you have children?)
    m sg

Salim: **ee, 3indi arba3 banaat.**
             (Yes, I have four girls.)

Ahmed: **ma sha'allah!**
             (Great!)

Salim: **w-inte mitzawwij?**
             (And you, are you married?)
             m sg

Ahmed: **la, aani ma mitzawwij.**
             (No, I am not married.)

Dialogue Two

Vocabulary

haadhi	this (*f*)
binti	my daughter
bintich	your (*f sg*) daughter
Hilwe	pretty (*f*)
shisimhe	what's her name
isimhe	her name
mitzawwije	married (*f*)
haadhe	this (*m*)
minu	who
ibni	my son
isme	his name
hadhole	these
Sadeeqaati	my friends (*f pl*)

Dialogue

Nisreen: **haadhi binti.**
(showing a photo) (This my daughter.)

Leila:	bintich Hilwe. shisimhe? (Your daughter is pretty. What's her name?) *f sg*
Nisreen:	isimhe amal. (Her name is Amal.)
Leila:	hiyye mitzawwije? (Is she married?)
Nisreen:	la, hiyye ma mitzawwije. (No, she is not married.)
Leila:	haadhe minu? (Who is this?) *m*
Nisreen:	haadhe ibni. isme fareed. (This is my son. His name is Fareed.)
Leila:	hadhole minu? (Who are these?)
Nisreen:	hadhole Sadiqaati. (These are my friends.) *f pl*

II. Notes on Vocabulary and Expressions

The general term for children independent of their gender is *awlaad*. It is the plural form of *weled* (boy).

The phrase *ma sha'allah* is a common courtesy expression used to show appreciation of God's bounty, usually in a friendly and secular context.

III. Useful Vocabulary

akh	brother
ab (usually addressed as *baabe*)	father
jidd (addressed as *jiddu*)	grandfather
jidde (addressed as *beebee*)	grandmother
zawj	husband
khaale	maternal aunt
ibin khaal (*m*)/**bit khaal** (*f*)	maternal cousin
khaal (addressed as *khaalu*)	maternal uncle
umm (addressed as *maame,* *yom,* or *yumme*)	mother
3amme	paternal aunt
ibin 3amm (*m*)/**bit 3amm** (*f*)	paternal cousin
3amm (addressed as *3ammu*)	paternal uncle
ukhut	sister
zawje	wife
Sadeeq (*m*)/**Sadeeqe** (*f*)	friend
3aazib (*m*)/**3aazbe** (*f*)	single

IV. Grammar

The possessive case using the preposition *3ind*

The possessive is formed by using the preposition *3ind* + pronoun suffix. It is the equivalent of the English verb "to have" in the present tense.

3indi	I have
3indek	you (*m*) have
3indich	you (*f*) have
3inde	he has
3id-he	she has

3id<u>ne</u>	we have
3id<u>kum</u>	you (*pl*) have
3id-<u>hum</u>	they have

Note that the *n* in *3ind* is dropped when the *d* is followed by a consonant, i.e. *3id-he*, *3id<u>ne</u>*, *3id<u>kum</u>*, *3id-<u>hum</u>*.

The gender of nouns

Nouns are either masculine or feminine. This rule also applies to objects. For example, *qelem* (pen) is masculine, and *janTe* (bag) is feminine. Many feminine nouns can be recognized by the ending *–e*.

The gender of a noun is often arbitrary. Some additional examples of masculine and feminine nouns:

ktaab	book (*m*)	**mraaye**	mirror (*f*)
maa3oon	plate (*m*)	**ti3laage**	hanger (*f*)
raadyo	radio (*m*)	**seyyaare**	car (*f*)
DHuwe	light (*m*)	**wereqe**	sheet of paper (*f*)
		Saboone	bar of soap (*f*)

If the noun has a physical gender, such as those relating to people, the feminine is often formed by adding the suffix *–e* to the masculine noun. For example:

Sadeeq (friend [*m*])	→	**Sadeeq<u>e</u>** (friend [*f*])
Tabeeb (doctor [*m*])	→	**Tabeeb<u>e</u>** (doctor [*f*])
muhandis (engineer [*m*])	→	**muhandis<u>e</u>** (engineer [*f*])

Gender agreement between nouns and adjectives

Unlike English, adjectives in Arabic have different forms, depending on the noun or pronoun they are modifying. Nouns and pronouns and their modifying adjectives always agree in gender.

Note also that the adjective comes after the noun. Some examples of masculine nouns modified by adjectives:

beautiful house	→ **biet Hilu**
	= **biet** (house) + **Hilu** (beautiful)
big book	→ **ktaab chibeer**
	= **ktaab** (book) + **chibeer** (big)
full plate	→ **maa3oon malyaan**
	= **maa3oon** (plate) + **malyaan** (full)
old radio	→ **raadyo 3ateeg**
	= **raadyo** (radio) + **3ateeg** (old)
strong light	→ **DHuwe qawi**
	= **DHuwe** (light) + **qawi** (strong)

Following are examples of feminine nouns qualified by adjectives. Note how the adjectives all end with the suffix –*e*:

big mirror	→ **mraaye chibeere**
	= **mraaye** (mirror) + **chibeere** (big)
broken hanger	→ **ti3laage meksoore**
	= **ti3laage** (hanger) + **meksoore** (broken)
old car	→ **seyyaare 3ateege**
	= **seyyaare** (car) + **3ateege** (old)
clean sheet of paper	→ **wereqe naDHeefe**
	= **wereqe** (sheet of paper) + **naDHeefe** (clean)
small bar of soap	→ **Saboone zgheire**
	= **Saboone** (bar of soap) + **zgheire** (small)

The same rules apply to nouns and adjectives that function as subject and predicate. The subject noun dictates the gender of the predicate adjective or noun.

Examples with a masculine subject noun:

aHmed mitzawwij.	Ahmed is married.
aHmed Tabeeb.	Ahmed is a doctor.

Additionally, some examples with a feminine subject noun. Again, note the use of the *–e* suffix:

nisreen mitzawwij<u>e</u>.	Nisreen is married.
nisreen Tabeeb<u>e</u>.	Nisreen is a doctor.

The plural of nouns

There are three main plural forms:

The regular masculine plural, which is formed by adding the suffix *–een* to the singular noun:

mudarris (teacher)	→	**mudarris<u>een</u>** (teachers)
muhandis (engineer)	→	**muhandis<u>een</u>** (engineers)

The regular feminine plural, which is formed by dropping the final *–e* of the singular and replacing it with the suffix *–aat*:

mudarris<u>e</u> (teacher)	→	**mudarris<u>aat</u>** (teachers)
muhandis<u>e</u> (engineer)	→	**muhandis<u>aat</u>** (engineers)

Irregular plurals, which occur in both masculine and feminine nouns, are also known as broken plurals. Examples:

Tabeeb (doctor)	→	**aTibbaa'** (doctors)
bneyye (girl)	→	**banaat** (girls)
weled (boy)	→	**awlaad/wilid** (boys/children)
janTe (bag)	→	**juneT** (bags)

The plural of nouns—regardless of the form—takes the same possessive endings as the singular (see Unit 2). For example:

kutub (books) + **-ne** ("we" suffix)
→ **kutubne** (our books)
mudarrisaat (teachers) + **-e** ("he" suffix)
→ **mudarrisaate** (his teachers)

awlaad (children) + **-hum** ("they" suffix)
→ **awlaad-hum** (their children)

Demonstrative pronouns and adjectives: "this/these"

The demonstrative pronouns "this/these" denote objects or people that are nearby the speaker. The Iraqi Arabic equivalents have three different forms: masculine, feminine, and plural.

haadhe	this (*m*)
haadhi	this (*f*)
hadhole	these (*pl*)

Singular demonstrative pronouns always agree with the gender of the noun, e.g.

haadhe ktaab.	This is a book.
haadhi bneyye.	This is a girl.

There is only one demonstrative pronoun for plural nouns regardless of the gender, e.g.

hadhole muhandiseen.	These are engineers (*m*).
hadhole muhandisaat.	These are engineers (*f*).

These demonstrative pronouns can also be used as demonstrative adjectives within a sentence, e.g.

aani aqre haadhe il-ktaab.	I am reading this book.
haadhi il-bneyye Hilwe.	This girl is pretty.
hadhole il-muhandisaat	These engineers are
ma mitzawwijaat.	not married.

Note that the noun modified by the demonstrative adjective is also modified by the article *il-*.

Negative sentences

Negative sentences are formed by placing *ma-* (not) before the relevant verb or adjective. Compare:

aani mitzawwij.	I am married.
aani ma mitzawwij.	I am not married.
inte mareeDH.	You are sick.
inte ma mareeDH.	You are not sick.

Interrogative sentences

To ask a question, one simply raises the intonation at the end of a sentence. For example:

inte mitzawwij.	You are married.
inte mitzawwij?	Are you married?
hiyye mareeDHe.	She is sick.
hiyye mareeDHe?	Is she sick?

V. Exercises

3.1 Fill in the blanks, using the suitable form of *3ind* to form the possessive with the word *waajib* (homework):

Example: _____ *waajib.* (you [*f sg*])
　　　　3indich waajib.

1. _____ *waajib.* (we)
2. _____ *waajib.* (she)
3. _____ *waajib.* (you [*pl*])
4. _____ *waajib.* (you [*m sg*])
5. _____ *waajib.* (they)

6. _____ *waajib.* (I)

7. _____ *waajib.* (he)

3.2 Convert the following masculine nouns and adjectives to the feminine:

1. *kaatib*   (writer)
2. *mumeththil*   (actor)
3. *muHaasib*   (accountant)
4. *naDHeef*
5. *thigeel*
6. *kareem*   (generous)

3.3 Underline the feminine words:

Tabeeb	*ktaab*
seyyaare	*maa3oon*
raadyo	*Saboone*
mu3allime	*wereqe*

3.4 Modify the predicate adjective or noun so that the sentence is grammatically correct.

Example: *il-ghurfe rekheeS* (*rekheeS* → cheap).
          il-ghurfe rekheeSe.

1. *hiyye chibeer.*
2. *ahmed Tabeeb.*
3. *nisreen mareeDH.*
4. *is-seyyaare maksoor.* (*maksoor* → broken)
5. *ir-raadyo 3ateeg.*

3.5 Change the following words to the plural:

1. *mitzawwije*
2. *mu3allim*

3. *seyyaare*
4. *Teyyaare*
5. *fallaaH* (→ farmer)
6. *Seideliyye*
7. *mektebe*
8. *muhandis*

3.6 Change the following sentences to the negative form.

Example: *aani ta3baan.* (I am tired.)
              aani ma ta3baan.

1. *huwwe farHaan.*
2. *leila nesheeTe.*   (*nesheeTe* → active)
3. *iHne mit'akhkhireen.*   (*mit'akhkhireen* → late)
4. *Sadeeqaati Hilwaat.*   (*Hilwaat* → pretty)
5. *ibni chibeer.*

UNIT 4
AT THE AIRPORT

I. Dialogues

Dialogue One

Vocabulary

jawaaz	passport
rajaa'an	please
tfaDHDHal	here (*m*), please (*polite response to a request*)
saa'iH	tourist (*m*)
ustaadh	professor (*m*)
zaa'ir	visiting (*m*)
wien	where
jaami3at baghdaad	Baghdad University
chem	how many
janTe	suitcase, bag
janTetien	two bags
ahlan beek	you (*m sg*) are welcome
maTaar	airport
shukran	thanks

Dialogue

Officer: **ij-jawaaz, rajaa'an.**
               (The passport, please.)

Tom: **tfaDHDHal.**
               (Here it is.)

Officer: **inte saa'iH?**
                   (Are you a tourist?)
                   m sg

Tom: **la, aani ustaadh zaa'ir.**
                   (No, I am a visiting professor.)

Officer: **wien?**
                   (Where?)

Tom: **b-jaami3at baghdaad.**
                   (At Baghdad University.)

Officer: **chem janTe 3indek?**
                   (How many bags do you have?)
                   m sg

Tom: **3indi janTetien.**
                   (I have two bags.)

Officer: **tfaDHDHal. ahlan beek b-maTaar**
(stamps and hands   **baghdaad.**
back passport)   (Here you are. Welcome to Baghdad Airport.)
                   m sg

Tom: **shukran.**
                   (Thanks.)

Dialogue Two

Vocabulary

juneT	suitcases
maaltek	yours (*m sg*)
maalti	mine (*used with a feminine noun*)

beli	yes
Hamre	red (*f*)
sode	black (*f*)
aku...?	is there...?
ei	any
kahrabaa'iyyaat	electric appliances
maku	there isn't/there aren't
ei shee	anything
it-taSreeH il-gumrugi	customs declaration

Dialogue

Officer: **hadhole ij-juneT maaltek?**
(Are these bags yours?)
m sg

Tom: **beli, hadhole ij-juneT maalti. 3indi janTetien: janTe Hamre, w-janTe sode.**
(Yes, these bags are mine. I have two bags: a red bag and a black bag.)

Officer: **aku ei kahrabaa'iyyaat bij-janTe il-Hamre?**
(Are there any electric appliances in the red bag?)

Tom: **la, maku.**
(No, there aren't.)

Officer: **3indek ei shee lit-taSreeH il-gumrugi?**
(Do you have anything to declare?)
m sg

Tom: **la, ma 3indi ei shee.**
(No, I don't have anything.)

II. Notes on Vocabulary and Expressions

Expressions of courtesy

The expression *rajaa'an* is a polite way of asking someone to do something for you. The word is used regardless of the person to whom one is speaking.

The expression *tfaDHDHal* is a polite way of offering something. It roughly translates as "Here you are." or "Here it is." The word's ending depends on the person addressed, i.e.

      tfaDHDHal   (*used when addressing a male*)
      tfaDHDHili   (*used when addressing a female*)
      tfaDHDHilu (*used when addressing two or more people*)

The phrase *ahlan beek* is the equivalent of saying "You're welcome." It is appropriate in both formal and informal situations. The second word changes depending on the number and gender of those to whom one is speaking, i.e.

      ahlan beek   (*used when addressing a male*)
      ahlan beech   (*used when addressing a female*)
      ahlan beekum (*used when addressing two or more people*)

Answering in the affirmative

In Iraqi Arabic, there are three equivalents to the English "yes." These are *ee*, *beli*, or *na3am*. The last is used in both formal and informal contexts.

III. Useful Vocabulary

Teyyaare	airplane
wuSool	arrival

maTaar baghdaad id-duweli	Baghdad International Airport
ilghaaʻ	cancellation
taʻkeed	confirmation
mughaadere	departure
tafteesh	inspection
tikit	ticket
piTaaqe	ticket
veeze	visa
taʻsheeret dukhool	visa

hna	here
hnak	there
jozi (m)/joziyye (f)	brown
riSaaSi (m)/riSaaSiyye (f)	gray
rumaadi (m)/rumaadiyye (f)	gray
akhDHar (m)/khaDHre (f)	green

IV. Grammar

The interrogative pronoun *wien* (where) and the preposition *b-* (in/at)

The preposition *b-* (in/at) is used when responding to questions beginning with the interrogative pronoun *wien* (where):

wien ij-jawaaz?	Where is the passport?
—**ij-jawaaz <u>b</u>ij-janTe.**	—The passport is in the bag.
wien il-mudarris?	Where is the teacher?
—**il-mudarris <u>b</u>il-medrese.**	—The teacher is at school.
wien kulliyyet iT-Tibb?	Where is the school of medicine?
—<u>**b**</u>**-jaami3at baghdaad.**	—At Baghdad University.

Note that the *b*-prefix is always affixed to the word it qualifies:

maTaar il-mooSil   →   **b-maTaar il-mooSil**
(Mosul airport)   (at Mosul airport)

il-ghurfe (the room)   →   **bil-ghurfe** (in the room)
is-seyyaare (the car)   →   **bis-seyyaare** (in the car)

The cardinal numbers: 1 to 10

Numbers in Iraqi Arabic differ from English in two respects: (1) they have different forms depending on whether they stand alone or with a noun; (2) there is a separate form for the dual (two).

1. The numbers when standing alone:

0	**Sifir**	6	**sitte**
1	**waaHid**	7	**sab3a**
2	**thnien**	8	**thmaanye**
3	**tlaathe**	9	**tis3a**
4	**arba3a**	10	**3ashre**
5	**khamse**		

2. When numbers stand with (complement) a noun, they undergo slight changes.

    The number for "one" has masculine and feminine forms that agree with the noun complemented. It also follows the noun instead of preceding it.

    one (1)   → **waaHid** (*m*) → **qelem waaHid** (one pen)

    wiHde (*f*) → **Soore wiHde** (one picture)

3. In addition to the singular and plural, Arabic also has the dual form, which, in Iraqi Arabic, is formed in masculine nouns by adding the suffix *–ien*, e.g.

qelem (a pen)   → **qelemien** (two pens)
baab (a door)   → **baabien** (two doors)
jawaaz (a passport)   → **jawaazien** (two passports)

As previously noted, most feminine nouns end with the suffix *-e*. In the dual form, the *-e* is dropped and replaced with the suffix *-tien*, e.g.

Soore (a picture)   → **Soortien** (two pictures)
seyyaare (a car)   → **seyyaartien** (two cars)

If the noun ends with *-Te*, the final -e is not dropped. The dual form suffix *-tien* is simply affixed, e.g.

janTe (a bag)   → **janTetien** (two bags)
khuTTe (a plan)   → **khuTTetien** (two plans)

4. The numbers 3 to 10 in combination with a noun are the same regardless of the noun's gender.

three (3)   → **tlath aqlaam** (three pens)
four (4)   → **arba3 aqlaam** (four pens)
five (5)   → **khamis aqlaam** (five pens)
six (6)   → **sit aqlaam** (six pens)
seven (7)   → **sabi3 aqlaam** (seven pens)
eight (8)   → **thmen aqlaam** (eight pens)
nine (9)   → **tisi3 aqlaam** (nine pens)
ten (10)   → **3ashir aqlaam** (ten pens)

Possessive suffixes and feminine nouns ending in –e

In the first-, second-, and masculine third-person singular, the
–e is dropped and a -t is added, followed by the appropriate
possessive pronoun suffix.

seyyaare (a car)

1st person (*m f sg*)	**seyyaar- + -t + -i**
	→ **seyyaarti** (my car)
2nd person (*m sg*)	**seyyaar- + -t + -ek**
	→ **seyyaartek** (your [*m sg*] car)
2nd person (*f sg*)	**seyyaar- + -t + -ich**
	→ **seyyaartich** (your [*f sg*] car)
3rd person (*m sg*)	**seyyaar- + -t + -e**
	→ **seyyaarte** (his car)

In the feminine third-person singular, and first-, second-, and
third-person plural, the -e is replaced with -et, followed by the
appropriate suffix.

3rd person (*f sg*)	**seyyaar- + -et + --he**
	→ **seyyaaret-he** (her car)
1st person (*m f pl*)	**seyyaar- + -et + -ne**
	→ **seyyaaretne** (our car)
2nd person (*m f pl*)	**seyyaar- + -et + -kum**
	→ **seyyaaretkum** (your [*pl*] car)
3rd person (*m f pl*)	**seyyaar- + -et + --hum**
	→ **seyyaaret-hum** (their car)

With feminine nouns ending in –te or –Te, the final –e becomes
–et in all persons, followed by the appropriate suffixes.

janTe (bag)

1st person (*m f sg*)	**janT- + -et + -i**
	→ **janTeti** (my bag)

2nd person (*m sg*)	jan**T**- + -et + -ek → jan**T**etek (your [*m sg*] bag)
2nd person (*f sg*)	jan**T**- + -et + -ich → jan**T**etich (your [*f sg*] bag)
3rd person (*m sg*)	jan**T**- + -et + -e → jan**T**ete (his bag)
3rd person (*f sg*)	jan**T**- + -et + --he → jan**T**et-he (her bag)
1st person (*m f pl*)	jan**T**- + -et + -ne → jan**T**etne (our bag)
2nd person (*m f pl*)	jan**T**- + -et + -kum → jan**T**etkum (your [*pl*] bag)
3rd person (*m f pl*)	jan**T**- + -et + --hum → jan**T**et-hum (their bag)

The interrogative pronoun *chem* (how many)

The word *chem* means "how many." Unlike English, the noun following *chem* is always singular, e.g.

chem janTe 3indek?	How many bags do you have?
chem su'aal 3indich?	How many questions do you have?
chem tuffaaHe 3idkum?	How many apples do you have?

The definite article *il-* with nouns and modifying adjectives

The definite article *il-* complements both the noun and the modifying adjective, e.g.

janTe Hamre (the red bag)	→	**ij-janTe il-Hamre** (a red bag)

biet chibeer	→	**il-biet ich-chibeer**
(a big house)		(the big house)

Remember that an assimilation occurs between the *il-* and certain consonants. See Unit 2 for details.

The possessive object pronoun *maal-*

The word *maal-* is used in combination with a noun to express ownership. In its conjugated forms the word is equivalent to the English possessive pronouns "mine," "yours," and "ours." The conjugation suffixes are the same as with other pronouns.

The conjugations of *maal-* with the masculine noun *qelem* (pen):

il-qelem maali.	The pen is mine.
il-qelem maalek.	The pen is yours (*m sg*).
il-qelem maalich.	The pen is yours (*f sg*).
il-qelem maale.	The pen is his.
il-qelem maal-he.	The pen is hers.
il-qelem maalne.	The pen is ours.
il-qelem maalkum.	The pen is yours (*pl*).
il-qelem maal-hum.	The pen is theirs.

The conjugations with the feminine noun **janTe** (bag):

ij-janTe maalti.	The bag is mine.
ij-janTe maaltek.	The bag is yours (*m*).
ij-janTe maaltich.	The bag is yours (*f*).
ij-janTe maalte.	The bag is his.
ij-janTe maalet-he.	The bag is hers.
ij-janTe maaletne.	The bag is ours.
ij-janTe maaletkum.	The bag is yours (*pl*).
ij-janTe maalet-hum.	The bag is theirs.

The word *aku* (there is/there are)

The word *aku* is the equivalent of "there is" or "there are." The word is the same regardless of the gender and number of the subsequent noun, e.g,

aku qelem.	There is a pen.
aku janTe.	There is a bag.
aku aTibbaa'.	There are doctors.

The word *aku* is also used to ask the questions "Is there...?" or "Are there...?" Remember that a question is asked by raising intonation at the end of the sentence:

aku qelem?	Is there a pen?
aku janTe?	Is there a bag?
aku aTibbaa'?	Are there doctors?

The negative of *aku* is *maku*.

maku qelem.	There is no pen.
maku janTe.	There is no bag.
maku aTibbaa'.	There are no doctors.

V. Exercises

4.1 Form questions using *wien*.

Example: *il-qelem bil-ghurfe.*
      → *wien il-qelem?*

1. *it-tikit bil-biet.*
2. *ir-raadyo bis-seyyaare.*
3. *il-ustaadh bij-jaami3a.*
4. *iT-Teyyaare bil-maTaar.*
5. *il-moze bich-chees.*   (*chees* → paper/plastic bag)

4.2 Fill in the blanks with the correct number.

Example: *3indi* _____ *as'ile.* (3)
→ *3indi tlath as'ile.*

1. *3indi* _____ *chlaab.*   (4) (*chlaab* → dogs)
2. *3indi* _____ *awraaq.*   (9) (*awraaq*
                                    → sheets of paper)
3. *3indi* _____ *juneT.*   (7)
4. *3indi* _____ *ikhwaan.*   (5) (*ikhwaan* → brothers)
5. *3indi* _____ *aSdiqaa'.*   (6) (*aSdiqaa'* → friends)
6. *3indi* _____ *kutub.*   (8)
7. *3indi* _____ *banaat.*   (3)

4.3 Change the following sentences using the dual masculine form.

Example: *3indi ibin waaHid.*
→ *3indi ibnien.*

1. *3indi maa3oon waaHid.*
2. *3indi moos waaHid.*   (*moos* → razor blade)
3. *3indi khaal waaHid.*
4. *3indi glaaS waaHid.*   (*glaaS* → glass)
5. *3indi cheTel waaHid.*   (*cheTel* → fork)

4.4 Change the following sentences using the dual feminine form.

Example: *3indi Sadeeqe wiHde.*
→ *3indi Sadeeqtien.*

1. *3indi khaashooge wiHde.*   (*khaashooge* → spoon)
2. *3indi mraaye wiHde.*
3. *3indi sichcheene wiHde.*   (*sichcheene* → knife)
4. *3indi purtuqaale wiHde.*   (*purtuqaale* → orange)
5. *3indi bieDHe wiHde.*   (*bieDHe* → egg)

4.5 Change the following sentences to questions using *chem*.

Example: *3indi arba3 seyyaaraat.*
  → *chem seyyaare 3indek?*

1. *3indi akh waaHid.*   (*akh* → brother)
2. *3indi khamis aqlaam.*
3. *3indi tisi3 kutub.*
4. *3indi koobien.*
5. *3indi tlath mu3allimeen.*

4.6 Fill in the blanks using the correct form of *maal*.

Example: *il-qelem* _____ (mine).
  → *il-qelem maali.*

1. *il-kaamire* _____.   (yours *m sg*; *kaamire*
                               → camera)
2. *ij-jawaaz* _____.   (ours)
3. *iT-Tabeeb* _____.   (his)
4. *iT-Tabeebe* _____.   (theirs)
5. *il-mudarris* _____.   (hers)
6. *il-mudarrise* _____.   (yours *pl*)
7. *it-tuffaaHe* _____.   (yours *f sg*; *tuffaaHe*
                               → apple)

4.7 Change the following sentences to the negative.

Example: *aku veeze.*
  → *maku veeze.*

1. *aku bieDH.*
2. *aku floos.*
3. *aku gumrug.*
4. *aku kahrabaa'iyyaat.*
5. *aku ei shee?*

4.8 Complete the following tables.

1.

Soore	a picture
_____	my picture
_____	your (*m sg*) picture
_____	your (*f sg*) picture
_____	his picture
_____	her picture
_____	our picture
_____	your (*pl*) picture
_____	their picture

2.

khuTTe	a plan
_____	my plan
_____	your (*m sg*) plan
_____	your (*f sg*) plan
_____	his plan
_____	her plan
_____	our plan
_____	your (*pl*) plan
_____	their plan

UNIT 5
GETTING AROUND

I. Dialogues

Dialogue One

Vocabulary

trooH	you (*m sg*) go
ootiel	hotel
arooH	I go
hnak	there
shged	how much
taakhudh	you (*m sg*) take
alif	thousand
deenaar	Iraqi currency
hwaaye	a lot
sabi3miyye w-khamseen	750
ustaadh	sir (*lit.* professor; see Unit 2)
kullish	very
qeleel	little
zien	OK then
thmanmiyye w-khamseen	850
meikhaalif	agreed
HuTT	put (*imperative m sg*)
Sandoog	car trunk, box
min feDHlek	please (*m sg*)
HaaDHir	OK
ashkurek	thank you (*to male addressee*)

Dialogue

Tom: **trooH l-ootiel baghdaad?**
(Do you go to Baghdad Hotel?)
m sg

Taxi driver: **ee, arooH hnak.**
(Yes, I go there.)

Tom: **shged taakhudh?**
(How much do you take?)
m sg

Taxi driver: **alif deenaar*.**
(1000 dinars.)

Tom :   **haadhe hwaaye. taakhudh sabi3miyye
w-khamseen deenaar?**
(This is a lot. Would you take 750 dinars?)
m sg

Taxi driver: **la ustaadh, haadhe kullish qeleel.**
(No, sir, this is very little.)

Tom: **zien, taakhudh thmanmiyye w-khamseen?**
(OK, then. Would you take 850?)
m sg

Taxi driver: **meikhaalif.**
(Agreed.)

Tom: **HuTT ij-juneT b-Sandoog is-seyyaare, min
feDHlek.**
(Please put the suitcases in the trunk.)

*The dinar amounts in this book do not reflect the actual price level in
Iraq. They are used for learning purposes only.

Taxi driver: **HaaDHir.**

         (OK.)

Tom: **ashkurek.**

         (Thank you.)

               m sg

Dialogue Two

Vocabulary

areed	I want
ashtiri	I buy
tikit murajja3	return ticket
treed	you (*m sg*) want
tsaafir	you (*m sg*) travel
qiTaar il-liel	night train
qiTaar in-nahaar	day train
asaafir	I travel
tishtiri	you (*m sg*) buy
dereje oola	first class
dereje siyaaHiyye	economy class
bawwaabet il-maHaTTe	the station gate
tshoof	you (*m sg*) see
hedheech	that (*f*)
binaaye	building
Safre	yellow (*f*)
3ala yemeen	to the right of

Dialogue

Tom: **areed ashtiri tikit murajja3 lil-baSre.**

        (I would like to buy a return ticket to Basra.)

Clerk: **chem tikit treed?**

        (How many tickets would you like to buy?)

               m sg

Tom: **areed tikit waaHid.**
           (I want one ticket.)

Clerk: **treed tsaafir b-qiTaar il-liel lo b-qiTaar in-nahaar?**
           (Would you like to travel on the night train or day train?)
           m sg

Tom: **areed asaafir b-qitaar il-liel.**
           (I would like to travel on the night train.)

Clerk: **treed tishtiri tikit dereje oola lo dereje siyaaHiyye?**
           (Would you like first class or economy class?)
           m sg

Tom: **dereje oola.**
           (First class.)

Clerk: **tfaDHDHal.**
           (Here.)

Tom: **ashkurek. wien bawwaabet il-maHaTTe, rajaa'an?**
           (Thank you. Where is the station's entrance gate, please?)
           m sg

Clerk: **tshoof hedheech il-binaaye iS-Safre?**
           (Do you see that yellow building?)
           m sg

Tom: **ee.**
           (Yes.)

Clerk: **il-bawwaabe 3ala yemeen il-binaaye.**
           (The gate is to the right of the building.)

II. Notes on Vocabulary and Expressions

Bargaining

It is always a good idea to check the taxi rates beforehand. If the driver is overcharging, it is quite acceptable to try to bring the price down.

Thank you

Besides *shukran* (thanks) you can also thank people using the full verb form:

ashkurek	I thank you (*m sg*)
ashkurich	I thank you (*f sg*)
ashkurkum	I thank you (*pl*)

Polite requests

After requesting something, it is polite to add a form of *min feDHlek* (please). The form changes depending on the gender and the number of persons addressed:

min feDHlek (*m sg*)
min feDHlich (*f sg*)
min feDHilkum (*pl*)

III. Useful Vocabulary

baisikil	bicycle
paS	bus
maaTorsikil	motorcycle
raakib	passenger
saayiq teksi	taxi driver

teksi	taxi
musaafir	traveler

ujre	fare
tikit ghier murajja3	one-way ticket
bi3eed	far
qareeb	near

IV. Grammar

More numbers

11	**da3ash**	16	**siTTa3ash**
12	**thna3ash**	17	**sbaTa3ash**
13	**tlatta3ash**	18	**thmunTa3ash**
14	**arbaTa3ash**	19	**tisaTa3ash**
15	**khumuSTa3ash**		

The tens from 20 to 90 have the same ending as nouns in the regular masculine plural (as in *mu3allimeen* "teachers").

20	**3ishreen**	60	**sitteen**
30	**tlaatheen**	70	**sab3een**
40	**arba3een**	80	**thmaaneen**
50	**khamseen**	90	**tis3een**

The numbers 21 to 29, 31 to 39, etc. are formed as follows:

single digit + conjunction *w-* (and) + tens

21	**waaHid w-3ishreen**	63	**tlaathe w-sitteen**
22	**thnien w-3ishreen**	78	**thmaanye w-sab3een**
39	**tis3a w-tlaatheen**	99	**tis3a w-tis3een**

Note that unlike English, numbers start with the smaller unit. For example, the one (*waaHid*) in twenty-one (*waaHid w-3ishreen*) comes first.

The numbers 100-1000:

100	**miyye**	600	**sitmiyye**
200	**meetien**	700	**sabi3miyye**
300	**tlethmiyye**	800	**thmanmiyye**
400	**arba3miyye**	900	**tisi3miyye**
500	**khamismiyye**	1000	**alif**

The numbers above 100 are spelled out with the *w-* and inserted between the hundreds, ones, and tens, e.g.

150	**miyye <u>w</u>-khamseen**
670	**sitmiyye <u>w</u>-sab3een**
345	**tlethmiyye <u>w</u>-khamse <u>w</u>-arba3een**

Hundreds standing with a noun

The hundreds, with the exception of 200, have a slightly different form when standing with a noun. For example:

meet kieloo	100 kilograms
khamismeet deenaar	500 dinars

The modified forms of the numbers:

100	**meet...**	600	**sitmeet...**
300	**tlethmeet...**	700	**sabi3meet...**
400	**arba3meet...**	800	**thmanmeet...**
500	**khamismeet...**	900	**tisi3meet...**

General comments on verbs

Verb conjugations are made by adding prefixes or suffixes to the verb root. At times, the vowels in the verb root also undergo changes.

In Iraqi Arabic the equivalent of the English verb base (e.g. "write") is the 3rd person masculine singular in the past tense. This is because it is free of any prefixes or suffixes. This is the way verbs are listed in this book, and the present-tense vowelling is featured in parentheses. For example:

kiteb (i) (write)

Sound verbs in the present tense

The majority of Arabic verbs have three root consonants, or radical letters, which are constant regardless of the conjugation. For example, the root consonants of the verb *shiker* (thank) are *sh-k-r*. These verbs are categorized as **sound verbs** in standard Arabic. The following table shows the conjugations in the present tense:

shiker (u) (thank)	
Singular	
I thank	**ashkur**
you (*m*) thank	**tishkur**
you (*f*) thank	**tishkureen**
he thanks	**yishkur**
she thanks	**tishkur**
Plural	
we thank	**nishkur**
you thank	**tishkuroon**
they thank	**yishkuroon**

Note that the root consonants *sh-k-r* stay the same throughout.

Sound verbs used in Units 1-12:

3iref (know)	**Hijez** (reserve)
3izem (invite)	**khiteb** (get engaged)
3uber (pass, cross)	**kiser** (break, turn)
DHiHak (laugh)	**kiteb** (write)
DHireb (beat)	**li3ab** (play)
difa3 (pay)	**liHag** (follow)
dikhel (enter)	**nizel** (go down)
dires (study)	**rikeDH** (run)
fihem (understand)	**risem** (draw)
fitaH (open)	**shiker** (thank)
fuSal (fire)	**shireb** (drink)
ghisel (wash)	**si'al** (ask)
gi3ad (sit)	**sima3** (hear)
gider (can)	**simaH** (allow)
gumez (jump)	**Siref** (spend)
Hijez (reserve)	**Tubekh** (cook)

Other verbs

Four other types of verbs are encountered in this unit's dialogues: hollow verbs, verbs with an initial *a-*, verbs ending in a doubled consonant, and derived verb forms.

Hollow verbs are verbs with a long vowel in the middle. Examples include *raaH* (go), *raad* (want), and *shaaf* (see). The present tense conjugations *trooH* (you go), *arooH* (I go), *areed* (I want), and *tshoof* (you see) appear in this unit's dialogues. The complete conjugation of these verbs in the present tense is discussed in Unit 6.

Verbs with an initial *a-*: For example, *akhadh* (take). The present tense conjugation *taakhudh* (you take) appears in Dialogue One. Other conjugations of this verb in the present tense are discussed in Unit 7.

Verbs ending in a doubled consonant: For example, *HaTT* (put). In Dialogue One, it is conjugated in the imperative (as a command) as *HuTT!* (put!). The conjugation of these verbs in the present tense and imperative is discussed in Unit 7.

Derived verb forms are discussed in Unit 9. Examples in the above dialogues are *ashtiri* (I buy) and *tsaafir* (you travel).

The verb plus the infinitive

In Arabic, the verb plus the infinitive, for example, "I want to rent a car," is formed by two conjugated verbs in the same person in the present tense. For example:

> **areed + ashtiri + tikit murajja3 lil-baSre**
> (I want) + (I buy) + (a ticket to Basra)
>
>> → **areed ashtiri tikit murajja3 lil-baSre.**
>> (I want to buy a ticket to Basra.)
>
> **treed + tishtiri + tikit dereje oola**
> (you want) + (you buy) + (a first-class ticket)
>
>> → **treed tishtiri tikit dereje oola?**
>> (Do you want to buy a first-class ticket?)

The verb for "want," *raad*, is discussed with its conjugations in the section on hollow verbs in the next unit.

The preposition *l-* (to/for)

The preposition *l-* (to/for) precedes the indirect object, e.g.

trooH l-ootiel baghdaad?	Are you going to Baghdad Hotel?
tom kiteb maktoob l-akhoo.	Tom wrote a letter to his brother.
areed aktib l-saalim.	I want to write to Salim.

However, when the preposition *l-* stands before a noun with definite article (*il-...*), the *l-* + *il-* become *lil-*, e.g.

areed ashtiri tikit	I want to buy a ticket
lil-baSre.	to Basra.

If the preposition *l-* precedes a noun with an assimilated article, e.g. *iT-Tabeeb*, the *l-* is assimilated with the initial *i-* and leaves the rest unchanged. For example:

Tom raaH liT-Tabeeb.	Tom went to the doctor.

The interrogative pronoun *shged* (how much)

In Unit 4, you learned the interrogative pronoun *chem* (how many). The other interrogative pronoun when asking about a quantity is *shged* (how much).

shged treed timmen?	How much rice do you want?
shged weqit 3indak?	How much time do you have?
shged akalit?	How much did you eat?

The use of "or" and "either or"

The general Iraqi term for "or" is *aw*, for example:

yaakhudh qiTaar aw paS.	He takes a train or a bus.

But when asking someone to choose between two things, *lo* is used instead:

treed tsaafir b-qiTaar	Would you like to travel
il-liel lo b-qiTaar	on the night train or
in-nahaar?	the day train?

taakhudh Teyyaare lo seyyaare?	Do you (want to) take a plane or a car?

The equivalent of either…or is *imma…aw.*

asaafir imma biT-Teyyaare aw bis-seyyaare.	I travel by either plane or car.

Demonstrative pronouns and adjectives: "that" and "those"

In Unit 3, the equivalents for the demonstrative pronouns/adjectives "this" and "these," which indicate nouns close to the speaker, were discussed. To indicate nouns that are away from the speaker, the equivalents of "that" and "those" are used. They have three forms:

hedhaak	that (*m*)
hedheech	that (*f*)
hedholaak	those (*pl*)

Like the singular demonstrative pronouns for "this," they always agree with the gender of the noun, e.g.

hedhaak ktaab.	That is a book.
hedheech bneyye.	That is a girl.

Similarly, the plural uses only one demonstrative pronoun, regardless of gender, e.g.

hedholaak muhandiseen.	Those are engineers (*m*).
hedholaak muhandisaat.	Those are engineers (*f*).

These demonstrative pronouns can also be used as demonstrative adjectives within a sentence, e.g.

hedhaak il-ktaab aHmer.	That book is red.
hedheech is-seyyaare Safre.	That car is yellow.
hedholaak il-musaafireen bil-qiTaar.	Those passengers are on the train.

V. Exercises

5.1 Write out the following numbers.

Example: 247 → *meetien w-sab3a w-arba3een*

1. 101
2. 45
3. 15
4. 151
5. 220
6. 33
7. 11
8. 459
9. 997

5.2 Fill out the following tables by conjugating the verbs in the present tense. Use the conjugation given for the 3rd person masculine singular as a guide.

1. **li3ab** (*play*)

Singular	
I play	
you (*m*) play	
you (*f*) play	
he plays	**yil3ab**
she plays	

Plural	
we play	
you play	
they play	

2. **kiteb** (*write*)

Singular	
I write	
you (*m*) write	
you (*f*) write	
he writes	**yiktib**
she writes	
Plural	
we write	
you write	
they write	

3. **dires** (*study*)

Singular	
I study	
you (*m*) study	
you (*f*) study	
he studies	**yidrus**
she studies	
Plural	
we study	
you study	
they study	

5.3 Fill in the blanks with the appropriate question word.

1. _____ *wereqe* (how many; *bil-*
   bil-ktaab? → in the)
2. _____ *3indek floos?* (how much)
3. _____ *tishreb mei?* (how much; *tishreb*
   → you [*m sg*] drink;
   mei → water)
4. _____ *moze bis-selle?* (how many; *bis-selle*
   → in the basket)
5. _____ *binaaye* (how many; *bil-medeene*
   bil-medeene? → in the city)

5.4 Translate the conjugations:

1. *til3aboon* (play)
2. *yiDH-Hak* (laugh)
3. *tuSruf* (spend)
4. *nishreb* (drink)
5. *tig3udoon* (sit)
6. *tisma3een* (hear)
7. *tiftaH* (open)
8. *ynaamoon* (sleep)
9. *aghsil* (wash)
10. *niktib* (write)

5.5 Fill in the blanks with the correct form of the preposition *l-* :

1. *leila tiktib* _____ *Tom.*
2. *aani arooH* _____ *baghdaad.*
   (*aani arooH* → I go)
3. *sam yrooH* _____ *il-baab.*
   (*sam yrooH* → Sam goes)
4. *aani aqre* _____ *il-aTfaal.*
   (*aani aqre* → I read; *il-aTfaal* → the children)
5. *ummi tsaafir* _____ *in-najaf.*
   (*ummi tsaafir* → my mother travels; *in-najaf* → Najaf)

5.6 Fill in the blanks with the correct demonstrative pronoun (*that/those*):

1. _____ *il-mudarriseen amreekaan.*
2. _____ *il-weled chibeer.*
3. _____ *is-seyyaare Safre.*
4. _____ *il-qelem maksoor.*
5. _____ *il-banaat yidrusoon.*

UNIT 6
AT THE HOTEL

I. Dialogues

Dialogue One

Vocabulary

aloo	hello (*used only on the phone*)
agder	I may, I can
aHjiz	I reserve
ghurfe	room
bit-telifon	on the phone
areed	I want, I would like
nefer	person
yom	day
treed-he	you (*m sg*) want it
Saar	OK (*lit.* done)
si3ir	price
su'aal	question
akheer	last
shwekit	when
nizool	check-in
Tal3a	check-out
findiq	hotel
saa3a	hour (*also equivalent to* o'clock)

Dialogue

Tom: **aloo, marHabe. min feDHlich, agder aHjiz ghurfe bit-telifon?**
(Hello, may I reserve a room on the phone, please?)

Receptionist: **na3am, tfaDHDHal.**
(Yes, please go ahead.)

Tom: **areed ghurfe mal nefer waaHid.**
(I want a room for one person.)

Receptionist: **chem yom treed-he?**
(For how many days do you want it?)
                    m sg

Tom: **arba3t ayyaam.**
(Four days.)

Receptionist: **Saar.**
(OK.)

Tom: **shged si3ir il-ghurfe?**
(What is the room's rate?)

Receptionist: **khamismeet deenaar*.**
(500 dinars.)

Tom: **su'aal akheer. shwekit in-nizool wiT-Tal3a min il-findiq?**
(One last question. When is check-in and check-out at the hotel?)

*The dinar amounts in this book do not reflect actual prices in Iraq.

Receptionist: **saa3a thna3ash.**
(12 o'clock.)

Tom: **shukran.**
(Thanks.)

Dialogue Two

Vocabulary

mesaa' il-khier	good evening
mesaa' in-noor	good evening (*in reply*)
maHjooze	reserved (*f sg*)
jaahze	ready (*f sg*)
ismek	your (*m sg*) name
tiqbeloon	you (*pl*) accept
ma3a il-asef	I am sorry
Sekk	check
kash	cash
id-dinye	the world
Haarre	hot (*f sg*)
tekyeef	air conditioning
ghuref	rooms
mukeyyefe	air-conditioned (*f sg*)
anaam	I sleep
arooH	I go
hesse	now
Tab3an	certainly, of course
miftaaH	key
tiSbaHeen 3ala khier	good night (*when addressing a female*)
tiSbaH 3ala khier	good night (*when addressing a male*)

Dialogue

Tom: **mesaa' il-khier.**
(Good evening.)

Receptionist: **mesaa' in-noor.**
(Good evening.)

Tom: **il-ghurfe il-maHjooze jaahze?**
(Is the reserved room ready?)

Receptionist: **ismek, rajaa'an?**
(Your name, please?)
m sg

Tom: **tom smith.**
(Tom Smith.)

Receptionist: **na3am, il-ghurfe jaahze.**
(Yes, the room is ready.)

Tom: **tiqbeloon kredit kard?**
(Do you accept credit cards?)
pl

Receptionist: **la, ma3a il-asef. imma Sekk aw kash.**
(No, I am sorry. Either check or cash.)

Tom: **id-dinye Haarre. aku tekyeef bil-ghurfe?**
(It's hot. Is there air conditioning in the rooms?)

Receptionist: **na3am, il-ghurfe mukeyyefe.**
(Yes, the rooms are air-conditioned.)

Tom: **areed anaam. agder arooH lil-ghurfe hesse?**
(I would like to sleep. May I go to the room now?)

Receptionist: **Tab3an. haadhe miftaaH il-ghurfe.**
(Certainly. This is the room key.)

Tom: **shukran. tiSbaHeen 3ala khier.**
(Thanks. Good night.)

Receptionist: **tiSbaH 3ala khier.**
(Good night.)

II. Notes on Vocabulary and Expressions:

Polite requests

A polite way of requesting something or asking for permission is to use the verb *agder* (I may, I can) or *nigder* (we may, we can) in the form of a question, as in:

> **agder arooH?** May I go?
> **nigder nrooH lis-seeneme?** May we go to the movies?

Remember that the two verbs have to agree in gender and number. (See also Unit 5, "Verb plus the infinitive.")

Greetings

In Iraqi Arabic, an initial greeting and the reply to it vary according to the time of day.

In the morning, the initial greeting is *SabaaH il-khier.* The appropriate response is *SabaaH in-noor.*

In the afternoon and early evening, the initial greeting is *mesaa' il-khier.* The appropriate response to this is *mesaa' in-noor.*

The Iraqi Arabic equivalent of "good night" changes according to the gender and number of the person or people being addressed. For example, in Dialogue Two, Tom says *tiSbaHeen 3ala khier* to the female receptionist, and she replies *tiSbaH 3ala khier*. The following are the proper forms of the expression:

tiSbaH 3ala khier.	(*when speaking to a male*)
tiSbaHeen 3ala khier.	(*when speaking to a female*)
tiSbaHoon 3ala khier.	(*when speaking to more than one person*)

Talking about the weather

The expression *id-dinye Haarre* (It's hot; *lit.* the world is hot) is common. Other weather expressions include *id-dinye baarde* (it's cold) and *id-dinye Teibe* (it's pleasant).

A note on *arba3t ayyaam* (four days)

The number *arba3* (four) in combination with the noun *ayyaam* (days), as it appears in Dialogue One, is an exception to the rule about numbers and nouns laid out in Unit 4. The letter *-t* is affixed to *arba3: arba3t̲ ayyaam*. This makes it easier to pronounce the words together.

III. Useful Vocabulary

riyoog	breakfast
si3ir il-liele	rate per night
Hajiz	reservation
khidmet il-ghuref	room service
tilfizyon	television

sareer mal neferien	double/queen/king bed
churpaaye mal neferien	double/queen/king bed
sareer mal nefer waaHid	twin/single bed
churpaaye mal nefer waaHid	twin/single bed
Hammaam	bathroom
baanyo	bathtub
tadfi'e markeziyye	central heating
doosh	shower
akhadh doosh	take a shower
akhadh hammaam	take a shower
twaaliet	toilet
maraaHeeDH	toilet
mei baarid	cold water
mei Haarr	hot water
shuqqe	apartment
flaat	apartment
eejaar	rent
mu'aththeth/mu'aththethe	furnished (*m*)/furnished (*f*)
ma mu'aththeth/	unfurnished (*m*)/
ma mu'aththethe	unfurnished (*f*)

IV. Grammar

Present tense of hollow verbs

Unlike sound verbs, which have three root consonants, hollow verbs have a long root vowel and two root consonants. The root vowel is always in the middle. Examples of hollow verbs include *raad* (want), *naam* (sleep), and *raaH* (go). The following table conjugates these verbs in the present tense.

Remember that hollow verbs—as all other verbs—are listed in the dictionary in the singular masculine third-person past conjugation (the "he" conjugation).

raad (ee)	(want)		naam (aa) (sleep)		raaH (oo) (go)	
Singular	I want	**areed**	I sleep	**anaam**	I go	**arooH**
	you (m) want	**treed**	you (m) sleep	**tnaam**	you (m) go	**trooH**
	you (f) want	**treedeen**	you (f) sleep	**tnaameen**	you (f) go	**trooHeen**
	he wants	**yreed**	he sleeps	**ynaam**	he goes	**yrooH**
	she wants	**treed**	she sleeps	**tnaam**	she goes	**trooH**
Plural	we want	**nreed**	we sleep	**nnaam**	we go	**nrooH**
	you want	**treedoon**	you sleep	**tnaamoon**	you go	**trooHoon**
	they want	**yreedoon**	they sleep	**ynaamoon**	they go	**yrooHoon**

Hollow verbs used in Units 1-12:

3aash (live)	**naam** (sleep)
baa3 (sell)	**raad** (want)
chaan (be)	**raaH** (go)
dhaab (melt)	**Saam** (fast, abstain from eating)
gaal (say)	**saaq** (drive)
gaam (get up)	**Saar** (become)
jaab (bring)	**shaaf** (see)
khaaf (fear, be afraid)	**shaal** (carry)
maat (die)	**zaar** (visit)

Nouns with adjectives

Nouns and their qualifying adjectives agree in gender and number, and both the noun and the qualifying adjective carry the article il- when the noun is definite. For example:

ghurfe maHjooze   a reserved room
il-ghurfe il-maHjooze   the reserved room

When a noun with the definite article is followed by an adjective without an article, they form a sentence, e.g.

il-ghurfe maHjooze.   The room is reserved.

Singular nouns, whether masculine or feminine, which denote inanimate objects, such as *ktaab m* (book) and *ghurfe f* (room), are treated as feminine singular when used in the plural, regardless of their gender in the singular, e.g.

il-ghurfe il-mukeyyefe → **il-ghuref il-mukeyyefe**
(the air-conditioned room)   (the air-conditioned rooms)

il-ktaab ij-jideed → **il-kutub ij-jideede**
(the new book)   (the new books)

The same rule applies when the noun and the adjective form a sentence:

il-ghurfe mukyyefe. → **il-ghuref mukeyyefe.**
(The room is   (The rooms are
air-conditioned.)   air-conditioned.)

il-ktaab jideed. → **il-kutub jideede.**
(The book is new.)   (The books are new.)

Nouns in the genitive (possessive) case

For nouns in the genitive (possessive) case, the following rules apply:

1. The possessing noun ("owner") takes the definite article; the noun that is possessed does not, e.g.

qelem il-weled   the boy's pen/the pen of the boy

2. The possessing noun always follows the noun that is possessed, e.g.

miftaaH + il-ghurfe   →   **miftaaH il-ghurfe**
([the] key) (the room)   (the room's key/the
                                    key of the room)

baab   +   il-biet   →   **baab il-biet**
([the] door)   (the house)   (the house's door/the
                             door of the house)

3. If the possessed noun is a feminine noun ending in –*e*, the ending is changed to –*et*. For example:

ghurfe   (room)   →   **ghurfet il-banaat**
                               (the girls' room)
janTe   (bag)   →   **janTet il-weled**
                               (the boy's bag)

However, if it is a feminine noun ending in -*a*, the ending changes to –*at*, e.g.

jaami3a (university)
→ **jaami3at il-baSre** (the University of Basra)

SafHa (page)
→ **SafHat il-ktaab** (the page of the book)

4. If the possessing noun is a person denoted by a proper name, or a noun with a possessive suffix, it is not preceded by the definite article *il-*. For example:

qelem aHmed   Ahmed's pen
janTet tom   Tom's bag
kutub 3ammi   my uncle's books

Pronoun suffixes attached to verbs as direct objects

Suffixes can be attached to the verb as a direct object, as in the sentence from Dialogue One:

chem yom treed-<u>he</u>?	How many days do you want <u>it</u> for?

The following are sample sentences featuring each pronoun:

-ni (me)
yzoor<u>ni</u>.	He visits <u>me</u>.
tshoof<u>ni</u>.	You see <u>me</u>.

-ek (you [*m sg*])
azoor<u>ek</u>.	I visit <u>you</u>.
tshoof<u>ek</u>.	She sees <u>you</u>.

-ich (you [*f sg*])
ashkur<u>ich</u>.	I thank <u>you</u>.
yzoor<u>ich</u>.	He visits <u>you</u>.

-e (him)
ashkur<u>e</u>.	I thank <u>him</u>.
yzoor<u>e</u>.	He visits <u>him</u>.

-he (her)
ashkur<u>he</u>.	I thank <u>her</u>.
tshoof<u>he</u>.	You see <u>her</u>.

-ne (us)
yishkur<u>ne</u>.	He thanks <u>us</u>.
tshoof<u>ne</u>.	She sees <u>us</u>.

-kum (you [*pl*])
yishkur<u>kum</u>.	He thanks <u>you</u>.
nshoof<u>kum</u>.	We see <u>you</u>.

- hum (them)
> **yishkur<u>hum</u>.**   He thanks them.
> **nzoor<u>hum</u>.**   We visit them.

Pronoun suffixes are discussed further in Unit 12.

The interrogative pronoun *shwekit* (when)

The pronoun *shwekit* (*lit.* what time?) is used in all time-related questions, such as:

> **shwekit maw3id**   When is the doctor's
>   **iT-Tabeeb?**   appointment?
> **shwekit naakul?**   When do we eat?
> **shwekit trooH?**   When are you (*m sg*) going?

The word *shwekit* is a variant of *weqit* (time). This pronunciation is commonly used in the middle and southern parts of Iraq, including Baghdad and Basra. In the northern parts, especially in the city of Mosul, it is pronounced *weqit* and *shweqit*.

V. Exercises

6.1 Conjugate the following hollow verbs in the present tense.

1. *shaaf* (see)

I	
you (*m*)	
you (*f*)	
he	*yshoof*
she	
we	
you (*pl*)	
they	

2. **khaaf** (fear)

I	
you (*m*)	
you (*f*)	
he	*ykhaaf*
she	
we	
you (*pl*)	
they	

3. **baa3** (sell)

I	
you (*m*)	
you (*f*)	
he	*ybee3*
she	
we	
you (*pl*)	
they	

4. **Saam** (fast)

I	
you (*m*)	
you (*f*)	
he	*ySoom*
she	
we	
you (*pl*)	
they	

5.   *3aash* (live)

I	
you (*m*)	
you (*f*)	
he	*y3eesh*
she	
we	
you (*pl*)	
they	

6.2 Translate the following into Iraqi Arabic.

1. they bring
2. he carries
3. you (*pl*) go
4. she wants
5. he becomes
6. I fast
7. you (*m sg*) sleep
8. you (*pl*) play
9. they die
10. we get up

6.3 Translate the following into Iraqi Arabic. New words are indicated on the right.

1. They see the film.   (*filim* → film)
2. You (*pl*) sell furniture.   (*athaath* → furniture)
3. He wants to eat.
4. I sleep early.   (*min weqit* → early)
5. You (*m sg*) go to the university.

6.4 Fill in the blanks with the correct suffix.

1. *ashoof* _____ .   (I see him.)
2. *ysheel* _____ .   (He carries you [*m sg*].)

3. *tilHag* _____ .   (You [*m sg*] follow me.)
4. *tzoor* _____ .   (She visits you [*f sg*].)
5. *ashkur* _____ .   (I thank her.)

6.5   Add the definite article *il-* as needed.

1. *ktaab sam*   (Sam's book)
2. *seyyaaret weled*   (the boy's car)
3. *biet jiddi*   (my grandfather's house)
4. *Tabeeb suzaan*   (Susan's doctor)
5. *deelaab ghurfe*   (the closet of the room;
                                          deelaab → closet)

6.6   Change the following to sentences by adding or deleting the definite article *il-*.

Example: *il-ktaab ij-jideed* → *il-ktaab jideed*

1. *il-biet ich-chibeer.*
2. *shaari3 khaali.*   (*khaali* → deserted)
3. *koob meksoor.*
4. *ir-raadyo il-ghaali.*
5. *maa3oon faarigh.*

6.7   Fill in the blanks using the adjective in parentheses in their correct forms.

Example: *weled* _____ (asleep) → *weled naayim*

1. *mudarriseen* _____   (good)
2. *aDHwiye* _____   (strong)
3. *dawaleeb* _____   (broken)
4. *Sadeeqaat* _____   (dear; *3azeeze* → dear)
5. *temreenaat* _____   (good; *temreen* → exercise)

6.8   Translate into Iraqi Arabic.

1.   He wants to wash the plate.
2.   I want to write.
3.   She wants to listen to the radio.
4.   We want to go to the movies.
5.   They want to sit.

UNIT 7
SHOPPING

I. Dialogues

Dialogue One

Vocabulary

kieloo	kilogram
tuffaaH	apples
aHmer	red (*m*)
aSfar	yellow
tHibb	you (*m sg*) like
laakh	other
khess	lettuce
il-yom	today
aHsen	the best
khosh	good
inTeeni	give me
raasien	two heads
putiete	potatoes
kieluwien	two kilograms
3ineb	grapes
abyeDH	white (*m*)
ma3a il-asef	regrettably
zien la3ad	OK then
shlon	how
reggi	watermelon
Hilu	sweet
fed	just
weSeT	medium size

ti'mur, 3ammi	very well, sir
khelli…	let…
aHuTT-he	I put them (*lit.* her; *see Grammar*)
Sandoog is-seyyaare	the trunk (of the car)
tislem	that's very nice of you

Dialogue

Salim: **areed kieloo tuffaaH.**
(I want a kilogram of apples.)

Grocer: **tuffaaH aHmer lo aSfar?**
(Yellow or red apples?)

Salim: **aHmer.**
(Red.)

Grocer: **tHibb shee laakh?**
(Would you like anything else?)
        m sg

Salim: **3indek khess zien?**
(Do you have good lettuce?)
        m sg

Grocer: **il-yom 3indi aHsen khess.**
(Today, I have the best lettuce.)

Salim: **khosh. inTeeni raasien khess, tlath kieloowaat putiete, w-kieluwien 3ineb abyeDH.**
(Good. Give me two heads of lettuce, three kilograms of potatoes, and two kilograms of white grapes.)

Grocer: **ma3a il-asef. ma 3indi 3ineb abyeDH.**
(I am sorry, I do not have white grapes.)

| Salim: | **zien la3ad, shlon ir-reggi?** |
| | (OK then, how is the watermelon?) |

| Grocer: | **aHmer w-Hilu.** |
| | (Red and sweet.) |

| Salim: | **areed fed tlath reggiyyaat weSeT.** |
| | (I just want three medium-size watermelons.) |

Grocer:	**ti'mur, 3ammi. khelli aHuTT-he b-Sandoog**
	is-seyyaare.
	(Very well, sir. Let me put them in the trunk.)

| Salim: | **tislem, shukran.** |
| | (That's very nice of you, thanks.) |

Dialogue Two

Vocabulary

tHibb	you (*m sg*) like
asaa3dek	I help you (*m sg*)
fed shee	something
qameeS	shirt
azreg	blue (*m*)
Hajim	size
ba3ad shee laakh	anything else
bejaame	pajamas
weSeT	medium
neeli	navy blue (*m*)
bes	only
w-alle	by God
biejee	beige (*m*)
meikhaalif	that's OK
majmoo3	total
baaqi	change (*lit.* the remaining)

Dialogue

Shopkeeper:	**tHibb asaa3idek b-fed shee?**
	(May I help you with anything?)
	m sg

Tom:	**beli, shukran. areed qameeS azreg, Hajim chibeer.**
	(Yes, thanks. I want a blue shirt, size large.)

Shopkeeper:	**tfaDHDHal. tHibb ba3ad shee laakh?**
	(Here you go. Would you like anything else?)
	m sg

Tom:	**3idkum bejaame neeli Hajim weSeT?**
	(Do you have navy pajamas, size medium?)
	pl

Shopkeeper:	**la w-alle, 3idne bes biejee.**
	(No, I am sorry. We have beige only.)

Tom:	**meikhaalif. shged il-majmoo3?**
	(That's OK. How much is the total?)

Shopkeeper:	**khamse w-3ishreen deenaar*.**
	(25 dinars.)

Tom:	**tfaDHDHal.**
	(Here you are.)
	m sg

Shopkeeper:	**shukran, w-haadhe il-baaqi.**
	(Thanks, and here is the change.)

---

*The dinar amounts in this book do not reflect the actual price level in Iraq. They are used for learning purposes only.

II. Notes on Vocabulary and Expressions

Apologizing using *ma3a il-asef*

This is a polite way of apologizing. The expression does not change with the gender or the number of people addressed.

The polite response to the request *ti'mur*

In stores and markets, one often hears a shopkeeper or sales-clerk say *ti'mur* in response to a request. It literally means, "Your request is an order." When addressing a man, it is occasionally followed by *ti'mur 3ammi* (Very well, sir).

The grocer calls Salim *3ammi* (*lit.* my [*paternal*] uncle). In this context, it just means "sir." Again, this is a respectful and amicable way of addressing strangers. However, it is not commonly used when addressing young people.

Similarly, elderly women may be addressed as *khaale* (*lit.* my [maternal] aunt).

The use of *khelli*

The word *khelli* is used to suggest or request permission for a particular action. It is similar to the English "let." Examples:

khelli nrooH lis-seeneme.	Let's go to the movies.
khelli nishreb gahwe.	Let's drink coffee.
khelli anaam hesse.	Let me sleep now.
khelli yishreb hwaaye mei.	Let him drink a lot of water.

The use of the expression *w-alle* (by God) in daily life

The name of God, or *alle*, is commonly invoked in everyday conversation. In sentences like Dialogue Two's *la w-alle, 3idne bes biejee* (No, I am sorry. We have beige only), no religious meaning is intended. The literal meaning of *w-alle* is "by God."

Another mundane expression that includes the name of *alle* is *la b-alle!*, which roughly translates as "You must be kidding!" It is used in response to hearing an extraordinary bit of news.

III. Useful Vocabulary

moz	bananas (*coll*)
baTTeekh	melon (*coll*)
Sandoog purtuqaal	box of oranges
khyaar	cucumber (*coll*)
tamur	dates (*coll*)
betinjaan	eggplant (*coll*)
3armooT	pears (*coll*)
TamaaTa	tomato (*coll*)
gaSSaab	butcher
baggaal	grocer
dukkaan	shop, store
maHall	shop, store
makhzen	shop, store
buTul mei	bottle of water
buTul Haleeb	bottle of milk
masHooq ghaseel	detergent
3uwed shikhkhaaT	matches
ma3joon asnaan	toothpaste
rekheeS	cheap (*m*)
ghaali	expensive (*m*)
taaze	fresh (*m* or *f*)
zgheyyir	small (*m*)

aswed	black (*m*)
akhDHar	green (*m*)
aSfar	yellow (*m*)

nafnoof	dress
fistaan	dress
panTiroon	pants
tannoore	skirt

IV. Grammar

Collective nouns

Many Arabic nouns have a collective, or multiple, form, especially foods. When indicating an individual food item, the feminine suffix *–e* is added to the collective form. The suffix *–yye* is added to collective nouns ending in *–i*. For example:

tuffaaH	apples
tuffaaHe	an (one) apple
moz	bananas
moze	a (one) banana
reggi	watermelons
reggiyye	a (one) watermelon

When indicating two items, the dual feminine ending *–tien* is used instead. For example:

reggitien	two watermelons
tuffaaHtien	two apples
moztien	two bananas

When counting three or more, the feminine plural ending *–aat* (or *-yyaat* for nouns ending in *–i*) is added, e.g.

3ashir reggiyyaat	ten watermelons
tlath tuffaaHaat	three apples
khamis mozaat	five bananas

In Dialogue One, the grocer offers to help carry the three watermelons to the car by saying *khelli aHuTT-he* (*lit.* let me put <u>her</u>). As food items are considered inanimate objects, the plural takes the feminine singular noun form. (See Unit 6.)

The interrogative pronoun *shlon* (how)

The question word *shlon* (*lit.* what color) is used to ask about the nature and quality of things. For example:

shlon ir-reggi?	How is the melon?
shlon ij-jaw?	How is the weather?
shlonek?	How are you?

The pronoun suffixes, discussed in Unit 2, are added to *shlon* when asking people how they are doing, e.g.

shlon<u>ek</u>**?**	How are you (*m sg*)?
shlon<u>ich</u>**?**	How are you (*f sg*)?
shlon<u>kum</u>**?**	How are you (*pl*)?

The use of *fed* and *fed shee*

The word *fed* can have two different functions in a sentence:

1.   By itself, it is an adverb meaning "just" or "only," e.g.

areed fed qelem.	I want just one pen.
areed fed arba3 tuffaaHaat.	I want only four apples.

2. The combination with the word *shee* means "something." For example:

areed ashreb fed shee.	I want to drink something.
khelli agool fed shee.	Let me say something.

The word *ba3ad*

In Dialogue Two, the shopkeeper asks Tom if he would like anything else:

tHibb <u>ba3ad</u> shee laakh?	Would you like anything <u>else</u>?

The word, when unmodified by pronoun suffixes, means "more," and does not change with the gender and number of the noun to which it refers. For example:

areed ba3ad Haleeb.	I want more milk.
nreed nubqe ba3ad yomien.	We want to stay two more days.
yinToon ba3ad floos.	They give more money.

When modified by pronoun suffixes, *ba3ad* means "still," e.g.

muneer w-leila ba3ad<u>hum</u> bil-mooSil.
(Munir and Leila are still in Mosul.)

The word *ba3ad* with pronoun suffixes and the English equivalents:

ba3ad<u>ni</u>...	I am still...
ba3d<u>ek</u>...	you (*m sg*) are still...
ba3d<u>ich</u>...	you (*f sg*) are still...

ba3d<u>e</u>...	he is still...
ba3ad-<u>he</u>...	she is still...
ba3ad<u>ne</u>...	we are still...
ba3ad<u>kum</u>...	you (*pl*) are still...
ba3ad-<u>hum</u>...	they are still...

Verbs with doubled consonants

Verbs with a doubled consonant at the end, such as *Habb* (love) or *HaTT* (put) are conjugated as follows:

	Habb (i) (*love*)		**HaTT (u)** (*put*)	
aani	I love	<u>a</u>Hibb	I put	<u>a</u>HuTT
inte	you (*m*) love	<u>t</u>Hibb	you (*m*) put	<u>t</u>HuTT
inti	you (*f*) love	<u>t</u>Hibb<u>een</u>	you (*f*) put	<u>t</u>HuTT<u>een</u>
huwwe	he loves	<u>y</u>Hibb	he puts	<u>y</u>HuTT
hiyye	she loves	<u>t</u>Hibb	she puts	<u>t</u>HuTT
iHne	we love	<u>n</u>Hibb	we put	<u>n</u>HuTT
intu	you love	<u>t</u>Hibb<u>oon</u>	you put	<u>t</u>HuTT<u>oon</u>
humme	they love	<u>y</u>Hibb<u>oon</u>	they put	<u>y</u>HuTT<u>oon</u>

Verbs with doubled consonants used in Units 1-12:

3add	(count)
dezz	(send)
geSS	(cut)
Habb	(love)
HaTT	(put)
jerr	(pull)
leff	(wrap)
sedd	(close)

Defective verbs ending in –e

Defective verbs end in -e instead of a third-root consonant. In the present tense, there are two key types of defective verbs:

1. Verbs with a final –e that changes to –i in the present tense, e.g. *niTe* (give) or *ije* (come).

niTe (*give*)		
aani	I give	an**T**i
inte	you (*m*) give	**t**inti
inti	you (*f*) give	**t**in**T**een
huwwe	he gives	yin**T**i
hiyye	she gives	**t**in**T**i
iHne	we give	**n**in**T**i
intu	you give	**t**in**T**oon
humme	they give	**y**in**T**oon

ije (*come*)		
aani	I come	a**j**i
inte	you (*m*) come	**t**i**j**i
inti	you (*f*) come	**t**i**j**een
huwwe	he comes	**y**i**j**i
hiyye	she comes	**t**i**j**i
iHne	we come	**n**i**j**i
intu	you come	**t**i**j**oon
humme	they come	**y**i**j**oon

Note that the only conjugations ending in –i are the "I [*aani*]," "you (*m sg*) [*inte*]," "he [*huwwe*]," "she [*hiyye*]," and "we [*iHne*]" forms. In the other forms, the conjugation ends the same way as in the conjugations of sound and hollow verbs. Also note that the conjugation prefixes in the present tense are the same as those for hollow verbs.

Defective verbs ending in –e in the past tense, and –i in the present tense, used in Units 1-12:

biche	(cry)
bide	(begin)
Hiche	(speak)
ije	(come)
lige	(find)
lighe	(cancel)
mile	(fill)
mishe	(walk)
niTe	(give)
rime	(shoot)

---

2. Verbs with a final –e that remains –e in the present tense, e.g. *qire* (read).

	qire (*read*)	
aani	I read	<u>a</u>qr<u>e</u>
inte	you (*m*) read	<u>ti</u>qr<u>e</u>
inti	you (*f*) read	<u>ti</u>qr<u>een</u>
huwwe	he reads	<u>yi</u>qr<u>e</u>
hiyye	she reads	<u>ti</u>qr<u>e</u>
iHne	we read	<u>ni</u>qr<u>e</u>
intu	you read	<u>ti</u>qr<u>oon</u>
humme	they read	<u>yi</u>qr<u>oon</u>

Except for the ending –e in the "I [*aani*]," "you (*m sg*) [*inte*]," "he [*huwwe*]," "she [*hiyye*]," and "we [*iHne*]" forms, there are no other differences between these and the present tense –i verbs in the previous sections.

Defective verbs ending in –e both in the present and in the past tense, used in Units 1-12:

buqe	(stay)
qire	(read)

Verbs with initial *a-*, *i-*, *u-*, or *w-*

1. In verbs with an initial *a-*, such as *akhadh* (take), see that *a-* changes to *aa-* in the present tense.

	akhadh (*take*)	
aani	I take	**aakhudh**
inte	you (*m*) take	**taakhudh**
inti	you (*f*) take	**taakhdheen**
huwwe	he takes	**yaakhudh**
hiyye	she takes	**taakhudh**
iHne	we take	**naakhudh**
intu	you take	**taakhdhoon**
humme	they take	**yaakhdhoon**

Note that in the conjugations ending in *–een* and *–oon*, the *u* in the middle is dropped.

Other initial *a-* verbs found in Units 1-12:

akal (eat)

2. Verbs with an initial *u-*, such as *umer* (command), add a glottal stop in the present tense (') after the *a* of the "I" form, and the *u* of all other conjugations.

	umer (*command*)	
aani	I command	**a'mur**
inte	you (*m*) command	**tu'mur**
inti	you (*f*) command	**tu'mureen**
huwwe	he commands	**yu'mur**
hiyye	she commands	**tu'mur**
iHne	we command	**nu'mur**
intu	you command	**tu'muroon**
humme	they command	**yu'muroon**

3. Verbs with an initial *w-*, such as *wuSel* (arrive), drop the *w* in the present tense, with the *u* generally becoming an *o*.

wuSel (*arrive*)		
aani	I arrive	**oSel**
inte	you (*m*) arrive	**toSel**
inti	you (*f*) arrive	**toSleen**
huwwe	he arrives	**yoSel**
hiyye	she arrives	**toSel**
iHne	we arrive	**noSel**
intu	you arrive	**toSloon**
humme	they arrive	**yoSloon**

Note that in the conjugations ending in *–een* and *–oon*, the *e* between *S* and *l* is dropped.

Other initial *w-* verbs in Units 1-12:

wugef (stand, stop)

V. Exercises

7.1 Conjugate the following verbs in the present tense.

1. **sedd** (close)

I close	
you (*m*) close	
you (*f*) close	
he closes	
she closes	**tsidd**
we close	
you (*pl*) close	
they close	

2. **leff** (wrap)

I wrap	
you (*m*) wrap	
you (*f*) wrap	
he wraps	
she wraps	
we wrap	
you (*pl*) wrap	**tliffoon**
they wrap	

3. **geSS** (cut)

I cut	**aguSS**
you (*m*) cut	
you (*f*) cut	
he cuts	
she cuts	
we cut	
you (*pl*) cut	
they cut	

7.2 Conjugate the following verbs in the present tense.

1. **bide** (begin)

I begin	
you (*m*) begin	
you (*f*) begin	
he begins	
she begins	
we begin	**nibdi**
you (*pl*) begin	
they begin	

2. **mile** (fill)

I fill	
you (*m*) fill	**timli**
you (*f*) fill	
he fills	
she fills	
we fill	
you (*pl*) fill	
they fill	

3. **lige** (find)

I find	
you (*m*) find	
you (*f*) find	
he finds	**yilgi**
she finds	
we find	
you (*pl*) find	
they find	

4. **buqe** (stay)

I stay	
you (*m*) stay	
you (*f*) stay	**tubqeen**
he stays	
she stays	
we stay	
you (*pl*) stay	
they stay	

5. **biche** (cry)

I cry	
you (m) cry	
you (f) cry	
he crys	
she crys	
we cry	
you (pl) cry	
they cry	**yibchoon**

7.3 Transform the following verb conjugations matching each given pronoun.

Example: *aani aHibb* → *humme* _____
→ *yHibboon*

1. *inti taakleen* → *intu* _____
2. *humme yijoon* → *huwwe* _____
3. *iHne naakhudh* → *aani* _____
4. *hiyye tu'mur* → *inte* _____
5. *huwwe yoSel* → *iHne* _____

7.4 Indicate the appropriate personal pronoun for each verb conjugation.

Example: *aqre* → *aani*

1. *njurr*
2. *taakhudh*
3. *timsheen*
4. *tHuTT*
5. *yilghi*
6. *t3iddoon*
7. *tinqudh*
8. *tiHchoon*

9. *nirmi*
10. *adizz*

7.5 Fill in the blanks with the Iraqi Arabic noun in the correct form.

Example: *3ashir* _____ (banana)   → *mozaat*

1. *tisi3* _____ (cucumber)
2. *aani ma aakul* _____. (watermelon)
3. *yishtiri* _____. (eggs)
4. _____ (two melons)
5. *geshsherit arba3* _____ (eggplant)
   (*geshsher* → peel)

7.6 Fill in the blanks appropriately using either *fed* or *fed shee*.

1. *tHibb taakul* _____ *hesse?*   (something)
2. *tHuTT* _____ *purtuqaale bich-chees.* (just)
3. *naakhudh* _____ *thmen mishmishaat.*   (just)
4. *yisma3* _____.   (something)
5. *yishreboon* _____ *baarid.*   (something)

7.7 Fill in the blanks using the correct form of *ba3ad*.

Example: selma _____ tibchi. → selma ba3ad-he tibchi.

1. *iHne* _____ joo3aaneen. (*joo3aan* → hungry)
2. *HuTTi* _____ *qelemien bij-janTe.*
3. *il-ghurfe* _____ *baarde.*
4. *treedoon tshoofoon* _____ *filmien?*
5. *il-banaat* _____ *bil-medrese.*

UNIT 8

FINDING YOUR WAY

I. Dialogues

Dialogue One

Vocabulary

wizaaret it-terbiye	Ministry of Education
il-3afu	pardon me, I am sorry
ma sima3it	I did not hear
sh-gilit	what you (*m sg*) said
shged tib3id	how far (*for use with feminine nouns*)
ya3ni	in other words, you mean
arooh il-he	I get to it
meshi	on foot
bit-ta'keed	certainly
bes	just, only
u3bur!	Pass (*m sg*)!
baanzeen khaane	gas station
maHall il-feeterchi	auto repair shop
ba3dien	then
imshi!	Walk (*m sg*)!
gubel	straight ahead
ila an	until
toSel	you (*m sg*) reach
aDHwiyet il-muroor	traffic lights
iksir!	Turn (*m sg*)!
yimne	right
Hawaali	about
deqaayiq	minutes

yisre	left
la tloof!	Do not turn (*m sg*)!
Hadeeqe 3aamme	public garden
gbaal	across from, in front of
shukran 3ala	thanks for
il-irshaadaat	directions
deqeeqe	exact (*f*)

Dialogue

Ahmed: **rajaa'an, wien wizaaret it-terbiye?**
            (Where is the Ministry of Education, please?)

Passer-by: **il-3afu, ma sima3it sh-gilit.**
            (I am sorry, I did not hear what you said.)
                                    m sg

Ahmed: **wizaaret it-terbiye, shged tib3id min hna?**
            (The Ministry of Education, how far is it from here?)

Passer-by: **ma hwaaye.**
            (Not far. [*lit.* Not much.])

Ahmed: **ya3ni, agder arooH il-he meshi?**
            (In other words, can I walk to it?)

Passer-by: **bit-ta'keed. bes u3bur haadhi il-baanzeen
            khaane w-maHall il-feeterchi. w-ba3dien imshi
            gubel ila an toSel aDHwiyet il-muroor.**
            (Certainly, you just pass this gas station and the
                        m sg
            auto repair shop. Then go straight ahead until you
            get to the traffic lights.)   *m sg*
            get to the traffic lights.)

Ahmed: **ee, w-ba3dien?**
            (Yes, and then?)

Passer-by: **iksir yimne, w-imshi Hawaali 3ashir deqaayiq.**
la tloof yimne aw yisre ila an tshoof Hadeeqe
3aamme. wizaaret it-terbiye binaaye chibeere
gbaal il-Hadeeqe.
(Turn right, and walk about ten minutes. Do not
turn right or left until you see a public garden.

m sg
The Ministry of Education is a big building across
from the garden.)

Ahmed: **shukran 3ala il-irshaadaat id-deqeeqe.**
(Thanks for the exact directions.)

Dialogue Two

Vocabulary

inTeeni!	Give (*m sg*) me!
hawiyye	ID card
ijaazet is-siyaaqe	driver's license
iftaH!	Open (*m sg*)!
Sandoog is-seyyaare	trunk of the car
sidd!	Close (*m sg*)!
gul-li!	Tell (*m sg*) me!
kielumetir	kilometer
shaari3	street
la tsooq!	Do not drive (*m sg*)!
ukhudh!	Take (*m sg*)!
taHweele	detour
sooq!	Drive (*m sg*)!
Hasab	according to
ishaaraat	signs
akhi	sir (*lit.* my brother)
fee-maan-illa	good-bye (*lit.* may you go with God's protection)

Dialogue

Officer: **inTeeni il-hawiyye w-ijaazet is-siyaaqe, rajaa'an,
            w-iftaH Sandoog is-seyyaare.**
            (Give me the ID card and driver's license, please,
            and open the trunk.)

Salim: **tfaDHDHal.**
            (Here they are.)

Officer: **shukran. sidd iS-Sandoog.**
            (Thanks. Close the trunk.)

Salim: **gul-li, chem kielumetir yib3id shaari3 ir-resheed
            3an hna?**
            (Tell me, how many kilometers away is Al-Rasheed
            Street from here?)

Officer: **Hawwaali kielumetrien.**
            (Around 2 kilometers.)

Salim: **agder aakhudh haadhe ish-shaari3?**
            (Can I take this street?)

Officer: **la. la tsooq b-haadhe ish-shaari3. ukhudh
            hedheech it-taHweele, w-sooq Hasab il-ishaaraat.**
            (No, do not drive on this street. Take that detour,
            and drive according to the signs.)

Salim: **shukran, akhi, fee-maan-illa.**
            (Thanks, sir. Good-bye.)

II. Notes on Vocabulary and Expressions

Thanking for something specific (*shukran 3ala...*)

To thank someone for something specific, say *shukran* (thanks), followed by *3ala* (for), and then the reason for one's gratitude.

> **shukran 3ala il-irshaadaat id-deqeeqe.**
> Thanks for the exact directions.

> **shukran 3ala in-naSeeHa.**
> Thanks for the advice.

Politely asking others to repeat something

The expression *il-3afu* (*lit.* pardon me) may be used in formal situations to request that something be repeated.

In casual situations, one might say *shinoo?* (What?) or *ha?*

Saying "good-bye"

Expressions for "good-bye" include *ma3a s-salaame* (may peace accompany you) and *fee-maan-illa* (may you go with God's protection). One replies by repeating *fee-maan-illa*. However, in casual circumstances, younger people may say *bei-baai* (bye-bye).

Addressing strangers

When talking to strangers, *akhi* (*lit.* my brother) is commonly used as a respectful and friendly address. One hears it on the street, when shopping, and in government offices. A woman may be addressed as *ukhti* (*lit.* my sister). The words *ikhwaan* (*lit.* brothers) or *khawaati* (*lit.* sisters) are used when speaking with two or more people.

III. Useful Vocabulary

darboone	alley
jisir	bridge
binaaye	building
ziwiyye	corner
madkhal	entrance
ma3mal	factory
mazra3a	farm
Tareeq khaariji	highway
biet	house
khareeTe	map
ittijaah waaHid	one-way (street)
mawqif seyyaaraat	parking lot
Tareeq	road
medrese	school
3uber ish-shaari3	cross the street
nefeq	tunnel
(ta3aal) waraaye!	Follow (*m sg*) me!
irja3!	Go (*m sg*) back!
yelle!	Let's go!
bi3eed	far (*m*)
saree3	fast
DHaayi3	lost (*adj m sg*)
qareeb	nearby
baTee'	slow (*m*)
sherq	east
shimaal	north
jinoob	south
gharb	west

IV. Grammar

The adverb *gubel* and the preposition *gbaal*

The words *gubel* and *gbaal* may sound rather similar. However, they have very different meanings.

The word *gubel*, which means "straight ahead," is an adverb, as in:

> **imshi gubel ila an toSel aDHwiyet il-muroor.**
> (Go straight ahead until you get to the traffic lights.)

(Another word for "straight ahead" is *ilal-amaam*, as in *ilal-amaam, sir!* [March forward!], the military command to march.)

The word *gbaal* is a preposition meaning "across from" or "in front of," as in:

> **wizaaret it-terbiye gbaal il-Hadeeqe.**
> (The Ministry of Education is in front of the garden.)

The use of *bes*

The word *bes* can have two different meanings:

1. An adverb in the sense of "just" or "only," e.g.

bes u3bur haadhi	Just pass this gas station.
il-baanzeen khaane.	
areed bes qelem waaHid.	I want just one pen.
bes areed arooH.	I just want to go.

    The difference between *bes* and *fed* (discussed in Unit 7) is that *bes* is more emphatic.

2. A conjunction similar to the English "but," e.g.

hesse weqit ghede bes	It is lunchtime now, but I
aani ma joo3aan.	am not hungry.

Another equivalent for "but" is *laakin*, e.g.

aHtaaj baanzeen laakin il-baanzeen-khaane masdoode.
(I need gas but the gas station is closed.)

Asking about distances

There are two ways of asking about a location:

1.　Using *wien*, the equivalent of the English "where," e.g.

wien wizaaret it-terbiye?　　Where is the Ministry
of Education?

2.　Using *shged yib3id* / *tib3id*, the equivalent of the phrase "how far is …," e.g.

shged yib3id ij-jisir min hna?
(How far is the bridge from here?)

shged tib3id wizaaret it-terbiye min hna?
(How far is the Ministry of Education from here?)

The words *yib3id* and *tib3id* are conjugations of the verb *yib3id* (be away). They are, respectively, the equivalents of "he is away" and "she is away." Use *yib3id* when the gender of the place noun being asked about is masculine. Use *tib3id* when the gender is feminine.

The imperative

The imperative is the form used when giving a command. Verbs in the imperative have three conjugations, one for each of the three forms of you: *inte*, *inti*, and *intu*. The following shows how to form the imperative for each of the different verb types.

1.   Sound verbs

Verb	you (m sg) [*inte*]	you (f sg) [*inti*]	you (pl) [*intu*]
kiser	**iksir**	**ikisri**	**ikisru**
3uber	**u3bur**	**u3ubri**	**u3ubru**
fitaH	**iftaH**	**ifitHi**	**ifitHu**

2.   Hollow verbs

Verb	you (m sg) [*inte*]	you (f sg) [*inti*]	you (pl) [*intu*]
jaab	**jeeb**	**jeebi**	**jeebu**
gaal	**gool**	**gooli**	**goolu**

With the verb *ygool* (say, tell), the equivalent for "Tell me!" is formed by adding the suffix –*li* (me) to the conjugation. The spelling and pronunciation of the verb also change slightly.

gool	→	**gul-li**
gooli	→	**gulli-li**
goolu	→	**gullu-li**

The phrase *gul-li* appears in this unit's Dialogue Two.

3.   Verbs with doubled consonants

Verb	you (m sg) [*inte*]	you (f sg) [*inti*]	you (pl) [*intu*]
sedd	**sidd**	**siddi**	**siddu**
HaTT	**HuTT**	**HuTTi**	**HuTTu**

4.   Defective verbs

Verb	you (m sg) [*inte*]	you (f sg) [*inti*]	you (pl) [*intu*]
mishe	**imshi**	**imshi**	**imshu**
niTe	**inTi**	**inTi**	**inTu**

5. Verbs with an initial *a-*

Verb	you (m sg) [*inte*]	you (f sg) [*inti*]	you (pl) [*intu*]
akhadh	**ukhudh**	**ukhdhi**	**ukhdhu**
akal	**ukul**	**ukli**	**uklu**

6. Verbs with an initial *w-*

Verb	you (m sg) [*inte*]	you (f sg) [*inti*]	you (pl) [*intu*]
wugef	**ogef**	**ogfi**	**ogfu**
wuSel	**oSel**	**oSli**	**oSlu**

The negative imperative

The negative imperative is formed by placing *la* before the verb. The verb is conjugated in the present tense, not the imperative. Examples:

la til3ab bish-shaari3!	Don't play in the street! (*addressing a male*)
la trooHeen hnak!	Don't go there! (*addressing a female*)
la taakloon b-haadhe il-maT3am!	Don't eat at this restaurant! (*addressing a group*)

The conjunction *ila an*

The equivalent of the conjunction "until" is *ila an*.

imshi ila an tshoof aDHwiyet il-muroor.	Walk until you see the traffic lights.

Pronouns and the preposition *l-*

In Unit 5, the use of the preposition *l-* (to, for) was demonstrated with nouns. An example:

areed aktib l-saalim.   I want to write to Salim.

It is used similarly with pronoun suffixes, e.g.

areed aktib le.   I want to write to him.

The use of *l-* with each of the pronoun suffixes, using the word *aTbukh* (I cook), is demonstrated below. Note that when the pronoun suffix begins with a consonant, *l-* becomes *il-*. With the "us" suffix *–ne*, it becomes *in-*.

aTbukh li.	I cook for me.
aTbukh lek.	I cook for you (*m sg*).
aTbukh lich.	I cook for you (*f sg*).
aTbukh le.	I cook for him.
aTbukh il-he.	I cook for her.
aTbukh in-ne.	I cook for us.
aTbukh il-kum.	I cook for you (*pl*).
aTbukh il-hum.	I cook for them.

V. Exercises

8.1 Translate the following in the imperative:

1. Walk! (*pl*)
2. Eat! (*m sg*)
3. Stay! (*f sg*)
4. Write! (*m sg*)
5. Stop! (*pl*)
6. Pull! (*m sg*)
7. Drive! (*f sg*)

8.2   Give the negative of each command

Example: rooHi hnak!
           → la trooHeen hnak!

1. *rooHu hnak!*
2. *sidd il-baab!*
3. *ukhdhi ij-janTe!*
4. *idukhli il-binaaye!*   (dikhel → enter)
5. *ugumzu!*   (gumez → jump)

8.3   Translate the following using *gubel* and *gbaal*.

1. Walk forward. (*addressed to a group of people*)
2. The school is across from the garden.
3. Don't stand in front of the fireplace. (*addressed to a boy or a man*; fireplace → *medfe'e*)
4. Go straight ahead until you reach the bus stop. (*addressed to a girl or a woman*; the bus stop → *mawqif il-paS*)
5. There is a car in front of the house.

8.4   Fill in the blanks with the appropriate word.

Example: _____ *areed arooH.* (just)
           → bes areed arooH.

1. *3ndi _____ qelem waaHid.* (only)
2. *ukul _____ tishba3.* (until)
3. *id-dinye Haarre _____ maku kahrabaa'.* (but)
4. *aani ashreb _____ koobien chai bil-yom.* (only; *bil-yom* → per day)
5. *urukDHu _____ toSloon il-3alaame.* (until; *3alaame* → sign)

8.5 Translate each of the following. If the indirect object is a noun, translate a second time with the indirect object changed to the appropriate pronoun. (Note: The new words in the parentheses are not necessarily the indirect objects of the sentences.)

Example: I go to the restaurant. (restaurant → *maT3am* [*m*])
    1) *arooH lil-maT3am.*
    2) *arooH le.*

1. I am cooking a chicken for you (*f sg*). (chicken → *dijaaje* [*f*])
2. We are coming to the school.
3. She is writing a letter to me.
4. He sells books to you (*f sg*).
5. He is walking to the gardens. (gardens → *Hadaayiq* [*f*])
6. We are sending an e-mail to the newspaper editors. (e-mail → *eemiel* [*m*]; the newspaper editors → *muHarrireen ij-jereede* [*m pl*])
7. Do you allow the kids to play here? (the kids → *aTfaal* [*m pl*])
8. She is drawing a beautiful picture for you (*m sg*).
9. I am buying pens for us.
10. Open the door for the guests. (*addressed to a boy or a man*; the guests → *il-khuTTaar* [*m pl*])

UNIT 9

ON THE TELEPHONE

I.   Dialogues

Dialogue One

Vocabulary

atkallam	I speak
wiyye	with
minu	who
mudeer	headmaster (*also* director)
medreset il-manSoor il-ibtidaa'iyye	al-Mansur Elementary School
ijtimaa3	business meeting
yintihi	ends (*i.e.* the meeting [*m noun*] ends)
saa3a wiHde w-nuSS	at 1:30 PM
Teyyib	OK then
mumkin tgoolee-le	can you (*f sg*) tell him
khaaber	he called
ynaaqish	he discusses
wiyyaak	with you (*m sg*)
mawDHoo3	subject
ta3yeen	hiring (*lit.* appointing)
mu3allimeen	teachers
raqam	number
mukarrar sab3a	seven-seven (*lit.* double seven)

Dialogue

Salim: **aloo, marHabe. agder atkallam wiyye seyyid muneer?**
(Hello, may I talk to Mr. Munir?)

Secretary: **minu HaDHirtek?**
(Who are you?)
m sg

Salim: **saalim salmaan, mudeer medreset il-manSoor il-ibtidaa'iyye.**
(Salim Salman, Headmaster of al-Mansur Elementary School.)

Secretary: **seyyid muneer 3inde ijtimaa3 hesse.**
(Mr. Munir has a meeting right now.)

Salim: **shwekit yintihi il-ijtimaa3, rajaa'an?**
(When does the meeting end, please?)

Secretary: **saa3a wiHde w-nuSS.**
(At 1:30 PM.)

Salim: **Teyyib, mumkin tgoolee-le saalim khaaber, w-yreed ynaaqish wiyyaak mawDHoo3 ta3yeen mu3allimeen.**
(OK then, would you tell him that Salim called,
f sg
and wants to discuss [with you] the subject of
m sg
hiring teachers.)

Secretary: **Teyyib, shged raqam telifon HaDHirtek?**
(OK, what is your phone number?)
m sg

Salim:	mukarrar sab3a, arba3a, tlaathe, thmaanye, Sifir, waaHid.
	(seven-seven-four-three-eight-zero-one.)

Secretary:	Teyyib seyyid saalim. ma3a s-salaame.
	(Very well, Mr. Salim. Good-bye.)

Dialogue Two

Vocabulary

3iyaade	doctor's office
maw3id	appointment
il-isboo3 ij-jaay	next week
Haaltek	your (*m sg*) condition
mista3jile	needing immediate attention
liesh	why
li-annahu	because
asewwi	I do
faHiS 3aam	general check-up
senewi	annual
taHleel demm	blood test
maHjooz	booked
sheher	month
neesaan	April
yaa	which
yom	day
il-arbi3aa'	Wednesday
saa3a khamse ille rubu3	at a quarter to five
3aadeten	usually
ashtughul	I work
saa3a khamse	five o'clock
tgheyyir	you (*m sg*) change
sitte w-nuSS	half past six
kullish zien	very good
muraaji3	patient
jideed	new
in-naqqaal	cell phone

Dialogue

Ahmed: **aloo, marHabe, 3iyyaadet id-diktor ibraheem il-Haarithi?**
(Hello, is this the office of Dr. Ibrahim al-Harithi?)

Secretary: **ee na3am, tfaDHDHal.**
(Yes, it is. How may I help you?)

Ahmed: **areed asewwi maw3id lil-isboo3 ij-jaay.**
(I would like to make an appointment for [the] next week.)

Secretary: **Haaltek mista3jile?**
(Does your condition need prompt attention?)
   m sg

Ahmed: **la.**
(No.)

Secretary: **liesh treed tshoof iT-Tabeeb?**
(Why do you want to see the doctor?)
   m sg

Ahmed: **li-annahu areed asewwi faHiS senewi 3aam, w-taHleel demm.**
(Because I would like to have an annual check-up, and a blood test.)

Secretary: **id-diktor maHjooz ila sheher neesaan.**
(The doctor is booked until April.)

Ahmed: **meikhaalif. yaa yom?**
(That's OK. What day [will he be available]?)

Secretary: **yom il-arbi3aa' 3ishreen bish-sheher zien?**
(Is Wednesday the 20th good for you?)

Ahmed: **beli, zien. yaa saa3a?**
              (Yes, it is. What time?)

Secretary: **saa3a khamse ille rubu3.**
              (At 4:45.)

Ahmed: **aani 3aadeten ashtughul ila saa3a khamse.**
              tigder tgheyyir il-maw3id?
              (I usually work till 5:00. Can you change the
              appointment?)   *m sg*
              appointment?)

Secretary: **sitte w-nuSS zien?**
              (Is 6:30 good?)

Ahmed: **kullish zien.**
              (Very good.)

Secretary: **HaDHirtek muraaji3 jideed?**
              (Are you a new patient?)
              m sg

Ahmed: **beli.**
              (Yes.)

Secretary: **Teyyib: ismek, w-raqam it-telifon, rajaaʻan.**
              (OK then, your name and phone number, please.)
              m sg

Ahmed: **aHmed manSoor, w-raqam in-naqqaal**
              thmaanye, sitte, mukarrar arba3a, khamse,
              mukarrar waaHid.
              (Ahmed Mansur, and my cell phone number is
              8644511.)

Secretary: **shukran. ma3a s-salaame.**
              (Thanks. Good-bye.)

II. Notes on Vocabulary and Expressions

Formal and polite address

In formal situations, one addresses a man with *HaDHirtek* instead of *inte* (you). A woman is addressed with *HaDHirtich* instead of *inti*.

The calendar

These are the months of the year in Iraqi Arabic:

kaanoon ith-thaani	January
shbaaT	February
adhaar	March
neesaan	April
eyyaar	May
Huzeiraan	June
tammooz	July
aab	August
eilool	September
tishreen il-awwel	October
tishreen ith-thaani	November
kaanoon il-awwel	December

The Islamic calendar is used in religious contexts. The most important Islamic months are:

ramaDHaan	the month of fasting (spelled *Ramadan* in the West)
dhul-Hijje	the month of pilgrimages to Mecca (*il-Hajj*)
muHarram	the first month in the calendar

It should be noted that the Islamic calendar is different from the Western calendar. Following the moon phase, the Islamic year also has 12 months but it is shorter than the solar year on which the Western calendar is based, with the result that Muslim holidays are usually 11 days earlier on the Western calendar each year.

Seasons of the year

rabee3	spring	**khareef**	fall
Sief	summer	**shite**	winter

Days of the week

is-sabit – Saturday	**il-arbi3aa'** – Wednesday
il-aHHad – Sunday	**il-khamees** – Thursday
ith-thinien – Monday	**ij-jum3a** – Friday
ith-thelaathaa' – Tuesday	

In Iraq, the first day of the week is *is-sabit*. The weekend is one day rather than two, and falls on *ij-jum3a*.

The word *yom* (day) may be used before the name of the day of the week, e.g. *yom il-khamees.*

All days, with the exception of *ij-jum3a*, are masculine nouns. Adjectives modifying them, of course, agree in gender, e.g.

ith-thinien ij-jaay	next Monday
ij-jum3a ij-jaaye	next Friday

Times of the day

fejir – dawn	**mughrub** – evening
SubuH – morning	**liel** – night
DHuhur – noon	**nuSS il-liel** – midnight
3aSir – afternoon	

III. Useful Vocabulary

uTle	holiday
saa3a	hour
deqeeqe	minute
faSil	season
thaaniye	second
isboo3	week
nihaayet il-isboo3	weekend
sene	year
yawmi	daily (*m*)
min weqit	early
il-faat	last (*m*)
mit'akhkhir	late
ba3dien	later
shehri	monthly (*m*)
il-khaTT mashghool	the line is busy
isboo3i	weekly (*m*)

IV. Grammar

Dropping and blending letters between words

Dropping and/or blending letters between words is quite common in Iraqi Arabic. There are few general rules, so, when these instances occur in this book, they are explained on an individual basis.

One such rule is when a word ending in -*n* is followed by a word beginning in *l*-. This occurs in Dialogue One, when Salim asks the secretary:

> **mumkin <u>tgoolee-le</u> saalim khaaber?**

The words *tgooleen* (you tell) and *le* (him) combine to create *tgoolee le*. The *-n* is dropped because of the difficulty of pronouncing the *l-* in conjunction with it.

Days of the month

When referring to a specific day of the month, the number is followed by the expression *bish-sheher* (of the month), as in:

3ashre bish-sheher	the 10th of the month
3ishreen bish-sheher	the 20th of the month

When stating the day of a specific month, the day comes first and the month second, e.g.

waaHid eyyaar	May 1st (*lit.* 1 May)
thmunTa3ash kaanoon il-awwel	December 18th (*lit.* 18 December)

Note that, unlike English, the cardinal numbers (1, 2, 3, etc.) are used instead of the ordinal numbers (1st, 2nd, 3rd, etc.).

(The years are discussed in Unit 10.)

Telling time

When asking the time, Iraqis say:

ibbiesh is-saa3a?	What hour is it?

When replying, one says *saa3a* (hour, o'clock, time) followed by the hour number, e.g.

saa3a wiHde	one o'clock
saa3a thintien	two o'clock
saa3a tlaathe	three o'clock

To ask about a specific time, one uses the word *shwekit* (when), e.g.

| **shwekit yibdi** | When does the program |
| **il-barnaamej?** | begin? |

The reply is the same as when asking about the hour. There is no equivalent to the English preposition "at" for adverbs of time, e.g.

yintihi il-ijtimaa3 saa3a	The meeting ends *at* 1:00.
wiHde.	
aHmad 3inde maw3id	Ahmed has an appointment
saa3a thintien.	*at* 2:00.

There is no equivalent for "AM" or "PM" in Iraqi Arabic.

The part of the day is sometimes added to the specific hour, e.g.

| **saa3a khamse iS-SubuH** | 5:00 in the morning |

The words for the fractions of the hour are:

| **rubu3** | quarter | **nuSS** | half |
| **thilith** | 20 minutes | **tlat-arbaa3** | three-quarters |

The conjunction *w-* (and) is used with fractions that are "after" or "past" the hour, e.g.

sitte w-khamse	6:05
sab3a w-3ashre	7:10
thmaanye w-rubu3	8:15
tis3a w-thilith	9:20
arba3a w-nuSS ille khamse	4:25
khamse w-nuSS	5:30
da3ash w-nuSS w-khamse	11:35

The word *ille* (to) is used with fractions that are "before," "until," or "to" the hour, e.g.

wiHde ille thilith	12:40
sitte ille rubu3	5:45
sab3a ille 3ashre	6:50
thmaanye ille khamse	7:55

The interrogative pronoun *yaa*

The interrogative pronoun *yaa* (which) has one form, regardless of gender and number, e.g.

yaa Sadeeqe tHibb azyad?	Which friend do you (*f sg*) like more?
yaa yom tinzil l-baghdaad?	Which day do you (*m sg*) go down to Baghdad?
yaa tuffaaHa treedeen?	Which apple do you (*f sg*) want?
yaa muterjimeen aHsen?	Which translators are better?

The interrogative pronoun *minu*

The interrogative pronoun *minu* (who) also has only one form. Examples:

minu yiji wiyyaaye?	Who comes with me?
minu Sadeeqaatek?	Who are your friends?

The interrogative pronoun *liesh* and the reply *li-annahu*

The word *liesh* means "why" in Iraqi Arabic. Replies generally begin with the preposition *li-annahu* (because). Examples:

liesh tiji mit'akhkhir?	<u>Why</u> do you come late?
li-annahu ma 3indi	<u>Because</u> I do not have
seyyaare.	a car.

liesh ma 3indich hawiyye?	<u>Why</u> don't you have an ID?
li-annahu il-hawiyye	<u>Because</u> the ID is lost.
DHaay3a.	

liesh tila3boon hna?	<u>Why</u> do you play here?
li-annahu maku hwaaye	<u>Because</u> there aren't a lot
seyyaaraat bish-shaari3.	of cars on the street.

The preposition *wiyye*

The preposition *wiyye* is the equivalent of the conjunction "with." Examples:

arooH <u>wiyye</u> Sadeeqti	I go to the movies <u>with</u>
lis-seeneme.	my girlfriend.
nrooH <u>wiyye</u> aSdiqaa'ne	We go to the movies <u>with</u>
lis-seeneme.	our friends.

As with other prepositions, pronoun suffixes can be attached to *wiyye*, e.g.

wiyyaa<u>ye</u>	with me
wiyyaa<u>k</u>	with you (*m sg*)
wiyyaa<u>ch</u>	with you (*f sg*)
wiyyaa	with him
wiyyaa<u>he</u>	with her
wiyyaa<u>ne</u>	with us
wiyyaa<u>kum</u>	with you (*pl*)
wiyyaa<u>hum</u>	with them

Note that the final *-e* of *wiyye* is dropped when adding pronoun suffixes.

Derived verbs

Arabic has several verb groups called *derived verbs*. These are verbs that are created by systematically adding letters or doubling the root consonants of the basic verbs discussed in previous units, thus extending or modifying the meaning of the basic verb. Although definition patterns can be established for some of the groups, it is recommended to treat derived verbs as vocabulary words in their own right when learning vocabulary. Examples:

Siref	spend (time, money)
Sarref	exchange money

kiser	break (*transitive verb, active meaning*)
inkiser	get broken, be broken (*intransitive verb, passive meaning*)

There are ten groups of derived verbs. In the dictionary sections of this book, as in Arabic grammar books, and some Arabic-English dictionaries, the groups of derived verbs are denoted with Roman numerals between I and X.

The following six are the most important derived verb groups.

Group II: The middle consonant is doubled. Examples:

gheyyer	change (something)
jadded	renew
Hawwel	transfer
sejjel	enroll
Sarref	exchange money
jarreb	try

In this group, verbs are transitive, i.e. they indicate an action performed on someone or something. For example: *jadded (yjaddid) ij-jawaaz* "renew the passport."

Group III: The long vowel *aa* is inserted between the first and the second consonant, e.g.

khaaber	call
naaqesh	discuss
waafeq	agree

In this group, verbs can be transitive, as in *naaqesh* (*ynaaqish*) *il-ktaab* "discuss the book," or intransitive, i.e. verbs without an object, as in *waafeq* (*ywaafuq*) "agree."

Group V: The middle root consonant is doubled, and an initial *t-* is added to the verb, e.g.

tgheyyer	change, alter
tkallam	speak
tSawwer	think, suppose

In this group, verbs are reflexive, i.e. the action reflects back on the subject noun. For example: *tgheyyer ij-jaw* "the weather changed."

Group VI: The long vowel *aa* is inserted between the first and the second consonant, and an initial *t-* is added. Examples:

tkhaaber	talk on the phone with
t3aaref	get acquainted with
t3aamel	bargain with

In this group, verbs indicate mutual action between the people involved in the action. The preposition *wiyye* "with" is usually used to indicate the mutual action. For example: *t3aamel wiyye il-baggaal* "he bargained with the shopkeeper."

Group VIII: The letter *t-* is inserted after the first root consonant. Examples include:

sh̲t̲ighel	work
sh̲t̲ire	buy
in̲t̲ihe	end

Some verbs in this group, such as *intihe* above, have an initial *i*. This is to ease pronunciation when the addition of the *t* by itself would make the word difficult to pronounce.

The verbs can be transitive, as in *shtire ktaab* "he bought a book," or intransitive as in *intihe il-filim* "the movie ended."

Group X: The prefix *(i)st-* is added to the verb. Examples:

i̲s̲ta3jel	hurry
s̲t̲emarr	continue
s̲t̲a3mal	use

In this group verbs can be transitive, as in *sta3mal is-seyyaare* (he used the car), or intransitive, as in *aHmed ista3jel* "Ahmad hurried."

The present tense of derived verbs

Below are examples of derived verb conjugations in the present tense. Note that certain vowel changes occur in the present tense.

To find out how to conjugate a derived verb in the present tense, please consult the dictionary included in this book, which lists the present tense in brackets.

		Group II Sarr**e**f (u)	Group III naaq**e**sh (i)	Group V tkallam (a)
Singular	aani	asarruf	anaaqish	atkallam
	inte	tSarruf	tnaaqish	titkallam
	inti	tsarrufeen	tnaaqsheen	titkall**i**meen
	huwwe	ySarruf	ynaaqish	yitkallam
	hiyye	tSarruf	tnaaqish	titkallam
Plural	ihne	nSarruf	**i**nnaaqish	nitkallam
	intu	tSarrufoon	tnaaqshoon	titkall**i**moon
	humme	ySarrufoon	ynaaqshoon	yitkall**i**moon

		Group VI tkhaaber (aa)	Group VIII shtigh**e**l (u)	Group X sta3m**a**l (i)
Singular	aani	atkhaaber	ashtughul	asta3mil
	inte	titkhaaber	tishtughul	tista3mil
	inti	titkhaabreen	tisht**a**ghleen	tista3mileen
	huwwe	yitkhaaber	yishtughul	yista3mil
	hiyye	titkhaaber	tishtughul	tista3mil
Plural	ihne	nitkhaaber	nishtughul	nista3mil
	intu	titkhaabroon	tisht**a**ghloon	tista3miloon
	humme	yitkaabrron	yisht**a**ghloon	yista3miloon

V. Exercises

9.1 Conjugate the verb in the present tense, in the person indicated.

1.	*steraaH (yistereeH)*	(we)
2.	*sejjel (ysejjil)*	(you *m*)
3.	*t3aaref (yit3aaref)*	(they)
4.	*naaqesh (ynaaqish)*	(I)
5.	*shtire (yishtiri)*	(you *pl*)
6.	*tgheyyer (yitgheyyer)*	(she)

9.2 Write out the time in Iraqi Arabic.

1. 2:30
2. 6:50
3. 11:35
4. 12:05
5. 3:40
6. 5:15

9.3 Write out the dates in Iraqi Arabic.

1. April 5th
2. September 17th
3. January 6th
4. February 14th
5. July 4th

9.4 Fill in the blanks by translating the indicated word in Iraqi Arabic.

1.	_____	*ktaab tHibboon azyad?*	(which)
2.	_____	*il-biet ma naDHeef?*	(why)
3.	_____	*yreed yishreb chai?*	(who)
4.	_____	*ayyaam tishtaghleen?*	(which)
5.	*intu* _____	*ta3baaneen il-yom?*	(why)

9.5 Replace the underlined words with *wiyye* and the appropriate pronoun.

Example: *aHmed yishtughul <u>wiyye iT-tebeeb</u>.*
                    aHmed yishtughul <u>wiyyaa</u>.

1. *areed anaaqish il-ktaab <u>wiyye iT-tullaab</u>.*
2. *zeki yil3ab <u>wiyye Leila</u>.*
3. *3indi maw3id <u>wiyye iT-Tabeeb</u> saa3a khamse w-nuSS.*
4. *minu yreed yrooH lis-seeneme <u>wiyye il-benaat</u>?*
5. *aani ma aqder ashtughul <u>wiyye il-muhandiseen</u>.*

9.6 Translate the following sentences into Iraqi Arabic.

1. In Iraq, Saturday is the first day of the week.
2. January is the first month of the year.
3. In the United States, Sunday is the first day of the week.
4. In Iraq, the banks are closed on Friday.
5. The children are in school until 2:00.

UNIT 10

MEDICAL AND PERSONAL CARE

I. Dialogues

Dialogue One

Vocabulary

is-salaamu 3aleikum	Hello (*lit.* May peace be upon you)
istereeH	Have a seat (*lit.* Have some rest)
alla bil-khier	*common male greeting* (*lit.* May God bless you)
min esh	from what
tishtiki	you (*m sg*) complain
zukaam	a cold
Sudaa3	headache
shedeed	strong (*m*)
bidet	started (*f*)
a3raaDH	symptoms
il-baarHa	yesterday
aqees Haraartek	I am taking your (*m sg*) temperature
sh-akhadhit	what did you (*m sg*) take
adwiye	medicine (*pl*)
shweyye	a little
3aalye	high (*f*)
DHaghTak	your (*m sg*) blood pressure
Tabee3i	normal (*m*)
gaHHa	cough
tish3ur	you (*m sg*) feel
alem	pain
Hunjurtek	your (*m sg*) throat

adhaanek	your (*m sg*) ears
Hassaasiyye min	allergy to
raachiete	prescription
laazim	must
duwe	medicine
b-intiDHaam	regularly
akil khefeef	light food
la tinse	do not forget (*m sg*)
tishreb	you (*m sg*) drink
sawaail	liquids
raaji3ni	come back (*m sg*) to [see] me

Dialogue

Tom: **is-salaamu 3aleikum, diktor.**
(Hello, doctor.)

Doctor: **wa 3aleikum is-salaam. itfaDHDHal istereeH.**
(Hello. Have a seat, please.)

(*Tom sits down*)

Doctor: **alla bil-khier.**
(*This has no equivalent in English; see note below*)

Tom: **alla bil-khier.**
(*This has no equivalent in English; see note below*)

Doctor: **min esh tishtiki il-yom?**
(What is the problem?; *lit.* What are you
complaining about today?) *m sg*
complaining about today?)

Tom: **3indi zukaam w-Sudaa3 shedeed.**
(I have a cold, and a bad [*lit.* strong] headache.)

Doctor: **shwekit bidet il-a3raaDH?**
(When did the symptoms start?)

Tom: **il-baarHa.**
(Yesterday.)

Doctor: **khelli aqees Haraartek. sh-akhadhit adwiye?**
(Let me take your temperature. What medicine did
you take?) *m sg*
you take?)
m sg

Tom: **bes aspiro.**
(Just aspirin.)

Doctor: **Haraartek shweyye 3aalye, bes DHaghTek
Tabee3i. 3indek gaHHa?**
(Your temperature is a little high, but your blood
  m sg   *m sg*
pressure is normal. Do you have a cough?)
                          m sg

Tom: **la.**
(No.)

Doctor: **tish3ur b-alem b-Hunjurtek?**
(Do you feel pain in your throat?)
      m sg   *m sg*

Tom: **ee.**
(Yes.)

Doctor: **tish3ur b-alem b-adhaanek?**
(Do you feel pain in your ears?)
      m sg   *m sg*

Tom: **ee.**
          (Yes.)

Doctor: **3indek Hassaasiyye min ei shee?**
           (Are you allergic to anything? [*lit.* Do you have an
              m sg   *m sg*
           allergy to anything?])

Tom: **beli, min il-pensileen.**
          (Yes, to penicillin.)

Doctor: **haadhi ir-raachiete. laazim taakudh id-duwe**
           b-intiDHaam, ukul akil khefeef, w-la tinse tishreb
           sawaail. raaji3ni il-isboo3 ij-jaay.
           (Here is the prescription. Take the medication
           regularly. Have some light food, and do not forget to
           drink liquids. Let me see you next week.)
                           m sg

Tom: **shukran, diktor.**
          (Thank you, Doctor.)

Dialogue Two

Vocabulary

guSSi-li	cut (*f sg*) for me
sha3ri	my hair
awwel marre	first time
tijeen	you (*f sg*) come
Saalon	hair salon, barbershop
moodiel	style
yemm	close to
chitif	shoulder
mdarrej	layered
awwelen	first
aghsile	I wash it (hair *m*)

shampu	shampoo
Teyyib	good
tidreen	you (*f sg*) know
akhooye	my brother
chaan yguSS sha3re	he used to have his hair cut
abooch	your (*f sg*) father
SaHeeH?	Is that right?
saakin	living in
mabrook!	Congratulations!
alle ybaarik beech	thanks (*lit.* may God bless you)
shlon-he	how is it (*f*)
geSSe	haircut
aHuTT-le	I put on it
sprei	spray
na3eemen	May you enjoy it
alle yin3im 3aliech	May God bless you

Dialogue

Leila: **guSSi-li sha3ri rajaaan.**
(Cut my hair, please.)

Hairdresser: **haadhi awwel marre tijeen liS-Saalon?**
(Is this the first time you've come to the shop?)
f sg

Leila: **beli.**
(Yes.)

Hairdresser: **shlon moodiel treedeen?**
(How do you want it cut?
f sg
[*lit.* What style do you want?])
f sg

Leila: **yemm ich-chitif, w-mdarrej.**
(Close to the shoulders, and layered.)

Hairdresser: **HaaDHir. khelli aghsile awwelen bish-shampu.**
(OK, let me shampoo it first.)

Leila: **Teyyib. tidreen akhooye chaan yguSS sha3re b-Saalon abooch?**
(Good. Do you know that my brother used to
f sg
have his hair cut at your father's shop?)
f sg

Hairdresser: **SaHeeH? wien akhooch hesse?**
(Is that right? Where is your brother now?)
f sg

Leila: **akhooye hesse mitzawwij w-saakin bil-mooSil.**
(My brother is married now and living in Mosul.)

Hairdresser: **mabrook!**
(Congratulations!)

Leila: **alle ybaarik beech.**
(Thanks.)

Hairdresser: **shlon-he il-geSSe?**
(How is the cut?)

Leila: **kullish ziene.**
(It's very good.)

Hairdresser: **khelli aHuTT-le shweyye sprei.**
(Let's put some spray on it.)

Leila: **shukran.**
(Thanks.)

| *Hardresser:* | **na3eemen.** |
| | (May you enjoy it.) |

| *Leila:* | **alle yin3im 3aliech.** |
| | (Thanks.) |

II. Notes on Vocabulary and Expressions

Greetings

A common greeting is *is-salaamu 3aleikum* (May peace be upon you). The appropriate reply is *wa 3aleikum is-salaam* (May peace be upon you, too). Both greeting and reply are the same, regardless of the number or gender of people addressed.

Inviting others to sit down

In Dialogue One, the doctor invites the patient to sit down by saying *istereeH* (*lit.* have some rest). This is considerably more polite than saying *ug3ud* (sit down).

The greeting *alla bil-khier*

It is common among Iraqi men to greet one another with the expression *alla bil-khier* (May God bless your day). One says it in reply, when the visitor, upon arriving, has sat down. The visitor repeats the greeting. It remains the same regardless of the number of men addressed.

Polite responses to good news

The Iraqi equivalent to "congratulations" is *mabrook* (May your bounty be blessed). The expression is the same regardless of the number or gender of those addressed.

However, the reply varies according to number and gender.

alle ybaarik beek	(*when speaking to a male*)
alle ybaarik beech	(*when speaking to a female*)
alle ybaarik beekum	(*when speaking to more than one person*)

The expression means "May God bless you."

The expression *na3eemen*

It is customary to say *na3eemen* (May you enjoy it) to someone who has just had a haircut. It is also customary to say it to a family member who has just taken a shower. The expression is the same regardless of one's gender, or whether one is alone or in a group. One either responds with *shukran* or with a different equivalent of "May God bless you":

alle yin3im 3aliek	(*when speaking to a male*)
alle yin3im 3aliech	(*when speaking to a female*)
alle yin3im 3aliekum	(*when speaking to more than one person*)

III. Useful Vocabulary

is3aaf	ambulance
Tawaari'	emergencies
musteshfe	hospital
marre bil-yom	once daily
Habbe	pill
martien bil-yom	twice daily
SiHHi	healthy, health-related (*m*)
mareeDH	sick (*m*)
ta3baan	tired (*m*)

Hallaaq (*f* **Hallaaqe**)	barber, hairdresser
mzeyyin	barber
zyaan	haircut (*for men*)
ghaseel melaabis	laundry
tanDHeef jaaff	dry cleaning
qunderchi	shoemaker
raggaa3	shoemaker
jaahiz	ready (*m*)
naDHDHaf	clean (*v*)
shaal	pick up (*v*)
SallaH	repair (*v*)

IV. Grammar

The prefix *sh-*

As can be seen throughout the book, question words (or inter-rogative pronouns) begin with the prefix *sh-*, e.g.

shged	how much (Unit 5)
shwekit	when, what time (Unit 6)
shlon	how; *lit.* what color (Unit 7)
shinoo	what (Unit 8)

When the prefix *sh-* is added to a verb, it is to ask what one is doing, e.g.

<u>**sh**</u>**-akhadhit adwiye?**	What medicine did you take?

When *sh-* is added to *aku* (there is), it forms the equivalent of the question "What is there?," or "What is it?," e.g.

<u>**sh**</u>**-aku?**	What is it?
<u>**sh**</u>**-aku bij-janTe?**	What is [there] in the bag?
<u>**sh**</u>**-aku maku?**	What's up? (*informal inquiry*)

The word *laazim* with a verb

The word *laazim* is used to indicate an obligation to do something. It is the equivalent of the English "must" or "have to," and comes before the verb, as in this example from this unit's Dialogue One:

laazim taakudh	You (*m sg*) must take the
id-duwe b-intiDHaam.	medicine regularly.

Note that *laazim* remains the same while the verb is conjugated, e.g.

laazim arooH hesse.	I must go now.
laazim trooHoon hesse.	You (*pl*) must go now.

Common irregular nouns and their possessive pronouns

In Unit 2, possessive pronoun suffixes were shown added to a word without changing it, as with *qelem*, e.g.

qelemi	my pen
qeleme	his pen
qelemhe	her pen

However, some common nouns, which usually designate family members, undergo changes when possessive pronouns are added. Two are included in Dialogue Two: *ab* (father) and *akh* (brother).

	ab	**akh**
my	**abooye**	**akhooye**
your (*m sg*)	**abook**	**akhook**
your (*f sg*)	**abooch**	**akhooch**

his	ab**oo**	akh**oo**
her	aboo**he**	akhoo**he**
our	aboo**ne**	akhoo**ne**
your (*pl*)	aboo**kum**	akhoo**kum**
their	aboo**hum**	akhoo**hum**

When the words *ab* and *akh* are used with a qualifying noun, the letter -*u* is added, e.g.

> **aHmed ab<u>u</u> dunya.** Ahmed is Dunya's father.
> **aHmed akh<u>u</u> muneer.** Ahmed is Muneer's brother.

In standard Arabic, the equivalent of "my brother" is *akhi*, rather than the Iraqi *akhooye*. Iraqis use *akhi* in the way Americans use "sir." It is an address heard in formal situations, such as in Unit 8, when it is used to address a police officer.

Ordinal numbers

In Iraqi Arabic, ordinal numbers (1st, 2nd, etc.) only go to 10. Cardinal numbers are used from then on.

Ordinal numbers have a gender, as shown in the table below.

	Masculine	*Feminine*
1st	**awwel**	**oola**
2nd	**thaani**	**thaaniye**
3rd	**thaalith**	**thaalthe**
4th	**raabi3**	**raab3a**
5th	**khaamis**	**khaamse**

6th	**saadis**	**saadse**
7th	**saabi3**	**saab3e**
8th	**thaamin**	**thaamne**
9th	**taasi3**	**taas3a**
10th	**3aashir**	**3aashre**

An ordinal number can be placed either before or after the noun.
If it comes before the noun, the masculine form is used, e.g.

> **haadhi awwel marre tijeen liS-Saalon?**
> (Is this the first time you've come to the shop?)

> **is-sabit awwel yom bil-isboo3.**
> (Saturday is the first day of the week.)

If an ordinal number comes after a noun, the genders must
agree, e.g.

> **dereje oola**   first class

If the definite article is used, it is used with both the noun and
the ordinal number, e.g.

> **ish-shaari3 ith-thaalith**   the third street
> **il-marre ir-raab3a**   the fourth time

Past tense

Unlike English, verbs in Arabic have only one past tense. The
conjugation patterns vary depending on the verb category
(sound verb, hollow verb, etc.). The conjugations for each verb
category are shown in the following tables. For help with deter-
mining which category a specific verb belongs to, see the Verb
Appendix on page 206.

Remember that unless you want to clearly identify or emphasize the subject, verbs are used without the personal pronouns.

1. Sound verbs

1.1 The conjugations for regular verbs with the vowel sequence *i-e* (*dires*) are shown in the following table.

	dires (study)		*shiker* (thank)		*ghisel* (wash)	
aani	I studied	**dires<u>it</u>**	I thanked	**shiker<u>it</u>**	I washed	**ghisel<u>it</u>**
inte	you (*m*) studied	**dires<u>it</u>**	you (*m*) thanked	**shiker<u>it</u>**	you (*m*) washed	**ghisel<u>it</u>**
inti	you (*f*) studied	**dires<u>ti</u>**	you (*f*) thanked	**shiker<u>ti</u>**	you (*f*) washed)	**ghisel<u>ti</u>**
huwwe	he studied	**dires**	he thanked	**shik<u>er</u>**	he washed	**ghisel**
hiyye	she studied	**dirs<u>et</u>**	she thanked	**shikr<u>et</u>**	she washed	**ghisl<u>et</u>**
iHne	we studied	**dires<u>ne</u>**	we thanked	**shiker<u>ne</u>**	we washed	**ghisel<u>ne</u>**
intu	you (*pl*) studied	**dires<u>tu</u>**	you (*pl*) thanked	**shiker<u>tu</u>**	you (*pl*) washed	**ghisel<u>tu</u>**
humme	they studied	**dirs<u>aw</u>**	they thanked	**shikr<u>aw</u>**	they washed	**ghisl<u>aw</u>**

Note that the *e* in the verb base is dropped in the *hiyye* and *humme* conjugations.

1.2 Irregular sound verbs with vowel sequence *i-e* (*shireb*) convert the *i* to a *u* in the *hiyye* and *humme* conjugations. Otherwise, the conjugations are the same as the regular *i-e* verbs shown above.

	3iref (know)		*shireb* (drink)		*Tileb* (demand)	
aani	I knew	**3iref<u>it</u>**	I drank	**shireb<u>it</u>**	I demanded	**Tileb<u>it</u>**
inte	you (*m*) knew	**3iref<u>it</u>**	you (*m*) drank	**shireb<u>it</u>**	you (*m*) demanded	**Tileb<u>it</u>**
inti	you (*f*) knew	**3iref<u>ti</u>**	you (*f*) drank	**shireb<u>ti</u>**	you (*f*) demanded	**Tileb<u>ti</u>**
huwwe	he knew	**3iref**	he drank	**shireb**	he demanded	**Tileb**
hiyye	she knew	**3<u>ur</u>fet**	she drank	**sh<u>ur</u>bet**	she demanded	**T<u>ul</u>bet**
iHne	we knew	**3iref<u>ne</u>**	we drank	**shireb<u>ne</u>**	we demanded	**Tileb<u>ne</u>**
intu	you (*pl*) knew	**3iref<u>tu</u>**	you (*pl*) drank	**shireb<u>tu</u>**	you (*pl*) demanded	**Tileb<u>tu</u>**
humme	they knew	**3<u>ur</u>f<u>aw</u>**	they drank	**sh<u>ur</u>b<u>aw</u>**	they demanded	**T<u>ul</u>b<u>aw</u>**

1.3 Regular sound verbs with the vowel sequence *i-a* (*difa3*) follow the same pattern as regular *i-e* verbs in the past tense. The only difference is that, in the *hiyye* conjugation, the ending is *–at* instead of *–et*.

	difa3 (pay)		*rija3* (return)		*simaH* (allow)	
aani	I paid	**difa3it**	I returned	**rija3it**	I allowed	**simaHit**
inte	you (*m*) paid	**difa3it**	you (*m*) returned	**rija3it**	you (*m*) allowed	**simaHit**
inti	you (*f*) paid	**difa3ti**	you (*f*) returned	**rija3ti**	you (*f*) allowed	**simaHti**
huwwe	he paid	**difa3**	he returned	**rija3**	he allowed	**simaH**
hiyye	she paid	**dif3at**	she returned	**rij3at**	she allowed	**simHat**
iHne	we paid	**difa3ne**	we returned	**rija3ne**	we allowed	**simaHne**
intu	you (*pl*) paid	**difa3tu**	you (*pl*) returned	**rija3tu**	you (*pl*) allowed	**simaHtu**
humme	they paid	**dif3aw**	they returned	**rij3aw**	they allowed	**simHaw**

1.4 Irregular sound verbs with the vowel sequence *i-a* (**DHiHak**) end in *–et* instead of *-at* in the *hiyye* conjugation, as in the following:

	DHiHak (laugh)		*li3ab* (play)		*si'al* (ask)	
aani	I laughed	**DHiHakit**	I played	**li3abit**	I asked	**si'alit**
inte	you (*m*) laughed	**DHiHakit**	you (*m*) played	**li3abit**	you (*m*) asked	**si'alit**
inti	you (*f*) laughed	**DHiHakti**	you (*f*) played	**li3abti**	you (*f*) asked	**si'alti**
huwwe	he laughed	**DHiHak**	he played	**li3ab**	he asked	**si'al**
hiyye	she laughed	**DHiHket**	she played	**li3bet**	she asked	**si'let**
iHne	we laughed	**DHiHakne**	we played	**li3abne**	we asked	**si'alne**
intu	you (*pl*) laughed	**DHiHaktu**	you (*pl*) played	**li3abtu**	you (*pl*) asked	**si'altu**
humme	they laughed	**DHiHkaw**	they played	**li3baw**	they asked	**si'law**

1.5 Following is the the conjugation of sound verbs with the vowel sequence *u-e* (**kuber**):

	kuber (grow)		**Subegh** (paint)		**wugef** (stand)	
aani	I grew	**kuberit**	I painted	**Subeghit**	I stood	**wugefit**
inte	you (*m*) grew	**kuberit**	you (*m*) painted	**Subeghit**	you (*m*) stood	**wugefit**
inti	you (*f*) grew	**kuberti**	you (*f*) painted	**Subeghti**	you (*f*) stood	**wugefti**
huwwe	he grew	**kuber**	he painted	**Subegh**	he stood	**wugef**
hiyye	she grew	**kubret**	she painted	**Subghet**	she stood	**wugfet**
iHne	we grew	**kuberne**	we painted	**Subeghne**	we stood	**wugefne**
intu	you (*pl*) grew	**kubertu**	you (*pl*) painted	**Subeghtu**	you (*pl*) stood	**wugeftu**
humme	they grew	**kubraw**	they painted	**Subghaw**	they stood	**wugfaw**

2. Hollow verbs

Hollow verbs follow a regular conjugation pattern in the past tense:

	gaal (say)		**naam** (sleep)		**raad** (want)	
aani	I said	**gilit**	I slept	**nimit**	I wanted	**ridit**
inte	you (*m*) said	**gilit**	you (*m*) slept	**nimit**	you (*m*) wanted	**ridit**
inti	you (*f*) said	**gilti**	you (*f*) slept	**nimti**	you (*f*) wanted	**ridti**
huwwe	he said	**gaal**	he slept	**naam**	he wanted	**raad**
hiyye	she said	**gaalet**	she slept	**naamet**	she wanted	**raadet**
iHne	we said	**gilne**	we slept	**nimne**	we wanted	**ridne**
intu	you (*pl*) said	**giltu**	you (*pl*) slept	**nimtu**	you (*pl*) wanted	**ridtu**
humme	they said	**gaalaw**	they slept	**naamaw**	they wanted	**raadaw**

Note that the equivalent of verb "to be" in the past is the hollow verb *chaan* (was). There is no present-tense equivalent for the verb "to be" in Arabic, because no verb is required (see Unit 2).

	chaan (was)	
aani	I was	chin**it**
inte	you (*m*) were	chin**it**
inti	you (*f*) were	chin**ti**
huwwe	he was	chaan
hiyye	she was	chaan**et**
iHne	we were	chin**ne**
intu	you (*pl*) were	chin**tu**
humme	they were	chaan**aw**

3. Verbs with doubled consonants

Verbs with doubled consonants follow a regular conjugation pattern in the past tense:

	geSS (cut)		*Habb* (love)		*leff* (wrap)	
aani	I cut	geSS**iet**	I loved	Habb**iet**	I wrapped	leff**iet**
inte	you (*m*) cut	geSS**iet**	you (*m*) loved	Habb**iet**	you (*m*) wrapped	leff**iet**
inti	you (*f*) cut	geSS**ieti**	you (*f*) loved	Habb**ieti**	you (*f*) wrapped	leff**ieti**
huwwe	he cut	geSS	he loved	Habb	he wrapped	leff
hiyye	she cut	geSS**et**	she loved	Habb**et**	she wrapped	leff**et**
iHne	we cut	geSS**iene**	we loved	Habb**iene**	we wrapped	leff**iene**
intu	you (*pl*) cut	geSS**ietu**	you (*pl*) loved	Habb**ietu**	you (*pl*) wrapped	leff**ietu**
humme	they cut	geSS**aw**	they loved	Habb**aw**	they wrapped	leff**aw**

4. Defective verbs ending in –e

The past-tense conjugation pattern for defective verbs ending in –e, with the exception of the *huwwe* conjugation, is the same as for verbs with doubled consonants.

	bide (start)		*lige* (find)		*niTe* (give)	
aani	I started	**bidiet**	I found	**ligiet**	I gave	**niTiet**
inte	you (*m*) started	**bidiet**	you (*m*) found	**ligiet**	you (*m*) gave	**niTiet**
inti	you (*f*) started	**bidieti**	you (*f*) found	**ligieti**	you (*f*) gave	**niTieti**
huwwe	he started	**bide**	he found	**lige**	he gave	**niTe**
hiyye	she started	**bidet**	she found	**liget**	she gave	**niTet**
iHne	we started	**bidiene**	we found	**ligiene**	we gave	**niTiene**
intu	you (*pl*) started	**bidietu**	you (*pl*) found	**ligietu**	you (*pl*) gave	**niTietu**
humme	they started	**bidaw**	they found	**ligaw**	they gave	**niTaw**

5.   Verbs with an initial vowel

Verbs with an initial vowel mostly follow the same pattern as regular *i-e* sound verbs (see 1.1. above).

	akal (eat)		*akhadh* (take)		*umer* (command)	
aani	I ate	**akalit**	I took	**akhadhit**	I commanded	**umerit**
inte	you (m) ate	**akalit**	you (m) took	**akhadhit**	you (m) commanded	**umerit**
inti	you (f) ate	**akalti**	you (f) took	**akhadhti**	you (f) commanded	**umerti**
huwwe	he ate	**akal**	he took	**akhadh**	he commanded	**umer**
hiyye	she ate	**aklet**	she took	**akhdhet**	she commanded	**umret**
iHne	we ate	**akalne**	we took	**akhadhne**	we commanded	**umerne**
intu	you (pl) ate	**akaltu**	you (pl) took	**akhadhtu**	you (pl) commanded	**umertu**
humme	they ate	**aklaw**	they took	**akhdhaw**	they commanded	**umraw**

Expressing a former habit

When indicating that one used to do something regularly, use the proper conjugation of *chaan* with the conjugation of the verb in the present tense. For example:

akhooye <u>chaan yguSS</u> sha3re b-Saalon abooch.
(My father <u>used to have</u> his hair <u>cut</u> at your father's shop.)

Other examples:

selma <u>chaanet</u> <u>tidrus</u> bil-liel.	Selma <u>used to study</u> at night.
<u>chaanaw yiSrufoon</u> hwaaye floos.	They <u>used to spend</u> a lot of money.

V. Exercises

10.1 Translate the following.

1. they opened
2. she ran
3. we saw
4. you (*pl*) found
5. he sent
6. I ate

10.2 Fill in the blanks using the correct form of the verb *chaan* and the accompanying verb.

Example: ukhti _____ wiyyaaye kull yom. (study)
    → *ukhti <u>chaanet tidrus</u> wiyyaaye kull yom.*

1. *leila _____ lis-seeneme marre wiHde bil-isboo3.* (go)
2. *aani _____ hwaaye.* (eat)
3. *huwwe _____ iT-Tabeeb b-intiDHaam.* (see)
4. *iHne _____ kutub min il-mektebe.* (buy; *mektebe* → bookstore)
5. *aHmed _____ bil-musteshfe.* (work)

10.3 Fill in the blanks using the correct form of ordinal number.

1. *shbaaT _____ sheher bis-sene.* (2nd)
2. *haadhi _____ marre ashoof il-filim.* (3rd)
3. *ir-reggiyye _____ chaanet ziene.* (1st)
4. *il-arbi3aa' _____ yom bil-isboo3.* (5th)
5. *il-medrese bil-binaaye _____.* (4th)

10.4 Fill in the blanks with the correct conjugation of the verb in Iraqi Arabic. Translate the final sentence into English.

Example: laazim _____ baachir. (you [*f sg*] go)
      → *laazim trooHeen baachir.*
      You must go tomorrow.

1. *laazim _____ hesse.* (you [*pl*] go)
2. *laazim _____ akhook.* (you [*m sg*] help)
3. *aani laazim _____ id-duwe.* (I take)
4. *iHne laazim _____ eemiel.* (we write)
5. *humme laazim _____ hesse.* (they travel)

10.5 Fill in the blanks with the correct form of *ab* or *akh*. Translate the answer into English.

Example: wien akhu nisreen?
      → *akhoohe b-amreeke.*
      Her brother is in America.

1. *ilhaam bint aHmed?* aHmed *_____.*
2. *wien abooch? _____ bil-baSre.*
3. *shlon akhook? _____ mareeDH.*
4. *shinoo shughl abookum? _____ muhandis.*
5. *minu abu leila w-salim? _____ id-diktor rasheed.*

10.6 Fill in the blanks with the appropriate question word (interrogative pronoun).

1. _____ *abook il-yom?*
2. _____ *maku?*
3. _____ *isim ish-shaari3?*
4. _____ *treedoon trooHoon?*
5. _____ *akalti wiyye il-3aSeer?*

UNIT 11
DOING BUSINESS

I. Dialogues

Dialogue One

Vocabulary

ajaddid	I renew
ijaaze	permit
isteeraad	import
imli	fill (out) (*imperative m sg*)
istimaare	form
khaanaat	entries
amli	I fill (out)
il-isim il-kaamil	full name
taareekh il-wilaade	date of birth
il-3inwaan il-bareedi	mailing address
taareekh	date
nefaadh	expiration
tawqee3	signature
titSewwer	do you (*m sg*) think/suppose
Teleb	application
raaH ykoon jaahiz	will be (*m sg*) ready
baachir	tomorrow
raaH nishtughul 3ala	we will work on
Telebaat	applications
raaH ykoon jaahiz	it (*m*) will be ready
raaH tkoon jaahze	it (*f*) will be ready
inshaalle	God willing
raaH aji	I will come
nihaayet il-isboo3 il-qaadim	end of next week

Dialogue

Ahmed: **shlon ajaddid ijaazet il-isteeraad?**
            (How do I renew the import permit?)

Official: **bes imli haadhi il-istimaare.**
            (Just fill out this form.)

Ahmed: **yaa khaanaat laazim amli?**
            (Which entries should I fill out?)

Official: **il-isim il-kaamil, taareekh il-wilaade, il-3inwaan**
            il-bareedi, raqam it-telifon, taareekh nefaadh
            il-ijaaze, it-tawqee3, w-taareekh il-yom.
            (Full name, date of birth, mailing address, phone
            number, expiration date of the permit, [your] signa-
            ture, and today's date.)

Ahmed: **titSewwer iT-Teleb raaH ykoon jaahiz baachir?**
            (Do you think the application will be ready
            tomorrow?)

Official: **la, ma atSewwer. raaH nishtughul 3ala Telebaat**
            il-isteeraad ba3ad chem yom, w-inshaalle raaH
            tkoon jaahze il-isboo3 ij-jaay.*
            (No, I don't think so. We will work on the import
            applications in a few days, and, God willing, they
            will be ready next week.)

*The word *Telebaat* (applications) is the plural of an inanimate
noun. As such, Arabic grammar dictates that it function as a feminine
singular noun rather than a plural. That is why the accompanying verb,
raaH tkoon, appears in the *hiyye (3rd-person f sg)* conjugation. For more
information, see Unit 6.

Ahmed: **zien la3ad, raaH aji nihaayet il-isboo3 il-qaadim.**
         yaa weqit aji aHsen, is-SubuH lo idh-DHuhur?
         (OK then, I shall come at the end of next week.
         Which time is better for me to come, morning
         or noon?)

Official: **il-3aSir aHsen weqit.**
           (The best time is in the afternoon.)

Ahmed: **shukran, fee-maan-illa.**
         (Thanks, good-bye.)

Official: **fee-maan-illa, akhi.**
           (Good-bye, sir.)

Dialogue Two

Vocabulary

asarruf	I cash
Sukook il-musaafireen	traveler's checks
waqqi3	sign (*imperative m sg*)
su'aal	question
idha	if
aftaH Hsaab	I open an account
beng	bank
aHawwil floos	transfer money
shekhsi	personal
il-ardun	Jordan
Tab3an	of course
tista3mil	you (*m sg*) use
ba3ad saa3tien	two hours later
yintihi	it (*m*) ends
dawaam	working hours
Hatte	so that, to, in order to
kaafi	enough

Dialogue

Tom: **rajaa'an areed aSarruf Sukook il-musaafireen.**
(I would like to cash traveler's checks, please.)

Teller: **sgedd treed tSarruf?**
(How much do you want to cash?)

Tom: **meetien w-khamseen alif deenaar.**
(250,000 dinar.)

Teller: **waqqi3 hna rajaa'an.**
(Sign here, please.)

Tom: **3indi su'aal: idha aftaH Hsaab bil beng maaletkum, agdar aHawwil floos l-haadhe il-Hsaab ish-shekhsi bil-ardun?**
(I have a question: If I open an account at your bank, can I transfer money to this personal account in Jordan?)

Teller: **Tab3an, idha timli haadhi il-istimaare hesse, tigder tista3mil il-Hsaab ba3ad saa3tien.**
(Certainly. If you fill [out] this form now, you can use the account in [*lit.* after] two hours.)

Tom: **shwekit yintihi id-dawaam il-yom?**
(What time do you close today? [*lit.* What time do the working hours end today?])

Teller: **saa3a thintien.**
(Two o'clock.)

Tom: **zien la3ad, il-yom ma 3indi weqit kaafi. raaH aji baachir Hatte aftaH il-Hsaab.**
(OK then. I do not have enough time today. I shall come tomorrow to open the account.)

II. Notes on Vocabulary and Expressions

The expression *inshaalle*

When discussing future plans or events, *inshaalle* (God willing) is a frequently used expression, regardless of the social or religious background of the speaker.

III. Useful Vocabulary

mekteb il-bareed	post office
faks	fax
DHaruf	envelope
waSil	receipt
Tawaabi3	stamps
maktoob	letter
difa3	pay (*v*)
eemiel	e-mail
kredit kard	credit card
3umle	currency
m3azzil	closed (*store*)
ba3ad baachir	day after tomorrow
awwel il-baarHa	day before yesterday
il-isboo3 il-faat	last week
istiraaHat il-ghede	lunch break
mfattiH	open (*store*)
muweDHDHefeen	employees
taSdeer	export
Hukoome	government
veeze	tourist visa
ta'sheere siyaaHiyye	tourist visa
muterjim	translator

IV. Grammar

Numbers over 1,000

All numbers over 1,000 follow the pattern:

thousand(s) + hundred(s) + single digits + tens

For example:

alif w-miyye	1100 (*lit.* one thousand and one hundred)
alif w-tisi3miyye w-tis3a w-tis3een	1999 (*lit.* one thousand and nine hundred and nine and ninety)

Note that, unlike English, numbers are not indicated in terms of hundreds, as in "eleven hundred" (1100). Likewise years are not spelled out in centuries. For example, 1999 is "one thousand and nine hundred, and nine and ninety," instead of "nineteen (hundred) ninety-nine."

Numbers: 2,000 to 10,000

alfien	2,000
tlattalaaf	3,000
arba3talaaf	4,000
khamistalaaf	5,000
sittalaaf	6,000
sabi3talaaf	7,000
thmantalaaf	8,000
tisi3talaaf	9,000
3ashirtalaaf	10,000

Examples of more complex numbers in this range:

thmantalaaf w-khamismiyye w-khamseen	8,550
alfien w-arba3a	2,004

Numbers: 10,000 to 1 million

3ishreen alif	20,000
tlaatheen alif	30,000
arba3een alif	40,000
khamseen alif	50,000
sitteen alif	60,000
sab3een alif	70,000
thmaaneen alif	80,000
tis3een alif	90,000
meet alif	100,000
meetien alif	200,000
tlethmeet alif	300,000
arba3meet alif	400,000
khamismeet alif	500,000
sitmeet alif	600,000
sabi3meet alif	700,000
thmenmeet alif	800,000
tisi3meet alif	900,000
milyon	1,000,000

An example of a more complex number in this range:

meetien w-khamse w-arba3een alif w-3ashre	245,010

Spelling out dates

The Arabic word for "date" is *taareekh*, e.g.

shinoo taareekh il-yom?	What is today's date?

You can also ask about the date by saying:

> **shged bish-sheher il-yom?**   What is the day of the
> or **il-yom shged bish-sheher?**   month today?

Unlike the American system, where the month precedes the day, dates in Arabic follow the order of day, month, and year. For example:

> **da3ash eyyaar, senet**   11/5/2003 (*lit.* 11 May of
> **alfien w-tlaathe**   the year 2003)

Note that the word *senet* (of the year) is inserted before the number.

Comparatives and superlatives

1. Comparative

The comparative is used to say that something/someone has more of a particular quality than something/someone else. In Iraqi Arabic, the comparative is formed by the comparative adjective followed by the preposition *min*, e.g.

> **Seyyaartich <u>aHsen min</u>**   Your car is <u>better than</u> mine.
> **seyyaarti.**

> **iDH-DHuhur**   Noon is <u>better than</u> the
> <u>**aHsen min**</u>   morning.
> **iS-SubuH.**

The comparative adjective has only one form regardless of the gender and number of the noun:

haadhe iT-Tabeeb akber min dhaak.	This doctor (*m*) is <u>older than</u> that one.
haadhi il-mu3allime azghar min dheech.	This teacher (*f*) is <u>younger than</u> that one.
hadhole il-muqaawileen aghle min hadholaak.	These contractors (*pl*) are <u>more expensive</u> than those.

2.   Superlative

The superlative is used when saying that something/someone has the most of a particular quality. While English has two different forms to convey comparative ("better") and superlative ("best"), Iraqi Arabic uses only one adjective. When the adjective is used as a superlative, it stands before the indefinite noun. For example:

Seyyaaret aHmed aHsen seyyaare.	Ahmed's car is <u>the best</u> car.
il-3aSir aHsen waqit.	The afternoon is <u>the best</u> time.
haadhe arkhaS ktaab.	This is <u>the cheapest</u> book (*m*).
haadhi azghar muhendise.	This is <u>the youngest</u> engineer (*f*).
hadhole aghle muqaawileen.	These are <u>the most expensive</u> contractors (*pl*).

Note that the forms of the adjective used in the superlative context also do not change with the number or gender of the nouns they are referring to.

The following chart lists the most common adjectives with their comparative and superlative forms.

	Adjective	Comparative/ Superlative
good	khosh, zien	aHsen
old (*object*)	qadeem	aqdem
	3ateeg	a3teg
new	jideed	ajded
fast	saree3	asra3
slow	baTee'	abTa'
old (*person*), big, great	chibeer	akbar
small, young	zgheyyir	azghar
cheap	rekheeS	arkhaS
expensive	ghaali	aghle
hot	Haarr	aHarr
cold	baarid	abred

Derived verbs in the past tense

The past-tense conjugations for the most important groups (II, III, V, VI, VIII, and X) is given below. For the present tense of derived verbs and their meaning patterns, see Unit 9.

Group II:

	Hawwel (transfer)		*qeddem* (introduce)	
aani	**I transferred**	**Hawwelit**	**I introduced**	qeddemit
inte	you (*m*) transferred	**Hawwelit**	you (*m*) introduced	**qeddemit**
inti	you (*f*) transferred	**Hawwelti**	you (*f*) introduced	**qeddemti**
huwwe	he transferred	**Hawwel**	he introduced	**qeddem**
hiyye	she transferred	**Hawwilet**	she introduced	**qeddimet**
iHne	we transferred	**Hawwelne**	we introduced	**qeddemne**
intu	you (*pl*) transferred	**Hawweltu**	you (*pl*) introduced	**qeddemtu**
humme	they transferred	**Hawwilaw**	they introduced	**qeddimaw**

	naDHDHaf (clean)	
aani	I cleaned	**naDHDHafit**
inte	you (*m*) cleaned	**naDHDHafit**
inti	you (*f*) cleaned	**naDHDHafti**
huwwe	he cleaned	**naDHDHaf**
hiyye	she cleaned	**naDHDHufet**
iHne	we cleaned	**naDHDHafne**
intu	you (*pl*) cleaned	**naDHDHaftu**
humme	they cleaned	**naDHDHufaw**

Note that the final vowel in the verb base changes in the *hiyye* and *humme* conjugations. The best way to keep track as to which vowel it changes to, is to remember the *huwwe* conjugation of the verb in the present tense. The conjugations for the above verbs are, respectively, *yHawwil*, *yqeddim*, and *ynaDHDHuf*. As can be seen, the final vowel of this conjugation matches the final vowel of the verb base for the past-tense *hiyye* and *humme* conjugations.

The verb entries in the dictionary sections of this book feature the present-tense *huwwe* conjugation in parentheses for easy reference.

Group III:

	jaaweb (reply)		khaaber (call)	
aani	I replied	jaawebit	I called	khaaberit
inte	you (m) replied	jaawebit	you (m) called	khaaberit
inti	you (f) replied	jaawebti	you (f) called	khaaberti
huwwe	he replied	jaaweb	he called	khaaber
hiyye	she replied	jaawbet	she called	khaabret
iHne	we replied	jaawebne	we called	khaaberne
intu	you (pl) replied	jaawebtu	you (pl) called	khaabertu
humme	they replied	jaawbaw	they called	khaabraw

	waafeq (agree)	
aani	I agreed	waafeqit
inte	you (m) agreed	waafeqit
inti	you (f) agreed	waafeqti
huwwe	he agreed	waafeq
hiyye	she agreed	waafqet
iHne	we agreed	waafeqne
intu	you (pl) agreed	waafeqtu
humme	they agreed	waafqaw

With Group III verbs, the final vowel of the verb base is dropped in the *hiyye* and *humme* conjugations.

Group V:

	t3allem (learn)		*t'ammel* (hope)	
aani	I learned	**t3allem<u>it</u>**	I hoped	**t'ammel<u>it</u>**
inte	you (*m*) learned	**t3allem<u>it</u>**	you (*m*) hoped	**t'ammel<u>it</u>**
inti	you (*f*) learned	**t3allem<u>ti</u>**	you (*f*) hoped	**t'ammel<u>ti</u>**
huwwe	he learned	**t3allem**	he hoped	**t'ammel**
hiyye	she learned	**t3all<u>imet</u>**	she hoped	**t'amm<u>ilet</u>**
iHne	we learned	**t3allem<u>ne</u>**	we hoped	**t'ammel<u>ne</u>**
intu	you (*pl*) learned	**t3allem<u>tu</u>**	you (*pl*) hoped	**t'ammel<u>tu</u>**
humme	they learned	**t3all<u>imaw</u>**	they hoped	**t'amm<u>ilaw</u>**

	tSewwer (suppose)	
aani	I supposed	**tSewwer<u>it</u>**
inte	you (*m*) supposed	**tSewwer<u>it</u>**
inti	you (*f*) supposed	**tSewwer<u>ti</u>**
huwwe	he supposed	**tSewwer**
hiyye	she supposed	**tSeww<u>iret</u>**
iHne	we supposed	**tSewwer<u>ne</u>**
intu	you (*pl*) supposed	**tSewwer<u>tu</u>**
humme	they supposed	**tSeww<u>iraw</u>**

With Group V verbs, note that the final vowel of the verb base becomes an *i* in the *hiyye* and *humme* conjugations. Unlike Group II verbs, there is no correspondence with the present-tense *huwwe* conjugation.

Group VI:

	t3aarek (fight)		*tSaadeq* (become friends)	
aani	I fought	**t3aarekit**	I became friends	**tSaadeqit**
inte	you (*m*) fought	**t3aarekit**	you (*m*) became friends	**tSaadeqit**
inti	you (*f*) fought	**t3aarekti**	you (*f*) became friends	**tSaadeqti**
huwwe	he fought	**t3aarek**	he became friends	**tSaadeq**
hiyye	she fought	**t3aarket**	she became friends	**tSaadqet**
iHne	we fought	**t3aarekne**	we became friends	**tSaadeqne**
intu	you (*pl*) fought	**t3aarektu**	you (*pl*) became friends	**tSaadeqtu**
humme	they fought	**t3aarkaw**	they became friends	**tSaadqaw**

	tshaarek (share)	
aani	I shared	**tshaarekit**
inte	you (*m*) shared	**tshaarekit**
inti	you (*f*) shared	**tshaarekti**
huwwe	he shared	**tshaarek**
hiyye	she shared	**tshaarket**
iHne	we shared	**tshaarekne**
intu	you (*pl*) shared	**tshaarektu**
humme	they shared	**tshaarkaw**

Group VI verbs, like those in Group III, drop the final vowel of the verb base in the *hiyye* and *humme* conjugations.

Group VIII:

	btisem (smile)		*shtighel* (work)	
aani	I smiled	**btisemit**	I worked	**shtighelit**
inte	you (*m*) smiled	**btisemit**	you (*m*) worked	**shtighelit**
inti	you (*f*) smiled	**btisemti**	you (*f*) worked	**shtighelti**
huwwe	he smiled	**btisem**	he worked	**shtighel**
hiyye	she smiled	**btismet**	she worked	**shtighlet**
iHne	we smiled	**btisemne**	we worked	**shtighelne**
intu	you (*pl*) smiled	**btisemtu**	you (*pl*) worked	**shtigheltu**
humme	they smiled	**btismaw**	they worked	**shtighlaw**

	intiDHer (wait)	
aani	I waited	**intiDHerit**
inte	you (*m*) waited	**intiDHerit**
inti	you (*f*) waited	**intiDHerti**
huwwe	he waited	**intiDHer**
hiyye	she waited	**intiDHret**
iHne	we waited	**intiDHerne**
intu	you (*pl*) waited	**intiDHertu**
humme	they waited	**intiDHraw**

Group VIII verbs drop the final vowel of the base verb in the *hiyye* and *humme* conjugations.

Group X:

	ista3jel (hurry up)		*sta3mal* (use)	
aani	I hurried up	**ista3jelit**	I used	**sta3malit**
inte	you (*m*) hurried up	**ista3jelit**	you (*m*) used	**sta3malit**
inti	you (*f*) hurried up	**ista3jelti**	you (*f*) used	**sta3malti**
huwwe	he hurried up	**ista3jel**	he used	**sta3mal**
hiyye	she hurried up	**ista3jilet**	she used	**sta3milet**
iHne	we hurried up	**ista3jelne**	we used	**sta3malne**
intu	you (*pl*) hurried up	**ista3jeltu**	you (*pl*) used	**sta3maltu**
humme	they hurried up	**ista3jilaw**	they used	**sta3milaw**

	stensekh (copy)	
aani	I copied	**stensekhit**
inte	you (*m*) copied	**stensekhit**
inti	you (*f*) copied	**stensekhti**
huwwe	he copied	**stensekh**
hiyye	she copied	**stensikhet**
iHne	we copied	**stensekhne**
intu	you (*pl*) copied	**stensekhtu**
humme	they copied	**stensikhaw**

Group X verbs change the final vowel of the verb base to an *i* in the *hiyye* and *humme* conjugations.

Future tense

Future action is indicated by adding *raaH* before a present-tense verb, e.g.

iT-Teleb <u>raaH ykoon</u> **jaahiz baachir.**	The application <u>will be</u> ready tomorrow.
tom <u>raaH yiji</u> baachir.	Tom <u>will come</u> tomorrow.
leila <u>raaH titkharraj</u> **is-sene ij-jaayye.**	Leila <u>will graduate</u> next year.
aSdiqaa'i <u>raaH</u> **<u>ysaafroon</u> il-isboo3** **ij-jaay.**	My friends <u>will travel</u> next week.

Note that *raaH* remains the same regardless of the conjugation of the accompanying verb.

The verb "to be" in the future tense

The Iraqi Arabic equivalent of "will be" is conjugated in the following table.

aani	I will be	**raaH akoon**
inte	you (*m sg*) will be	**raaH tkoon**
inti	you (*f sg*) will be	**raaH tkooneen**
huwwe	he will be	**raaH ykoon**
hiyye	she will be	**raaH tkoon**
iHne	we will be	**raaH nkoon**
intu	you (*pl*) will be	**raaH tkoonoon**
humme	they will be	**raaH ykoonoon**

Basic conditional sentences using *idha*

The word *idha* is the equivalent of "if." It usually indicates a conditional situation and can be used with different verb tenses. Examples:

> **idha aftaH Hsaab bil beng, agdar aHawwil floos?**
> (If I open an account, can I transfer money?)

> **idha timli haadhi il-istimaare hesse, tigder tista3mil il-Hsaab ba3ad saa3tien.**
> (If you fill out this form now, you can use the account in two hours.)

> **idha aakhudh qiTaar il-liel, raaH akoon hnak iS-SubuH.**
> (If I take the night train, I will be there in the morning.)

> **idha treed titkallam wiyye il-mudarris, rooH hesse!**
> (If you want to speak to the teacher, go now!)

V. Exercises

11.1 Translate each of the following verb conjugations.

1. they supposed
2. she smiled
3. you (*f*) cleaned
4. I hurried up
5. we answered
6. he shared

11.2 Write out the dates in Iraqi Arabic.

1. April 30, 1990
2. July 7, 2002
3. June 12, 1867
4. September 5, 1935
5. January 2, 2005

11.3 Write out the numbers in Iraqi Arabic.

1. 25,670,100
2. 956,401
3. 760,000
4. 853,099
5. 1,444,176

11.4 Fill in the blanks, selecting from the following regular or comparative adjectives and superlatives:

aqdem min, arkhaS, azghar, ghaali, akbar min, asra3 min, abred min, baTee', abTa' min, aHsen min

1. *leila _____ Taalibe.*
2. *aHmed yimshi _____ muneer.*
3. *idh-dheheb hwaaye _____.*
4. *ma 3indi floos, ishtiriet _____ janTe.*
5. *haadhi il-binaaye _____ hadheech.*
6. *ish-shite _____ min iS-Sief.* (the summer → *iS-Sief*)
7. *il-muroor _____.* (traffic → *il-muroor*)
8. *il-reggiyye _____ it-tuffaaHa.*
9. *iT-Teyyaare _____ is-seyyaare.*
10. *inshaalle ij-jaw baachir ykoon _____ il-yom.*

11.5 Change the following sentences into the future tense, using the adverbs of time given.

Example: aani bil-medrese hesse.   [*baachir*]
    → *aani raaH akoon bil-medrese baachir.*

1. *leila w-muneer raaHaw*
   lis-seeneme il-baarHa.   [*il-isboo3 ij-jaay*]
2. *aHmed yigi il-yom.*   [*il-khamees*]
3. *iHne naakul saa3a wiHde.*   [*saa3a sab3a*]
4. *intu khaabertu iS-SubuH?*   [*baachir*]
5. *selma Hawwilet floos*
   il-baarHa.   [*ba3ad yomien*]
6. *intu chintu bil-biet il-baarHa?*   [*baachir*]

11.6 Translate the following sentences.

1. If I open an account now, can I transfer money tomorrow?
2. If you (*m sg*) take this train, you will be there at 5:00.
3. If we go now, we will see her.
4. If the bookstore is open, we will buy books.
5. If she writes a letter, she has to buy stamps.

UNIT 12
SOCIALIZING

I.   Dialogues

Dialogue One

Vocabulary

minu?	who is this?
umm karam	*respectful address to a mother* (*lit.* mother of Karam)
abu dunya	*respectful address to a father* (*lit.* father of Dunya)
ij-jahaal	the children
il-Hamdu lillah	thank God
3eedkum mubaarek	have a blessed feast
mawjood	he is available
laH-DHe	a moment
Saar zamaan	it's been a long time
shifnaakum	we saw you (*pl*)
3aa'ile	family
ee welle	yes, indeed (*lit.* yes, by God)
mashghooleen	busy (*pl*)
akhbaarkum	your (*pl*) news
khier!	I hope everything is well!
sh-Saar?	what happened?
tweffet	she passed away
ma3a shadeed il-asaf	I am terribly sorry
il-beqiyye b-Hayaatkum	our condolences
khiTeb	he got engaged

awwel il-baarHa	the day before yesterday
haay id-dinye	this is life (*used in reference to both good and bad fortune*)
sh-nigder nsewwi?	What can we do? (*used in reference to bad fortune*)
yi3jibkum	you (*pl*) like (*lit.* it pleases you)
nit3ashshe siwe	have dinner together
mat3am	restaurant
ij-jum3a ij-jaayye	next Friday
bit-ta'keed	certainly
shukran 3ala id-da3we	thanks for the invitation
mamnoon	you are welcome

Dialogue

(Note: The family relationships are as follows: Ahmed and his wife are the parents of Dunya. Salim and his wife are the parents of Karam. The use of the titles *abu* (father) and *umm* (mother) with a child's name is discussed further in the lesson.)

Ahmed: **aloo marHabe, minu? umm karam?**
(Hello, who is this? Umm Karam?)

Salim's wife: **ee beli. ahlan abu dunya, shlonek w-shlon umm dunya wij-jahaal?**
(Yes, welcome, Abu Dunya. How are you, and how are Umm Dunya and the kids?)

Ahmed: **zieneen. il-Hamdu lillah, 3eedkum mubaarek.**
(We are all fine, thank God. May you have a blessed feast.)

Salim's wife: **w-3eedek mubaarek.**
(The same to you.)

Ahmed: **abu karam mawjood?**
(Is Abu Karam available?)

Salim's wife: **beli, fed laH-DHe.**
(Yes, he is. Just a second.)

Salim: **ahlan abu dunya, Saar zamaan min
shifnaakum, inte wil-3aa'ile.**
(Hello, abu-Dunya. It has been a long time
since we last saw you and the family.)

Ahmed: **ee welle chinne hwaaye mashghooleen.**
(Yes, you are right. We were quite busy.)

Salim: **shinoo akhbaarkum?**
(What's new?)

Ahmed: **welle akhbaarne ziene w-ma ziene.**
(Well, our news is good and bad.)

Salim: **khier! sh-Saar?**
(I hope it's good. What happened?)

Ahmed: **ukhut umm dunya ich-chibeere tweffet
gabul chem sheher.**
(Umm Dunya's eldest sister passed away a
few months ago.)

Salim: **la, ma3a shadeed il-asaf. il-beqiyye
b-Hayaatkum.**
(Oh, no, I am terribly sorry. Our condolences.)

Ahmed: **w-Hayaatkum il-baaqye.**
(Thanks.)

Salim: **wil-akhbaar iz-ziene?**
(And the good news?)

Ahmed:	**akhooye iz-zgheyyir khiTeb awwel il-baarHa.** (My youngest brother got engaged the day before yesterday.)
Salim:	**mabrook mabrook!** (Congratulations!)
Ahmed:	**alle ybaarik beek. eeh, haay id-dinye. sh-nigder nsewwi. agool, yi3jibkum nit3ashshe siwe bil-mat3am ij-jum3a ij-jaayye?** (Thanks. Well, this is life, what can we do. Listen, would you all like to have dinner together at the restaurant next Friday?)
Salim:	**bit-ta'keed. shukran 3ala id-da3we.** (Certainly. Thanks for the invitation.)
Ahmed:	**mamnoon. nshoofkum yom ij-jum3a.** (You are welcome. See you on Friday.)
Salim:	**inshaalle. ma3a s-salaame.** (God willing. Good-bye.)

Dialogue Two

Vocabulary

Hijezne	we reserved
miez	table
ashkhaaS	persons
Hammaamaat	bathrooms
3ala yesaar	to the left
madkhal	entrance
da-arooH	I am going
tweSSoon	you (*pl*) order

qaa'imet il-akil	menu
is-seyyidaat awwalen	ladies first
dolme	dish of stuffed vegetables
zalaaTe	salad
ashreb	I drink
leffet kabaab	sandwich of grilled ground meat
Turshi	pickles
khuDHer	(fresh) herbs
sh-tHibbeen	what would you like
liben shineene	yogurt drink
hem	also
nefis ish-shee	the same thing
beere	beer
timmen	rice
margat baamye	okra stew cooked with lamb and tomato sauce
khilaal rubu3 saa3a	within a quarter of an hour
wejbe shehiyye	delicious meal
il-Hsaab	the bill
kullish Teyyib	very delicious
khidme	service
mumtaaze	excellent (*f*)
gaarsone	waitress
bakhsheesh	tip

Dialogue

Ahmed and his wife Nejle, and Salim and his wife Farida are in a restaurant.

Ahmed: **Hijezne miez l-arba3 ashkhaaS.**
(We reserved a table for four.)

Waitress: **il-miez jaahiz. itfaDHDHalu.**
(The table is ready. Follow me.)

Farida: **rajaa'an, wien il-Hammaamaat?**
(Where are the bathrooms, please?)

Waitress: **3ala yesaar il-madkhal.**
(To the left of the entrance.)

Farida : **aani da-arooH lil-hammaam, tijeen wiyyaaye?**
(to Nejle) (I am going to the bathroom. Do you want to
come with me?)

Nejle: **la, arooH ba3dien.**
(No, I'll go [*lit.* I go] later.)

***

Waitress: **yi3jibkum tweSSoon ei shee min qaa'imet
il-akil?**
(Would you like to order anything from the menu?)

Salim: **is-seyyidaat awwalen.**
(Ladies first.)

Nejle: **dolme w-zalaaTe. w-areed ashreb pipsi,
rajaa'an.**
(Dolma and salad. I would like a Pepsi to drink,
please.)

Farida: **leffet kabaab wiyye Turshi w-khuDHer.**
(A kebab sandwich, with pickles and herbs.)

Waitress: **sh-tHibbeen tishrebeen wiyyaahe?**
(What would you like to drink with it?)

Farida: **liben shineene.**
(A yogurt drink.)

Ahmed: **aani hem aHibb aweSSi nefis ish-shee, bes areed ashreb beere wiyye il-akil.**
(I would also like to order the same thing, but would like a beer to drink with the food.)

Salim: **aani areed timmen w-margat baamye, wiyye liben shineene.**
(I would like rice and okra stew, with a yogurt drink.)

Waitress: **il-akil raaH ykoon jaaHiz khilaal rubu3 saa3a. wejbe shehiyye.**
(The food will be ready in 15 minutes. We wish you a delicious meal.)

***

Ahmed: **il-Hsaab, rajaa'an.**
(The bill, please.)

Waitress: **itfaDHDHal. inshaalle 3ijebkum il-akil?**
(Here it is. I hope you liked the food [*lit.* the food pleased you]?)

Ahmed: **kullish Teyyib, wil-khidme chaanet mumtaaze.**
(It was very delicious, and the service was excellent.)

Nejle:
(*whispering to Ahmed*) **inTi il-gaarsone khosh bakhsheesh.**
(Give the waitress a good tip.)

II. Notes on Vocabulary and Expressions

The use of *abu* and *umm* as titles: a respectful way of addressing parents

It is the custom among Iraqis to call their friends by the names of their eldest son or daughter. For example, in Dialogue One, Salim's wife is called *umm karam* (*lit.* the mother of Karam), and Ahmed is called *abu dunya* (*lit.* the father of Dunya).

Responses to bad news

When learning of the passing away of a person, it is customary to say the equivalent of "our condolences" to their loved ones. It varies according to gender and number.

> **il-beqiyye b-Hayaatek** (*used when addressing a male*)
> **il-beqiyye b-Hayaatich** (*used when addressing a female*)
> **il-beqiyye b-Hayaatkum** (*used when addressing two or more people*)

The response also depends on the number and gender of the person being spoken to:

> **w-Hayaatek il-baaqye** (*used when addressing a male*)
> **w-Hayaatich il-baaqye** (*used when addressing a female*)
> **w-Hayaatkum il-baaqye** (*used when addressing two or more people*)

Exchanging courtesies during the month of Ramadan and other religious holidays

At the beginning of Ramadan, the Islamic month of fasting, people greet each other by saying

ramaDHaan kareem.   Ramadan is generous (or gracious).

During religious holidays, a common courtesy is "May your feast be blessed. It changes with the number and gender of the person being spoken to:

3eedek mubaarek	(*used when addressing a male*)
3eedich mubaarek	(*used when addressing a female*)
3eedkum mubaarek	(*used when addressing two or more people*)

The response, the equivalent of "You are wished the same," also changes.

w-3eedek mubaarek	(*used when addressing a male*)
w-3eedich mubaarek	(*used when addressing a female*)
w-3eedkum mubaarek	(*used when addressing two or more people*)

Another courtesy during holidays is "May your days be happy":

ayyaamek sa3eede	(*used when addressing a male*)
ayyaamich sa3eede	(*used when addressing a female*)
ayyaamkum sa3eede	(*used when addressing two or more people*)

III. Useful Vocabulary

riyoog	breakfast
3ashe	dinner
ghede	lunch
boi	waiter
DHief (*pl* **DHyoof**)	guest
Hafle	party
thaaniyen	secondly
zaar	visit (*v*)
3iris	wedding
3izem	invite (*v*)
abu il-biet	host
umm il-biet	hostess
Saam	fast (during Ramadan) (*v*)
fuToor	major meal during Ramadan, eaten after sunset
suHoor	small meal during Ramadan, eaten before sunrise

IV. Grammar

Uses and functions of *nefis*

The word *nefis* (literally "soul" or "spirit") is used in Iraqi Arabic as either an adjective, meaning "the same," or as a reflexive pronoun.

1. *nefis* used as an adjective:

   When used as an adjective *nefis* does not change according to the noun's gender or number. Also, the noun it qualifies is always preceded by the definite article.

nefis ish-shee	the same thing
nefis il-ghurfe	the same room
nefis il-wilid	the same boys
nefis il-banaat	the same girls

2. *nefis* used as a reflexive pronoun:

   When *nefis* is used as a reflexive pronoun, it is modified by the appropriate pronoun suffix. Note that *nefis* becomes *nefs* when the suffix begins with a vowel.

nefsi	myself
nefsek	yourself (*m*)
nefsich	yourself (*f*)
nefse	himself
nefis-he	herself
nefisne	ourselves
nefiskum	yourselves
nefis-hum	themselves

3. When the prefix *b-* stands before *nefis* and a pronoun suffix, it means "by [one]self."

b-nefsi	by myself
b-nefsek	by yourself (*m*)
b-nefsich	by yourself (*f*)
b-nefse	by himself
b-nefis-he	by herself
b-nefisne	by ourselves
b-nefiskum	by yourselves
b-nefis-hum	by themselves

Present-tense verbs and direct object pronouns

In Unit 6, pronoun suffixes were shown attached to a verb in the singular. The verb underwent no modification. However, this is not the case with all verb conjugations suffixes. Some suffixes modify the verb ending in the present-tense form of the "you" (*f sg*), "you" (*pl*), and "they" conjugations, which all end in a syllable with a long vowel:

tishkureen	you (*f sg*) thank
tishkuroon	you (*pl*) thank
yishkuroon	they thank

Following is the full conjugation of the verb *shiker* (thank) with all pronouns. Note that some instances are for demonstration purposes only.

-ni (me)

ashkurni	I thank me
tishkurni	you (*m sg*) thank me
tishkureeni	you (*f sg*) thank me
yishkurni	he thanks me
tishkurni	she thanks me
nishkurni	we thank me
tishkurooni	you (*pl*) thank me
yishkurooni	they thank me

As can be seen, the endings of the "you" (*f sg*), "you" (*pl*), and "they" conjugations are contracted to -*ni*.

-ek (you [*m sg*])

ashkurek	I thank you
tishkurek	you (*m sg*) thank you
tishkureek	you (*f sg*) thank you
yishkurek	he thanks you

tishkur<u>ek</u>	she thanks you
nishkur<u>ek</u>	we thank you
tishkuroo<u>k</u>	you (*pl*) thank you
yishkuroo<u>k</u>	they thank you

Note that the final -*n* of the verb is dropped in "you" (*f sg*), "you" (*pl*), and "they" and is replaced by the -*k* of the suffix.

<u>-ich</u> (you [*f sg*])

ashkur<u>ich</u>	I thank you
tishkur<u>ich</u>	you (*m sg*) thank you
tishkuree<u>ch</u>	you (*f sg*) thank you
yishkur<u>ich</u>	he thanks you
tishkur<u>ich</u>	she thanks you
nishkur<u>ich</u>	we thank you
tishkuroo<u>ch</u>	you (*pl*) thank you
yishkuroo<u>ch</u>	they thank you

Note that the final -*n* of the verb is dropped in "you" (*f sg*), "you" (*pl*), and "they" and replaced by the -*ch* of the suffix.

<u>-e</u> (him)

ashkur<u>e</u>	I thank him
tishkur<u>e</u>	you (*m sg*) thank you
tishkur<u>ee</u>	you (*f sg*) thank him
yishkur<u>e</u>	he thanks him
tishkur<u>e</u>	she thanks him
nishkur<u>e</u>	we thank him
tishkur<u>oo</u>	you (*pl*) thank him
yishkur<u>oo</u>	they thank him

The verb conjugations "you" (*f sg*), "you" (*pl*), and "they" do not take this suffix, instead the final -*n* is dropped.

-he (her)

ashkur**he**	I thank her
tishkur**he**	you (*m sg*) thank her
tishkuree**he**	you (*f sg*) thank her
yishkur**he**	he thanks her
tishkur**he**	she thanks her
nishkur**he**	we thank her
tishkuroo**he**	you (*pl*) thank her
yishkuroo**he**	they thank her

The final *-n* of the verb in "you" (*f sg*), "you" (*pl*), and "they" is dropped and the suffix *–he* is added.

-ne (us)

ashkur**ne**	I thank us
tishkur**ne**	you (*m sg*) thank us
tishkuree**ne**	you (*f sg*) thank us
yishkur**ne**	he thanks us
tishkur**ne**	she thanks us
nishkur**ne**	we thank us
tishkuroo**ne**	you (*pl*) thank us
yishkuroo**ne**	they thank us

The final *–n* of the verb is contracted to *–ne* in "you" (*f sg*), "you" (*pl*), and "they."

-kum (you [*pl*])

ashkur**kum**	I thank you (*pl*)
tishkur**kum**	you (*m sg*) thank you (*pl*)
tishkuree**kum**	you (*f sg*) thank you (*pl*)
yishkur**kum**	he thanks you (*pl*)
tishkur**kum**	she thanks you (*pl*)
nishkur**kum**	we thank you (*pl*)
tishkuroo**kum**	you (*pl*) thank you (*pl*)
yishkuroo**kum**	they thank you (*pl*)

The final *–n* of the verb is dropped in "you" (*f sg*), "you" (*pl*), and "they" and the suffix *–kum* is added.

-hum (them)

ashkur<u>hum</u>	I thank them
tishkur<u>hum</u>	you (*m sg*) thank them
tishkuree<u>hum</u>	you (*f sg*) thank them
yishkur<u>hum</u>	he thanks them
tishkur<u>hum</u>	she thanks them
nishkur<u>hum</u>	we thank them
tishkuroo<u>hum</u>	you (*pl*) thank them
yishkuroo<u>hum</u>	they thank them

The final *–n* of the verb is dropped in the "you" (*f sg*), "you" (*pl*), and "they" conjugations and the suffix *–hum* is added.

Past-tense verbs and direct object suffixes

Verbs in the past tense take the same direct object suffixes as verbs in the present tense. The numerous changes undergone by particular verbs are beyond the scope of this book. However, the following example with the verb *3iref* (know) can serve as a basic pattern.

3iref<u>ni</u>	he knew me
3iref<u>ek</u>	he knew you (*m sg*)
3iref<u>ich</u>	he knew you (*f sg*)
3iref<u>e</u>	he knew him
3iref<u>he</u>	he knew her
3iref<u>ne</u>	he knew us
3iref<u>kum</u>	he knew you (*pl*)
3iref<u>hum</u>	he knew them

Continuous tense using the prefix *da-*

In Iraqi Arabic, the present continuous tense for an ongoing activity is formed by adding the prefix *da-* to the verb in the present tense, e.g.

aani <u>da-ashreb</u> chai hesse.	I <u>am drinking</u> tea now.
aHmed <u>da-yidrus</u> hendese.	Ahmed <u>is studying</u> engineering.

The continuous tense is also used in questions with the interrogative prefix *sh-*, e.g.

sh-da-asewwi?	What am I doing?
sh-da-tiktibbeen?	What are you (*f sg*) writing?
sh-da-yiqroon?	What are they reading?

V. Exercises

12.1 Fill in the blanks using the correct form of *nefis* as a reflexive pronoun:

1. *leila w-selma _____ raaHaw lis-seeneme.*
2. *aani _____ ma a3ruf.*
3. *intu _____ laazim tiqroon il-ktaab.*
4. *zeki _____ kiteb il-eemiel.*
5. *iHne _____ raaH nzoorhe.*

12.2 Fill in the blanks using the correct form of *nefis*, by itself or with the prefix *b-*.

1. *aani shifit _____ il-filim arba3 marraat.*
2. *jiddi raaH liT-Tabeeb _____. (jiddi → my grandfather)*
3. *humme ista3milaw _____ il-ktaab.*
4. *laazim yrooHoon lil-medrese _____.*
5. *iHne saaferne l-baghdaad _____.*

12.3 Answer the following questions by replacing the verb "do" (*sewwe* [*ysewwi*]) with the verb in brackets. For the proper conjugation of the verb in the present tense, use the dictionary. Then translate the answer into English.

Example: dunya, sh-da-tsewween? –(*naDHDHaf*)
 → *aani da-anaDHDHuf il-hammaam.*
 I am cleaning the bathroom.

1.	*sh-da-tsewwi, aHmed?*	(*akal*)
2.	*sh-da-tsewwi leila?*	(*dires Tibb*)
3.	*sh-da- tsewwoon?*	(*qire*)
4.	*sh-da-tsewween?*	(*khaaber ummi*)
5.	*sh-da-nsewwi?*	(*shireb gahwe*)

12.4 Attach the appropriate direct object pronoun suffixes to the following verbs and translate

Example: ySaddig (*aani*)
 → *ySaddigni* (he believes me)

1.	*azoor*	(*intu*)
2.	*tshoofeen*	(*huwwe*)
3.	*yinToon*	(*iHne*)
4.	*tisma3oon*	(*aani*)
5.	*tu3rufeen*	(*humme*)
6.	*yis'aloon*	(*inte*)
7.	*Hadhdher*	(*inti*)
8.	*yidizzoon*	(*hiyye*)
9.	*saa3ad*	(*aani*)
10.	*khaaber*	(*iHne*)
11.	*tHibboon*	(*hiyye*)

12.5 Translate the following text into Iraqi Arabic, using the dictionary for unfamiliar words:

Leila, do you want to come to the bookstore with me? I have to buy a dictionary, and maybe you will also see the new books there. It is the biggest bookstore in Baghdad, and the books are not expensive. The building is on Rashid Street. Just walk on the street until you reach the post office; then, turn left. Let's meet tomorrow at 2:30 in the afternoon in front of the bookstore. If you come late, it doesn't matter. I will wait there.

12.6 Translate the following text into English, using the dictionary for unfamiliar words:

muneer w-ibraheem aSdiqaa' min iT-Tfoole. chaanaw yidrusoon w-yil3aboon siwiyye. raaHaw l-kulliyyet il-adaab, qisim it-taareekh, w-tkharrijaw min ij-jaami3a senet alif w-tisi3miyye w-khamse w-tis3een. muneer HaSSel waDHeefe b-baghdaad, w-tzawwej ukhut ibraheem, w-humme kullish sa3eeden siwiyye. ibraheem rija3 lij-jaami3a Hatte yidrus lid-diktoraa w-yitkheSSeS b-taareekh il-3iraaq il-qadeem. huwwe hesse ustaadh b-jaami3at il-mooSil.

KEY TO EXERCISES

Unit 1

1.11
<u>hemm</u>ien
sa<u>feer</u>
<u>faa</u>diye
<u>nagh</u>me
3<u>areeDH</u>
<u>shoo</u>fi
<u>ku</u>tub
3<u>ateeg</u>
<u>fi</u>hem
<u>khe</u>lli n<u>rooH</u>

Unit 2

2.1
1.   **aani** farHaane
2.   **iHne** farHaneen
3.   **huwwe** farHaan
4.   **inte** farHaan
5.   **hiyye** farHaane
6.   **inti** farHaane
7.   **intu** farHaneen
8.   **humme** farHaneen

2.2
1.   hiyye min ingiltere
2.   iHne min kenede

3. inti min almaanye
4. huwwe mudeer
5. humme min roosye
6. inte muterjim
7. aani mareeDH
8. intu min il-yaabaan

2.3
1. ktaab**kum**
2. biet**-hum**
3. qaamoos**ich**
4. koob**i**
5. beled**ne**
6. mudarris**-he**
7. weled**ek**
8. bareed**e**

2.4
1. **inti** min maSir
2. **huwwe** min franse
3. **iHne** min almaanye
4. **intu** min lubnaan
5. **humme** min turkiye
6. **aani** min spaanye
7. **hiyye** min baghdaad
8. **inte** min amreeke

2.5
1. in-naar
2. il-kursi
3. ich-chemche
4. is-sur3a
5. il-weqit
6. il-Haraare
7. il-liel
8. iDH-DHaruf
9. id-derub
10. il-qamees

Unit 3

3.1
1. **3idne** waajib
2. **3id-he** waajib
3. **3idkum** waajib
4. **3indek** waajib
5. **3id-hum** waajib
6. **3indi** waajib
7. **3inde** waajib

3.2
1. kaatibe
2. mumeththile
3. muHaasibe
4. naDHeefe
5. thigeele
6. kareeme

3.3
seyyaare, mu3allime, Saboone, wereqe

3.4
1. hiyye **chibeere**
2. ahmed **Tabeeb**
3. nisreen **mareeDHe**
4. is-seyyaare **maksoore**
5. ir-raadyo **3ateeg**

3.5
1. mitzawwijaat
2. mu3allimeen
3. seyyaaraat
4. Teyyaaraat
5. fallaaHeen
6. Seideliyyaat

7. mektebaat
8. muhandiseen

3.6
1. huwwe ma farHaan
2. Leila ma nesheeTe
3. iHne ma mitakhkhireen
4. Sadeeqaati ma Hilwaat
5. ibni ma chibeer

Unit 4

4.1
1. **wien** it-tikit?
2. **wien** ir-raadyo?
3. **wien** il-ustaadh?
4. **wien** iT-Teyyaare?
5. **wien** il-moze?

4.2
1. 3indi **arba3** chlaab
2. 3indi **tisi3** awraaq
3. 3indi **sabi3** juneT
4. 3indi **khamis** ikhwaan
5. 3indi **sit** aSdiqaaʻ
6. 3indi **thmen** kutub
7. 3indi **tlath** banaat

4.3
1. 3indi **maa3oonien**
2. 3indi **moosien**
3. 3indi **khaalien**
4. 3indi **glaaSien**
5. 3indi **cheTelien**

4.4
1. 3indi **khaashoogtien**
2. 3indi **mraaytien**
3. 3indi **sichcheentien**
4. 3indi **purtuqaaltien**
5. 3indi **bieDHtien**

4.5
1. chem **akh** 3indek?
2. chem **qelem** 3indek?
3. chem **ktaab** 3indek?
4. chem **koob** 3indek?
5. chem **mu3allim** 3indek?

4.6
1. il-kaamire **maaltek**
2. ij-jawaaz **maalne**
3. iT-Tabeeb **maale**
4. iT-Tabeebe **maalet-hum**
5. il-mudarris **maalhe**
6. il-mudarrise **maaletkum**
7. it-tuffaaHe **maaltich**

4.7
1. **maku** bieDH
2. **maku** floos
3. **maku** gumrug
4. **maku** kahrabaa'iyyaat
5. **maku** ei shee

4.8
1.
Soor**ti**
Soor**tek**
Soor**tich**
Soor**te**
Soor**et-he**
Soor**etne**

Soore**tkum**
Soore**t-hum**

2.
khuTT**eti**
khuTT**etek**
khuTT**etich**
khuTT**ete**
khuTTe**t-he**
khuTT**etne**
khuTTet**kum**
khuTTe**t-hum**

Unit 5

5.1

101	=	miyye w-waaHid
45	=	khamse w-arba3een
15	=	khumuSTa3ash
151	=	miyye w-waaHid w-khamseen
220	=	meetien w-3ishreen
33	=	tlaathe w-tlaatheen
11	=	da3ash
459	=	arba3amiyye w-tis3a w-khamseen
997	=	tisi3miyye w-sab3a w-tis3een

5.2

	Singular	Plural
play	al3ab 1st	nil3ab 1st
	til3ab 2nd *m*	til3aboon 2nd
	til3abeen 2nd *f*	
	yil3ab 3rd *m*	yil3aboon 3rd
	til3ab 3rd *f*	

write	aktib 1ˢᵗ	niktib 1ˢᵗ
	tiktib 2ⁿᵈ *m*	tiktiboon 2ⁿᵈ
	tiktibeen 2ⁿᵈ *f*	
	yiktib 3ʳᵈ *m*	yiktiboon 3ʳᵈ
	tiktib 3ʳᵈ *f*	
study	adrus 1ˢᵗ	nidrus 1ˢᵗ
	tidrus 2ⁿᵈ *m*	tidrusoon 2ⁿᵈ
	tidruseen 2ⁿᵈ *f*	
	yidrus 3ʳᵈ *m*	yidrusoon 3ʳᵈ
	tidrus 3ʳᵈ *f*	

5.3
1. **chem** wereqe bil-ktaab?
2. **shged** floos 3indek?
3. **shged** mei tishreb?
4. **chem** moze bis-selle?
5. **chem** binaaye bil-medeene?

5.4
1. You play (2ⁿᵈ *pl*)
2. He laughs (3ʳᵈ *sg m*)
3. You spend (2ⁿᵈ *sg m*), or she spends (3ʳᵈ *sg f*)
4. We drink (1ˢᵗ *pl*)
5. You sit (2ⁿᵈ *pl*)
6. You hear (2ⁿᵈ *sg f*)
7. You open (2ⁿᵈ *sg m*), or she opens (3ʳᵈ *sg f*)
8. They sleep (3ʳᵈ *pl*)
9. I wash (1ˢᵗ *sg*)
10. We write (1ˢᵗ *pl*)

5.5
1. leila tiktib **l-tom**
2. aani arooH **l-baghdaad**
3. sam yrooH **lil-bab**
4. aani aqre **lil-aTfaal**
5. ummi tsaafir **lin-najaf**

5.6
1. **hedholaak** il-mudarriseen amreekaan. (Those teachers are Americans)
2. **hedhaak** il-weled chibeer. (That boy is big)
3. **hedheech** is-seyyaare Safre (That car *f* is yellow)
4. **hedhaak** il-qelem maksoor (That pen *m* is broken)
5. **hedholaak** il-banaat yidrusoon (Those girls study)

Unit 6

6.1

	Singular	*Plural*
shaaf (see)	ashoof 1st	nshoof 1st
	tshoof 2nd *m*	tshoofoon 2nd
	tshoofeen 2nd *f*	
	yshoof 3rd *m*	yshoofoon 3rd
	tshoof 3rd *f*	
khaaf (be afraid)	akhaaf 1st	nkhaaf 1st
	tkhaaf 2nd *m*	tkhaafoon 2nd
	tkhaafeen 2nd *f*	
	ykhaaf 3rd *m*	ykhaafoon 3rd
	tkhaaf 3rd *f*	
baa3 (sell)	abee3 1st	nbee3 1st
	tbee3 2nd *m*	tbee3oon 2nd
	tbee3een 2nd *f*	
	ybee3 3rd *m*	ybee3oon 3rd
	tbee3 3rd *f*	
Saam (fast)	asoom 1st	nSoom 1st
	tSoom 2nd *m*	tSoomoon 2nd
	tSoomeen 2nd *f*	
	ySoom 3rd *m*	ySoomoon 3rd
	tSoom 3rd *f*	
3aash (live)	a3eesh 1st	n3eesh 1st
	t3eesh 2nd *m*	t3eeshoon 2nd
	t3eesheen 2nd *f*	
	y3eesh 3rd *m*	y3eeshoon 3rd
	t3eesh 3rd *f*	

6.2
1. yjeeboon
2. ysheel
3. trooHoon
4. treed
5. ySeer
6. aSoom
7. tnaam
8. til3aboon
9. ymootoon
10. ngoom

6.3
1. **yshoofoon** il-filim
2. **tbee3oon** athaath
3. **yreed** yaakul
4. **anaam** min weqit
5. **trooH** lij-jaami3a

6.4
1. ashoof**e**
2. ysheel**ek**
3. tilHag**ni**
4. tzoor**ich**
5. ashkur**he**

6.5
1. ktaab sam
2. seyyaaret il-weled
3. biet jiddi
4. Tabeeb suzaan
5. deelaab il-ghurfe

6.6
1. il-biet chibeer
2. ish-shaari3 khaali
3. il-koob meksoor

4.   ir-raadyo ghaali
5.   il-maa3oon faarigh

6.7
1.   mudarriseen **zieneen**
2,   aDHwiye **qawiyye**
3.   dawaleeb **meksoore**
4.   Sadeeqaat **3azeezaat**
5.   temreenaat **ziene**

6.8
1.   yreed yighsil il-maa3oon
2.   areed aktib
3.   treed tisma3 ir-raadyo
4.   nreed nrooH lis-seeneme
5.   yreedoon yig3udoon

Unit 7

7.1

	Singular	*Plural*
sedd (close)	asidd 1st	nsidd 1st
	tsidd 2nd *m*	tsiddoon 2nd
	tsiddeen 2nd *f*	
	ysidd 3rd *m*	ysiddoon 3rd
	tsidd 3rd *f*	
leff (wrap)	aliff 1st	nliff 1st
	tliff 2nd *m*	tliffoon 2nd
	tliffeen 2nd *f*	
	yliff 3rd *m*	yliffoon 3rd
	tliff 3rd *f*	
geSS (cut)	aguSS 1st	nguSS 1st
	tguSS 2nd *m*	
	tguSSeen 2nd *f*	tguSSoon 2n
	yguSS 3rd *m*	
	tguSS 3rd *f*	yguSSoon 3rd

7.2

	Singular	Plural
bide (begin)	abdi 1st	nibdi 1st
	tibdi 2nd *m*	tibdoon 2nd
	tibdeen 2nd *f*	
	yibdi 3rd *m*	yibdoon 3rd
	tibdi 3rd *f*	
mile (fill)	amli 1st	nimli 1st
	timli 2nd *m*	timloon 2nd
	timleen 2nd *f*	
	yimli 3rd *m*	yimloon 3rd
	timli 3rd *f*	
lige (find)	algi 1st	nilgi 1st
	tilgi 2nd *m*	tilgoon 2nd
	tilgeen 2nd *f*	
	yilgi 3rd *m*	yilgoon 3rd
	tilgi 3rd *f*	
buqe (stay)	abqe 1st	nubqe 1st
	tubqe 2nd *m*	tubqoon 2nd
	tubqeen 2nd *f*	
	yubqe 3rd *m*	yubqoon 3rd
	tubqe 3rd *f*	
biche (cry)	abchi 1st	nibchi 1st
	tibchi 2nd *m*	tibchoon 2nd
	tibcheen 2nd *f*	
	yibchi 3rd *m*	yibchoon 3rd
	tibchi 3rd *f*	

7.3
1. taakloon
2. yiji
3. aakhudh
4. tu'mur
5. noSel

7.4
1. njurr → **iHne**
2. taakhudh → **inte/hiyye**
3. timsheen → **inti**
4. tHuTT → **inte/hiyye**
5. yilghi → **huwwe**
6. t3iddoon → **intu**
7. tinqudh → **inte/hiyye**
8. tiHchoon → **intu**
9. nirmi → **iHne**
10. adizz → **aani**

7.5
1. tisi3 **khyaaraat**
2. aani ma aakul **reggi**
3. yishtiri **bieDH**
4. **beTeekhtien**
5. geshsherit arba3 **betinjaanaat**

7.6
1. tHibb taakul **fed shee** hesse?
2. tHuTT **fed** purtuqaale bich-chees
3. naakhudh **fed** thmen mishmishaat
4. yisma3 **fed shee**
5. yishreboon **fed shee** baarid

7.7
1. iHne **ba3adne** joo3aaneen
2. HuTTi **ba3ad** qelemien bij-janTe
3. il-ghurfe **ba3ad-he** baarde
4. treedoon tshoofoon **ba3ad** filmien?
5. il-banaat **ba3ad-hum** bil-medrese

Unit 8

8.1
1. imshu
2. ukul
3. ubqi
4. iktib
5. ogfu
6. jurr
7. sooqi

8.2
1. la **trooHoon** hnak!
2. la **tsidd** il-baab!
3. la **taakhdheen** ij-janTe!
4. la **tidkhuleen** il-binaaye!
5. la **tugmuzoon**!

8.3
1. imshu **gubel**
2. il-medrese **gbaal** il-Hadeeqe
3. la togaf **gbaal** il-medfe'e
4. rooHi **gubel** ila an toSleen mawqif il-paS
5. aku seyyaare **gbaal** il-biet

8.4
1. 3ndi **bes** qelem waaHid
2. ukul **ila an** tishba3
3. id-dinye Haarre **laakin** maku kahrabaa'
4. aani ashreb **bes** koobien chai bil-yom
5. urukDHu **ila an** toSloon il-3alaame

8.5
1. aTbukh lich dijaaje
2. niji lil-medrese; niji il-he
3. tiktib li maktoob

4.   ybee3 lich kutub
5.   yimshi lil-Hadaayiq; yimshi il-he
6.   ndizz eemiel l-muHarrireen ij-jereede; ndizz il-hum emiel
7.   tismaH lil-aTfaal yil3aboon hna? tismaH il-hum
      yil3aboon hna?
8.   tirsim lek Soore Hilwe
9.   ashtiri in-ne (a)qlaam
10.   iftaH il-baab lil-khuTTaar; iftaH ilhum il-baab

Unit 9

9.1

1.   nistereeH
2.   tsejjil
3.   yit3aarfoon
4.   anaaqish
5.   tishtiroon
6.   titgheyyer

9.2
1.   2:30 saa3a thintien w-nuSS
2.   6:50 saa3a sab3a ille 3ashre
3.   11:35 saa3a da3ash w-nuSS w-khamse
4.   12: 05 saa3a thna3ash w-khamse
5.   3:40 saa3a arba3a ille thilith
6.   5:15 saa3a khamse w-rubu3

9.3
1.   khamse neesaan
2.   sbaTa3ash eilool
3.   sitte kaanoon ith-thaani
4.   arbaTa3ash shbaaT
5.   arba3a tammooz

9.4
1. **yaa** ktaab tHibboon azyad?
2. **liesh** il-biet ma naDHeef?
3. **minu** yreed yishreb chai?
4. **yaa** ayyaam tishtaghleen?
5. **intu** liesh ta3baaneen il-yom?

9.5
1. areed anaaqish il-ktaab **wiyyaahum**
2. zeki yil3ab **wiyyaahe**
3. 3indi maw3id **wiyyaa** saa3a khamse w-nuSS
4. minu yreed yrooH lis-seeneme **wiyyaahum**
5. aani ma aqder ashtughul **wiyyaahum**

9.6
1. bil-3iraaq is-sabit awwel yom bil-isboo3
2. kaanoon ith-thaani awwel sheher bis-sene
3. b-amreeke il-aHHad awwel yom bil-isboo3
4. bil-3iraaq il-binoog masdoode yom ij-jum3a
5. il-awlaad bil-medrese ila saa3a thintien

Unit 10

10.1
1. fitHaw
2. rikDHet
3. shifne
4. ligietu
5. dezz
6. akalit

10.2
1. leila **chaanet trooH** lis-seeneme marre wiHde bil-isboo3
2. aani **chinit aakul** hwaaye
3. huwwe **chaan yshoof** iT-Tabeeb b-intiDHaam

4. iHne **chinne nishtiri** kutub min il-mektebe
5. aHmed **chaan yishtughul** bil-musteshfe

10.3
1. shbaaT **thaani** sheher bis-sene
2. haadhi **thaalith** marre ashoof il-filim
3. ir-reggiyye **il-oola** chaanet ziene
4. il-arbi3aa' **khaamis** yom bil-isboo3 (5th)
5. il-medrese bil-binaaye **ir-raab3a**

10.4
1. laazim **trooHoon** hesse. You (*pl*) have to go now.
2. laazim **tsaa3id** akhook. You (*m sg*) have to help your brother.
3. aani laazim **aakhudh** id-duwe. I have to take the medicine.
4. iHne laazim **niktib** eemiel. We have to write an e-mail.
5. humme laazim **ysaafroon** hesse. They have to travel now.

10.5
1. aHmed **aboohe**. Ahmed is her father.
2. **abooye** bil-baSre. My father is in Basra.
3. **akhooye** mareeDH. My brother is sick.
4. **aboone** muhandis. Our father is an engineer.
5. **aboohum** id-diktor rasheed. Their father is Dr. Rasheed.

10.6
1. **shlon** abook il-yom?
2. **sh-aku** maku?
3. **shinoo** isim ish-shaari3?
4. **shwekit** treedoon trooHoon?
5. **sh-akalti** wiyye il-3aSeer?

Unit 11

11.1
1. tSewwiraw
2. btismet

3. naDHDHafti
4. ista3jelit
5. jaawebne
6. tshaarek

11.2
1. tlaatheen neesaan, senet alif w-tisi3miyye w-tis3een
2. sab3a tammooz, senet alfien w-thnien
3. thna3ash Huzeiraan, senet alif w-thmanmiyye w-sab3a w-sitteen
4. tis3a eyaar, senet alif w-tisi3miyye w-khamse w-tlaatheen
5. waahid shbaaT, senet alfien w-khamse

11.3
1. khamse w-3ishreen milyon w-sitmiyye w-sab3een alif w-miyye
2. tisi3miyye w-sitte w-khamseen alif w-arba3miyye w-waahid
3. sabi3miyye w-sitteen alif
4. thmanmiyye w-tlaathe w-khamseen alif w-tis3a w-tis3een
5. milyon w-arba3miyye w-arba3a w-arba3een alif w-miyye w-sitte w-sab3een

11.4
1. leila **azghar** Taalibe.
2. aHmed yimshi **abTa' min** muneer.
3. idh-dheheb (gold) hwaaye **ghaali**.
4. ma 3indi floos, ishtiriet **arkhaS** janTe.
5. haadhi il-binaaye **aqdem min** hadheech.
6. ish-shite (winter) **abred min** iS-Sief (summer).
7. il-muroor (traffic) **baTee'**.
8. il-reggiyye **akbar min** it-tuffaaHa.
9. iT-Teyyaare **asra3 min** is-seyyaare.
10. inshaalle ij-jaw baachir ykoon **aHsen min** il-yom.

11.5

1. leila w-muneer **raaH yrooHoon** lis-seeneme il-isboo3 ij-jaay.
2. aHmed **raaH yigi** il-khamees.
3. iHne **raaH naakul** saa3a sab3a.
4. intu raaH **tkhaabroon** baachir?
5. selma **raaH tHawwil** floos ba3ad yomien.
6. intu **raaH tkoonoon** bil-biet baachir?

11.6

1. idha aftaH Hsaab hesse agder aHawwil floos baachir?
2. idha taakhudh haadhe il-qiTaar raaH tkoon hnak saa3a khamse.
3. idha nrooH hesse raaH nshoofhe.
4. idha il-mektebe mfattiHe raaH nishtiri kutub.
5. idha tiktib maktoob laazim tishtiri Tawaabi3.

Unit 12

12.1

1. leila w-selma **nefis-hum** raaHaw lis-seeneme.
2. aani **nefsi** ma a3ruf.
3. intu **nefiskum** laazim tiqroon il-ktaab.
4. zeki **nefse** kiteb il-eemiel.
5. iHne **nefisne** raaH nzoorhe.

12.2

1. aani shifit **nefis** il-filim arba3 marraat.
2. jiddi raaH liT-Tabeeb **b-nefse**.
3. humme ista3milaw **nefis** il-ktaab.
4. laazim yrooHoon lil-medrese **b-nefis-hum**.
5. iHne saaferne l-baghdaad **b-nefisne**.

12.3

1. aani **da-aakul**. I am eating.
2. leila **da-tidrus** Tibb. Leila is studying medicine.

3.   iHne **da-niqre**. We are reading.
4.   aani **da-akhaabur** ummi. I am calling my mother.
5.   iHne **da-nishreb** gahwe. We are drinking coffee.

12.4

1.   azoorkum (I visit you *pl*)
2.   tshoofee (you *f sg* see him)
3.   yinToone (they give us)
4.   tisma3ooni (you *pl* hear me)
5.   tu3rufeehum (you *f sg* know them)
6.   yis'alook (they ask you *m sg*)
7.   Hadhdherich (he warned you *f sg*)
8.   yidizzoohe (they send her)
9.   saa3adni (he helped me)
10. khaaberne (he called us)
11. tHibboohe (you *pl* love her)

12.5

leila, treedeen tijeen lil-mektebe wiyyaaye? aani laazim ashtiri
qaamoos, w-yimkin inti hemmen raaH tshoofeen kutub
jideede hnak. hiyye akbar mektebe b-baghdaad, wil-kutub ma
ghaalye. il-binaaye b-shaari3 ir-rasheed. bes imshi bish-
shaari3 ila an toSleen mekteb il-bareed, ba3dien ikisri yisre.
khalli niltiqi baachir saa3a thintien w-nuSS il-3aSir, gbaal
il-mektebe. idha tijeen mit'akhkhire, ma yhimm, aani raaH
antiDHir hnak.

12.6

Munir and Ibrahim are friends since childhood. They used to
study and play together. They went to the College of Arts, the
history department, and graduated from the university in 1995.
Munir obtained a job in Baghdad and married Ibrahim's sister,
and they are very happy together. Ibrahim returned to the university to study for a doctorate, and he specializes in the
history of ancient Iraq. He is now a professor at the University
of Mosul.

VERB APPENDIX FOR THE CONJUGATION OF SOUND VERBS IN THE PAST TENSE

1. Regular i-e *verbs*

	dires (study)		*shiker* (thank)	
aani	I studied	**dires<u>it</u>**	I thanked	**shiker<u>it</u>**
inte	you *m* studied	**dires<u>it</u>**	you *m* thanked	**shiker<u>it</u>**
inti	you *f* studied	**dires<u>ti</u>**	you *f* thanked	**shiker<u>ti</u>**
huwwe	he studied	**dires**	he thanked	**shik<u>er</u>**
hiyye	she studied	**dirs<u>et</u>**	she thanked	**shikr<u>et</u>**
iHne	we studied	**dires<u>ne</u>**	we thanked	**shiker<u>ne</u>**
intu	you *pl* studied	**dires<u>tu</u>**	you *pl* thanked	**shiker<u>tu</u>**
humme	they studied	**dirs<u>aw</u>**	they thanked	**shikr<u>aw</u>**

3idem	execute	kireH	hate
3ijeb	like	kiser	break
3ileg	switch on	kiteb	write
3iSer	squeeze	libes	wear
3iTes	sneeze	lizem	catch
3izem	invite	milek	own
dhiker	mention	niqedh	rescue
difen	bury	niqel	transport
dikhel	enter	niSeb	install
fihem	understand	nishef	dry
fishel	fail	nisher	spread
ghireg	drown	nizef	bleed
ghisel	wash	qibel	accept
gider	be able to	qileq	worry
HiDHer	attend	qiSed	mean
hijem	attack	qitel	kill
Hijez	reserve	rigeS	dance
Hilem	dream	rikeDH	run
Hileq	shave	risem	draw
Hireg	burn	rizem	pack
Hizer	guess	shihed	testify
khidem	serve	sijen	imprison
khileq	create	Tired	expel
khitem	seal	tirek	leave
kidheb	lie		

2.   *Irregular* **i-e** *verbs*

	3iref (know)		*shireb* (drink)	
aani	I knew	**3irefit**	I drank	**shirebit**
inte	you *m* knew	**3irefit**	you *m* drank	**shirebit**
inti	you *f* knew	**3irefti**	you *f* drank	**shirebti**
huwwe	he knew	**3iref**	he drank	**shireb**
hiyye	she knew	**3urfet**	she drank	**shurbet**
iHne	we knew	**3irefne**	we drank	**shirebne**
intu	you *pl* knew	**3ireftu**	you *pl* drank	**shirebtu**
humme	they knew	**3urfaw**	they drank	**shurbaw**

DHireb	hit	**sileb**	hold up
khiTeb	deliver a speech	**Tileb**	demand
rihem	fit	**wiSef**	describe
rikeb	ride		

3. Regular i-a verbs

	difa3 (pay)		rija3 (return)	
aani	I paid	**difa3<u>it</u>**	I returned	**rija3<u>it</u>**
inte	you (*m*) paid	**difa3<u>it</u>**	you (*m*) returned	**rija3<u>it</u>**
inti	you (*f*) paid	**difa3<u>ti</u>**	you (*f*) returned	**rija3<u>ti</u>**
huwwe	he paid	**difa3**	he returned	**rija3**
hiyye	she paid	**dif3<u>at</u>**	she returned	**rij3<u>at</u>**
iHne	we paid	**difa3<u>ne</u>**	we returned	**rija3<u>ne</u>**
intu	you (*pl*) paid	**difa3<u>tu</u>**	you (*pl*) returned	**rija3<u>tu</u>**
humme	they paid	**dif3<u>aw</u>**	they returned	**rij3<u>aw</u>**

fitaH	open	**shiba3**	be full
jima3	collect	**shiraH**	explain
mina3	prevent	**sibaH**	swim
misaH	erase	**sima3**	hear
nibaH	bark	**wiga3**	fall
niza3	take off	**zira3**	plant
qita3	disconnect		

4.   *Irregular* **i-a** *verbs*

	DHiHak (laugh)		*li3ab* (play)	
aani	I laughed	**DHiHak<u>it</u>**	I played	**li3ab<u>it</u>**
inte	you (*m*) laughed	**DHiHak<u>it</u>**	you (*m*) played	**li3ab<u>it</u>**
inti	you (*f*) laughed	**DHiHak<u>ti</u>**	you (*f*) played	**li3ab<u>ti</u>**
huwwe	he laughed	**DHiHak**	he played	**li3ab**
hiyye	she laughed	**DHiHk<u>et</u>**	she played	**li3b<u>et</u>**
iHne	we laughed	**DHiHak<u>ne</u>**	we played	**li3ab<u>ne</u>**
intu	you (*pl*) laughed	**DHiHak<u>tu</u>**	you (*pl*) played	**li3ab<u>tu</u>**
humme	they laughed	**DHiHk<u>aw</u>**	they played	**li3b<u>aw</u>**

si'al	ask	**liHag**	follow
si3al	cough	**TiHan**	grind
shi3ar	feel	**wi3ad**	promise
3iradDH	show		

5. *Regular* u-e *verbs*

	kuber (grew)		*Subegh* (paint)	
aani	I grew	**kuberit**	I painted	**Subeghit**
inte	you (*m*) grew	**kuberit**	you (*m*) painted	**Subeghit**
inti	you (*f*) grew	**kuberti**	you (*f*) painted	**Subeghti**
huwwe	he grew	**kuber**	he painted	**Subegh**
hiyye	she grew	**kubret**	she painted	**Subghet**
iHne	we grew	**kuberne**	we painted	**Subeghne**
intu	you (*pl*) grew	**kubertu**	you (*pl*) painted	**Subeghtu**
humme	they grew	**kubraw**	they painted	**Subghaw**

3uber	cross	**rubeT**	tie
DHumen	guarantee	**shumer**	throw
fuSel	fire	**Tubekh**	cook
gumez	jump	**umer**	command
khubeT	mix	**wugef**	stand
nufeDH	shake	**wuSel**	reach
qubeDH	capture, get paid		

IRAQI ARABIC-ENGLISH DICTIONARY

Arrangement of Entries

Arabic words appear in romanized form throughout this book. As such, this dictionary lists them in alphabetical order according to the roman alphabet. The letter "3" (pronounced *ain*) is treated as a letter between "a" and "b". Arabic letters rendered as double consonants in English, for example *th* and *sh*, are given their own heading. The alphabetization follows this order:

a - 3 - b - ch - d - dh - DH - e - f - g - gh - h - H - i -
j - k - kh - l - m - n - o - p - q - r - s - S - sh - t -T -
th - u - v - w - y - z

Adjectives are generally listed in their singular masculine form. For the reader's convenience, the feminine and/or plural forms are largely included. The irregular ones in particular have these forms noted.

Iraqi Arabic verbs are listed as follows: 3rd person masculine singular in the past tense, followed by the present tense in brackets: *kiteb (yiktib)*. For derived verbs, the group is given in Roman numerals, e.g *zeyyed (yzeyyid) II* (For an overview of the most important derived verb groups, see Unit 9).

In the Iraqi Arabic-English section of the dictionary, words and idioms usually preceded by the article *il-* are listed under the first letter of the noun. For example, the city of Basra is listed under "b," i.e. *baSre (il-baSre)*.

a

aab August *n*

aakhir ish-sheher at the end of the month *adv*

aale instrument *n*

aamir (umeraa') prison warden; commander (*army*) *n*

aani I *pron*

aanise (aanisaat) Miss *n*

a3DHam greatest *adj*; ~ **min** greater than *adj*

a3la Hadd maximum, highest level *n*

a3le highest, upper *adj*; ~ **min** higher than *adj*

a3len (yi3lin) IV announce *v*

a3raaDH *pl* symptoms *n*

a3teg (min) older (than) (*object*) *adj*

a3dhaa' tanaasuliyye genitals *n*

ab (abaa') father *n*

ab3ad farther *adj*; beyond *prep*

abed ever *adv*

abeden never *adv*

abred (min) colder (than) *adj*

abTa' (min) slower (than) *adj*

abul-bareed postman *n*

abul-booriyyaat plumber *n*

abyeDH (*f* bieDHe) white *adj*

adhaar March *n*

aDHlam (*f* DHalme) dark *adj*

aDHwiyet il-muroor traffic lights *n pl*

afghaan (il-afghaan) *coll* Afghan(s) *n*

afghaanistaan Afghanistan *n*

afraad (il-afraad) personnel *n*

afreeqi (*pl* afaariqe) African *adj*

afreeqye Africa *n*

aghle (min) more expensive (than) *adj*

aghlebiyye majority *n*

aHarr (min) hotter (than) *adj*

ahemiyye importance *n*

aHHad (il-aHHad) Sunday *n*

ahlan welcome *n*; ~ **wa sahlan** welcome; ~ **beek** you're welcome (see also Unit 4)

aHmer (*f* Hamre) red *adj*

aHsen best *adj*; ~ **min** better than *adj*

ajded (min) newer (than) *adj*

ajhize equipment *n*; **ajhizet inSaat sirriyye** hidden microphone

ajjer (y'ajjir) II rent *v*

ajnebi (*pl* ajaanib) alien, foreign *adj*; foreigner *n*

akadeemi academic *adj*

akal (yaakul) eat *v*

akbar (**min**) bigger/older (than) *adj*

akh (ikhwaan) brother *n*

akhadh (yaakhudh) take *v*; ~ **doosh** take a shower *v*; ~ **Hammaam** take a
  bath/shower *v* ~ **reheene** take hostage *v*

akhaff (**min**) lighter (than) *adj*

akhbaar news *n*

akhDHar (*f* khaDHre) green *adj*

akheer last, final *adj*

akheeren finally *adv*

akhi *way of addressing a male stranger* (*lit.* my brother)

akhle (yikhli) IV evacuate *v*

akil *coll* food *n*

akkad (y'akkid) II emphasize *v*

akraad *coll* Kurds *n*

ak-thar min more than *prep*; **il-ak-thariyye** the majority *n*

aku there is/are

alem pain *n*

alif (alaaf) thousand *adj*

alla bil-khier may God bless your day (*greeting among men*)

alle ybaarik beek may God bless you (*a response to* **mabrook**
  [Congratulations!])

alle yin3im aliek May God bless you (*a response to* **na3eemen** [May you
  enjoy.])

almaani German *adj, n*

almaanye Germany *n*

aloo hello (*telephone only*)

amaan safety, security *n*

ameen honest, safe *adj*

amel hope *n*

amin security *n*

amreeke America, United States *n*

amreeki (*pl* amreekaan) American *adj*

amur (awaamir) order, command *n*

anaani selfish *adj*

angas (**min**) worse (than) *adj*

anhe (yinhi) IV end *v trans*

anqaS (**min**) less (than) *prep*

anqedh (yinqudh) IV save *v*

anSe (**min**) lower (than) *adj*

antej (yintij) IV produce *v*
aqall (min) less (than) *adv*
aqdem (min) older (than) (*object*) *adj*
aqrab (min) closer (than) *adj*
arba3 four (*with a noun*) *adj*
arba3a four (*standing alone*) *adj*
arba3een forty *adj*; ~ **alif** forty thousand *adj*
arba3meet four hundred (*with noun*) *adj*; ~ **alif** four hundred thousand *adj*
arba3miyye four hundred (*standing alone*) *adj*
arba3talaaf four thousand *adj*
arbaTa3ash fourteen *adj*
arbi3aa' (il-arbi3aa') Wednesday *n*
ardun (il-ardun) Jordan *n*
arduni Jordanian *adj, n*
areq insomnia *n*
ariDH (araaDHi) land *n*
arkhaS (min) cheaper (than) *adj*
armal (araamil) widower *n*
armale (araamil) widow *n*
asaasi basic *adj*
aSder (yiSdur) IV issue *v*
aseer Harub (asra Harub) P.O.W. (prisoner of war) *n*
aSfar (*f* Safre) yellow *adj*
ashger (*f* shegre *pl* shugur) blond *adj*
ashi33a X-ray *n;* **akhadh** ~ take an X-ray *v*
aslaak shaa'ike barbed wire *n*
aSli original *adj*
asliHa dherriyye nuclear weapons *n pl*
asmer (*f* samre *pl* sumur) brunette *adj*
asra3 (min) faster (than) *adj*
asses (y'assis) II establish *v*
aswa' (min) worse *adj*
aswaaq supermarket *n*
aswed (*f* sode) black *adj*
athaath furniture *n*
ather jeriH (athaar jrooH) scar *n*
athnaa' during *prep*
aTresh (*f* Tarshe *pl* Turshaan) deaf *adj*
aTwel (min) longer (than) *adj*
aw or *conj*
awket (min) earlier (than) *adv*
awlaad children *n*
awwel (*f* oola) first *adj*; ~ **il-baarHa** day before yesterday *adv*

ayyaamek sa3eede *courtesy exchange during religious holidays* (*lit.* may your days be happy)
az3aj (yiz3ij) IV disturb *v*
azghar (min) younger/smaller (than) *adj*
azme crisis *n*
azreg (*f* zarge) blue *adj*
azyad (min) more (than) *adv*

3 (ain)

3aa'ile (3awaa'il) family *n*
3aad (y3eed) repeat *v*
3aade shahriyye (il-3aade ish-shahriyye) menstruation *n*
3aadeten usually *adv*
3aadi ordinary, regular; usual *adj*
3aadil (*f* 3aadle) just *adj*
3aaf (y3oof) leave *v*
3aahre prostitute *n*
3aajil (*f* 3aajle) urgent *adj*
3aalem world *n*
3aalemi international *adj*
3aali (*f* 3aalye) high; loud *adj*
3aalim (*pl* 3ulemaa') scientist *n*
3aamil (*pl* 3awaamil) factor *n*; (*pl* 3ummaal) laborer, worker *n*; ~ **fenni** technician *n*; ~ **beddaale** operator *n*
3aamm general; public *adj*
3aamood (a3mide) column *n*
3aaqir (3aaqre) sterile, infertile *adj*
3aar shame *n*
3aareDH (y3aariDH) III disagree *v*
3aash (y3eesh) exist, live *v*
3aashet il-ayaadi *compliment to a cook* (*lit.* Long live the hands that cooked this food.)
3aashir (*f* 3aashre) tenth *adj*
3aaSife (3awaaSif) storm *n*
3aaSime (3awaaSim) capital (*city*) *n*
3aaTil (*f* 3aaTle *pl* 3aaTleen) unemployed; out of order (*machine*) *adj*
3aawen (y3aawin) III aid, help *v*
3aaz (y3ooz) be lacking *v*
3aazib (*f* 3aazbe *pl* 3uzzaab) single (*not married*) *adj*
3abbaare ferry *n*
3abber (y3abbur) II express *v*

3ada except *prep*; **ma ~** except for *prep*
3adaale justice *n*
3adasaat laaSiqe contact lens *n*
3add (y3idd) count *v*
3aded (a3daad) number *n*
3adese lens *n*
3adhaab ordeal *n*
3adhdhab (y3adhdhib) II torture *v*
3aDHeem great *adj*
3aDHele muscle *n*
3adhraa' virgin *n*
3aDHum (3DHaam) bone *n*
3adil (*f* 3adle) even, straight, flat, level *adj*
3adu (a3daa') enemy *n*
3adwe infection *n*
3afu (il-3afu) pardon me; sorry
3ajeeb ghareeb unbelievable *adj*
3ajooze (*pl* 3ajaayiz) old (*woman*) *adj, n*
3akis contrast, opposite *n*
3al ak-thar mostly *adv*
3al gaa3 on the ground *adv*
3ala on, on top of, over, upon *prep*; **~ ghafle** suddenly *adv*; **~ kull Haal** at any rate *adv*; **~ SafHa** aside, apart *adv*; **~ Tool** all along, always *adv*; **~ yemeen** to the right of *adv*
3alaamaat iT-Tareeq *pl* road signs *n*
3alaame mark; sign *n*
3aleikum is-salaam May peace be upon you (*greeting in reponse to* is-salaamu 3aleikum)
3alem (a3laam) flag *n*
3amali practical *adj*
3amaliyye operation, surgery *n*; **3amaliyyet naqil id-demm** blood transfusion *n*
3ameeq deep *adj*
3amel (a3maal) act; function; labor, work *n*
3amm (paternal) uncle; father-in-law *n*
3amme (parental) aunt *n*
3ammi my uncle; Sir (*respectful address for strangers older than the speaker*)
3amood faqari spine *n*
3an on (*about*) *prep*; **~ Tareeq** via *prep*
3aqebe obstacle *n*
3aqeem infertile *adj*
3aqid (3uqood) contract *n*

3aqil mind *n*
3aqliyye mentality *n*
3arab *coll* Arabs *n*
3arebi Arab(ic) *adj*
3areeDH broad, wide *adj*
3areeDHe (3araayiDH) petition *n*
3arees groom *n*
3areg perspiration, sweat *n*; liquor made from dates *n*
3ariDH (3urooDH) show (*theater*) *n*; review *n*
3arke fight *n*
3armooT *coll* pears *n*
3aroos(e) bride *n*
3aSaaye (3iSi) stick *n*
3aSebi nervous *adj*; **ij-jihaaz il-** ~ nervous system *n*
3aSeer juice *n*
3asel honey *n*
3ashe dinner *n*
3ashir ten *adj* (*with a noun*)
3ashirtalaaf ten thousand *adj*
3ashre ten *adj* (*standing alone*)
3askeri military *n*
3aSi (3uSaat) rebel *n*
3aSir afternoon *n*
3ateeg old (*object*) *adj*
3aTshaan thirsty *adj*
3ayyen (y3ayyin) II appoint *v*
3ayyine sample *n*
3azeez dear *adj*
3azil isolation *n*
3eed holiday (*religious*) *n*; ~ **meelaad** birthday *n*; ~ **meelaad sa3eed!** Happy birthday!
3eedek mubaarek *courtesy exchanged during religious holidays* (*lit.* May your feast be blessed.)
3ibr across *prep*
3idde (3uded) gear, equipment; hardware *n*
3idem (yi3dim) execute *v*
3idwaan aggression *n*
3idwaani hostile *adj*
3ieb (3yoob) flaw *n*
3ien (3yoon) eye *n*
3ieni *informal address* (*lit.* My eye.)
3ijeb (yi3jib) like *v*
3ikis (3koos) elbow *n*

3ilaaj medication; therapy *n*
3ilaaqe relationship *n*; connection *n*; ~ **jinsiyye** intercourse (sexual) *n*
3ilbe (3ileb) container *n*
3ileg (yi3lig) switch on; light (*fire*) *v*
3ilich chewing gum *n*
3ilim (3iloom) science *n*
3ilmi scientific *adj*
3ilu height (*building*) *n*
3inaaye care *n*; ~ **murekkeze** intensive care *n*; ~ **SiHHiyye** health care *n*
3ind have *prep* + suffix (see Unit 2)
3ineb *coll* grapes *n*
3injaaS *coll* plum(s) *n*
3inwaan (3anaaween) address; title *n*; ~ **baariz** headline *n*; ~ **bareedi** mailing address *n*
3iraaq (il-3iraaq) Iraq *n*
3iraaqi Iraqi *adj, n*
3iraDH (yi3ruDH) show *v*
3iref (yu3ruf) know *v*
3iris (a3raas) wedding *n*
3ishreen twenty *adj*; ~ **alif** twenty thousand *adj*
3iSer (yi3Sur) squeeze *v*
3iSyaan insurgency *n*
3iTes (yi3Tus) sneeze *v*
3iyaade clinic, doctor's office *n*
3izem (yi3zim) invite *v*
3oodet shikhkhaaT match (*wooden*) *n*
3raak fighting *n*
3uber (yu3bur) pass *v*; ~ **ish-shaari3** cross the street *v*
3uboodiyye slavery *n*
3uboor transit *n*; ~ **il-mushaat** zebra crossing *n*
3uDHu (a3DHaa') member; organ (body) *n*
3umaan Oman *n*
3umle currency *n*
3umoole commission *n*
3umur age *n*
3unf violence *n*
3unSur (3anaaSir) component, element; race *n*
3unSuri *m* racial *adj*
3unSuriyye racism *n*
3uqoobe (3uqoobaat) penalty, punishment *n*; sanction *n*
3usur haDHum indigestion *n*
3uTle (3uTel) holiday; vacation *n*
3uTur (3uToor) perfume *n*

b

b- at, by, in *prep*
baa3 (ybee3) sell *v*
baab (abwaab, beebaan) door *n*
baachir tomorrow *adv*
baag (yboog) steal, rob *v*
baakhire (bawaakhir) ship *n*
baalqon balcony *n*
baanyo bathtub *n*
baanzeen gasoline *n*; ~ **khaane** gas station *n*
baaqi change (*money*); remaining amount *n*
baarHa (il-baarHa) yesterday *adv*
baarid (*f* baarde) cold, cool *adj*; (*pl* bawaarid) soft drink *n*
baas (yboos) kiss *v*
baaTini internal (*medical*) *adj*
baawe3 (ybaawi3) III look *v*
ba3ad more *adj*; yet *adv*; after (*time*) *prep*; ~ **baachir** day after tomorrow
    adv; ~ **shee laakh** something else; one more thing *pron*; anything else
    (*in questions*) *pron*
ba3de (*f* ba3ad-he) still *adv*
ba3dien after that, later, then *adv*
ba3ooDHe (ba3ooDH) mosquito *n*
baggaal (bgageel) grocer, shopkeeper *n*
baghdaad Baghdad *n*
bahaaraat spices *n*
baHar (buHoor) sea *n*
baHith (biHooth) research *n*
baHr (il-baHr) il-abyeDH il-mutewaSSiT Mediterranean Sea *n*; **il-baHr**
    il-aHmer Red Sea *n*
baHrien (il-baHrien) Bahrain *n*
baHriyye marine corps; navy *n*
baisikil (baisiklaat) bicycle *n*
bakhsheesh tip *n*
balloo3a (balaalee3) septic tank *n*
baqqe (ybaqqi) II keep *v*
bareed mail *n*
barmeel (baraameel) barrel *n*
barri wild (*animals, plants*) *adj*; by land *adj*
baseeT simple *adj*
baSre (il-baSre) Basra *n*
baTaale unemployment *n*
baTal (abTaal) hero *n*

baTee' (baTee'e) slow *adj*
baTTaal out of work *adj*
baTTaaniyye blanket *n*
baTTeekh *coll* musk melon *n*
bawwaab doorman *n*
bawwaabe gate *n*
bawwaag robber *n*
bazzoon (bazaazeen) cat *n*
bechi *coll* cry *n*
beddel (ybeddil) II exchange (*money*) *v*; change *trans v*
bedir full moon *n*
bee hwaaye bahaaraat spicy *adj*
bee'e environment *n*
bee'i ecological *adj*
beebee grandmother *n*
beer (aabaar, byaare) water well *n*
beere *coll* beer *n*
begge mosquito *n*
bejaame pajamas *n*
beled (buldaan) country *n*
beledi municipal *adj*
belem (blaame) boat *n*
beli yes *adv*
beljeeke Belgium *n*
beljeeki Belgian *adj, n*
benefseji purple *adj*
beng (binoog) bank *n*
beqere cow *n*
beqiyye (il-beqiyye b-Hayaatek) my/our condolences (*speaking to a man*)
beree' (*pl* abriyaa') innocent *adj*
berid cold *n*
beriTaani British *adj*
beriTaanye Great Britain *n*
berre outside *adv*
bes just, only *adv*
betinjaan *coll* eggplant *n*
beyyen (ybeyyin) II appear, indicate, seem *v*
bi- at, by, in *prep*
bi3eed far *adj*
bi3eer (bi3raan) camel *n*
biche (yibchi) cry *v*
bidaaye beginning, start *n*
bide (yibdi) begin, start *v*

biDHaa3a goods *n*
bi-DH-DHabuT precisely *adv*
bidoon without *prep*; ~ **tawaqquf** non-stop *adv*
biedDH *coll* egg *n*
biejee beige *adj*
bien among, between *prep*
biet (byoot) house, home *n*
bil-3aafye *response to* **3aashet il-ayaadi** (*compliment to a cook*)
bil-3aalem kulle worldwide *adv*
bil-fi3il indeed *adv*
bil-ijmaa3 unanimous *adj*
bil-magloobi upside down *adv*
bil-qimme at the top *adv*
bil-waajib on duty *adj*
bil-waaqi3 actually *adv, conj*
bil-weqit il-muhadded on time *adv*
bilyon (belaayeen) billion *n*
binaa' construction *n*; structure *n*
binaaye building *n*
bine (yibni) build *v*
bint (banaat) daughter *n*
b-intiDHaam regularly *adv*
biskit (basaakit) cookie *n*
bismaar (besaameer) nail (*metal*) *n*
bistaan (besaateen) orchard *n*
bit akh niece (*daughter of brother*) *n*
bit 3amm/3amme cousin (*paternal*) *n f*
bit khaal/khaale cousin (*maternal*) *n f*
bit ukhut niece (*daughter of sister*) *n*
bit-ta'keed certainly *adv*
bit-tijaaH towards *prep*
bkhuSooS about, concerning *prep*
blooze blouse *n*; ~ **Soof** sweater *n*
bneyye (banaat) girl *n*
boge robbery *n*
boi (boyaat) waiter *n*
bol urine *n*
bose kiss *n*
boSTechi postman *n*
brek brake *n*; **daas** ~ (ydoos ~) brake *v*
brunz bronze *n*
brunzi bronze *adj*
b-suhoole easily *adv*

b-sur3a quickly, rapidly *adv*
bSaaT (buSuT) rug *n*
b-Soore 3aamme generally *adv*
b-Soore ra'eesiyye mainly *adv*
btisem (yibtisim) VIII smile *v*
buHaire lake *n*
bukhaar steam, vapor *n*
bundiqiyye (benaadiq) rifle *n*
bunye (il-bunye it-taHtiyye) infrastructure *n*
buq3a (buqa3) spot, stain *n*
buqe (yubqe) remain, stay *v*
burhaan (beraaheen) proof *n*
burij (abraaj) tower *n*
buTul (bTaale) bottle *n*
b-waasTet via *prep*
byalogi biological *adj*

ch

chaan be *v past tense*
cha3ab (ch3oobe) heel; bottom *adj, n*
chai tea *n*
chakiete (chakietaat) jacket *n*
chakooch (chewaakeech) hammer *n*
chees (chyaase) paper/plastic bag *n*; ~ **mal nom** sleeping bag *n*
cheff (chfoof) glove *n*
chelib (chlaab) dog *n*
chem how many *interr*; several *adj*; some *adj, pron*
chemche ladle *n*
chenne (chenaayin) daughter-in-law *n*
cherchef (cheraachif) sheet (*bed*) *n*
cherikh (chrookh) wheel *n*
cheTel (cheTelaat) fork *n*
chibde liver *n*
chibeer (*pl* kbaar) big, large; considerable *adj*
chief because *conj*
chillaab (chillaabaat) hook *n*; **chillaabtien** pliers *n*
chilwe (chelaawi) kidney *n*
chiswe men's swimsuit *n*
chitif (chtoof) shoulder *n*
churpaaye bed *n*; ~ **mal nefer waaHid** twin/single bed; ~ **mal neferien**
      queen/king bed

d

daa'im constant *adj*
daa'imen always *adv*
daa'imi permanent *adj*
daa'ire (dawaa'ir) circle *n*; government office *n*; ~ **kahrabaa'iyye** circuit *n*
daa'iri circular *adj*
daafi (*f* daafye) warm *adj*
daakhil interior *n*
daakhili interior *adj*
daar neshir (door neshir) publishing house *n*
daate bies database *n*
da3am (yid3im) support *v*
da3ash eleven *adj*
da3im support *n*
da3we (da3waat) invitation *n*
dabbaabe armored car, tank *n*
dakhkhen (ydakhkhin) II smoke *v*
damaar destruction *n*
dam3a (dmoo3) tear *n*
dammar (ydammur) II destroy *v*
daqeeq bil-mawaa3eed punctual *adj*
daqqaq (ydaqqiq) II check *v*
darboone (daraabeen) alley *n*
darras (ydarris) II teach *v*
dawaam working hours *n*; ~ **kaamil** full-time *adj*
debel double *adj*
deelaab (dawaaleeb) closet, cabinet *n*
deemuqraaTi democratic *adj*
deemuqraaTiyye democracy *n*
deen (diyaanaat) religion *n*
deenaar (denaaneer) dinar (*Iraqi currency*) *n*
deeni religious *adj*
deezil diesel *n*
deffe (ydeffi) II warm, heat *trans v*
defter (defaatir) notebook *n*
dehhen (ydehhin) II grease *v*
dekhel income *n*
deleel evidence *n*; guide, guidebook, directory *n*
dellaal realtor *n*
demm blood *n*; **taHleel** ~ blood test *n*; **naqil id-~** blood transfusion *n*
denboos (denaabees) pin *n*
denimaark (id-denimaark) Denmark *n*

denimaarki Danish *adj*
deqeeq exact *adj*
deqeeqe (deqaayiq) minute *n*
derej ladder *n*; staircase *n*
dereje grade *n*; ~ **oola** first class *n*; ~ **siyaaHiyye** tourist class *n*
derejet il-Haraare temperature *n*
deris (droos) lesson *n*
dernefees screwdriver *n*
derub (deraabeen) road *n*
derzen (deraazin) dozen *n*
dewaajin *coll* poultry *n*
dewwer (ydewwir) II search *v*
dezz (ydizz) send *v*
di3a (yid3u) invite *v*
diblomaasi diplomat *n*
dien (diyoon) debt, credit *n*
difaa3 defense *n*
difa3 (yidfa3) pay *v*; push *v*
difen (yidfin) bury *v*
dihin fat, grease *n*
dijaaj *coll* chicken *n*
dijitel digital *adj*
dijle Tigris *n*
dikhel (yidkhul) enter *v*
diktator dictator *n*
diktor doctor *n*
diktoraa doctorate *n*
dimashq Damascus *n*
dinye (id-dinye) the world *n*; **id-dinye baarde** it's cold today; ~ **Haarre** it's hot today; ~**Teibe** it's pleasant today
dire (yidri) know *v*
dires (yidrus) study *v*
distoor constitution *n*
dmaagh brain *n*
dolme stuffed vegetables *n pl*
dondirme ice cream *n*
doolaar (doolaaraat) dollar *n*
doosh shower *n*
dor (adwaar) role *n*
dosheg (dwaashig) mattress *n*
dramateeki dramatic *adj*
dugme (digam) button *n*
dukhkhaan smoke *n*

dukkaan (dakaakeen) shop, store *n*
duwe (adwiye) drug (*medicine*) *n*
duweli international *adj*
duwwiere round, circle *n*

dh

dhaab (ydhoob) melt *v*
dhaakire memory (*ability*) *n*
dhaat ir-ri'e pneumonia *n*
dhak (*f* dheech) that *pron*
dharbe strike *n*
dhawq (adhwaaq) taste *n*
dheheb gold *n*
dhehebi golden *adj*
dheker male *n*
dherri nuclear *adj*
dhibbaane (dhibbaan) fly *n*
dhiel (dhyoole) tail *n*
dhiker (yidhkur) mention *v*
dhikra memory, remembrance *n*
dhure corn *n*

DH

DHaabuT (DHubbaaT) (military) officer *n*
DHaaf (yDHeef) add *v*
DHaag (yDHoog) taste *v*
DHaaHiye (DHawaaHi) suburb *n*
DHaayi3 lost *adj*
DHa3eef (*pl* DH3aaf) weak *adj*
DHaghiT pressure *n*
DHaHiyye (DHaHaaya) victim *n*
DHajeej noise *n*
DHakhum (*f* DHakhme) huge, vast *adj*
DHalme *f* dark *adj*; darkness *n*
DHamaan guarantee *n*
DHammaade bandage *n*
DHareebe (DHaraayib) tax *n*
DHarer damage *n*
DHaroori essential *adj*; necessary *adj*

DHaruf (DHuroof) circumstance *n*; envelope *n*
DHeher back *n*
DHeyya3 (yDHeyyi3) II lose *v*
DHeyyig (*f* DHeyge) narrow *adj*
DHi3eef (*pl* DH3aaf) thin *adj*; weak *adj*
DHidd anti-, against *adj*
DHief (DHyoof) guest, visitor *n*
DHiHak (yiDH-Hak) laugh *v*
DHil shade *n*
DHireb (yiDHrub) beat, hit, strike *v*; ~ **ooti** iron *v*; ~ **ubre** inject *v*
DHuhur noon *n*
DHumen (yiDHmun) guarantee *v*
DHuwe (aDHwiye) lamp, light (*artificial*) *n*; ~ **in-nahaar** daylight *n*

e

edaa' performance *n*
edeb literature *n*; good manners *n*; ~ **siz** impolite, impudent *adj*
edebi literary *adj*
edewaat *pl* tools *n*; ~ **iHtiyaaTiyye** spare parts *n pl*
ee yes *adv*
eed (eedenaat) hand *n*; arm *n*
eejaabi positive *adj*
eejaar rent *n*
eemaan faith *n*
eemiel (eemelaat) e-mail *n*; **dezz** ~ send an e-mail *v*
eeqaa3 rhythm *n*
eeraan Iran *n*
eeraani Iranian *adj, n*
ei any *adj*; ~ **shee** anything *pron*; ~ **waaHid** anyone *pron*
eidz AIDS *n*
eilool September *n*
eliketroni electronic *adj*
erlende Ireland *n*
erlendi Irish *adj, n*
esed (isoode) lion *n*
eyyaar May *n*

f

faa'ide (fawaa'id) benefit; interest rate *n*
faaja' (yfaaji') III surprise someone *v*

faaneele tee-shirt, undershirt *n*
faare (feeraan) mouse *n*
faarigh (*f* faarghe) empty *adj*
faat (*f* faayte) previous *adj*; **il-faat** (*f* il-faatet) the last (*most recent*) *adj*
faatiH (*f* faatHa) light (*color*) *adj*
faayel (faayelaat) file *n*
fa33aaliyye action *n*
faDHaa' space *n*; ~ **khaariji** outer space *n*
faDHee3 (*f* faDHee3a) horrible, terrible *adj*
faHel male (*animal*) *n*
faHiS check-up (*medical*) *n*
fakhoor (fakhoore) proud (*in a positive sense*) *adj*
faks (faksaat) fax *n*; **dezz** ~ send a fax *v*
fallaaH (filih, falaaleeH) farmer *n*
faqeer (*pl* fuqeraa') poor *adj*
fardat Hidhaa' (aHdhiye) shoe *n*
fareeq (fireq) team *n*
farHaan happy *adj*
fari3 (froo3) branch *n*
fariq difference *n*
farq il-3umle exchange rate *n*
faSeeH standard Arabic (*language*) *n*
faSil (fuSool) chapter *n*; season *n*
faSoolye *coll* beans *n*
fawaakih *coll* fruit *n*
fech jaw *n*
fed just, only *adv*; ~ **marre** once *adv*; ~ **shee** something *pron*; ~ **waaHid**
    someone *pron*
fee-maan-illa good-bye *n*
fei shade *n*
fejir dawn *n*
fejjer (yfejjir) II blow up *v*
fejwe gap *n*
fekh (afkhaakh) trap *n*
fekker (yfekkir) II think *v*
felesTeen Palestine *n*
felesTeeni Palestinian *adj, n*
felle great *adj*
fenn art *n*
fennaan artist *n*
feqere paragraph *n*
ferd (afraad) individual *n*
ferdi individual; odd (*number*) *adj*

feshel failure *n*
fetHe opening *n*
fetre period (time) *n*
fettesh (yfettish) II search *v*
fewwet (yfewwit) II miss (*an airplane, etc.*) *v*
feyeDHaan (feyeDHaanaat) flood *n*
fi3li actual *adj*
fihem (yifhem) understand *v*
fikhaariyyaat pottery *n*
fikre (afkaar) idea; thought *n*
fikri intellectual *adj*
filfil *coll* pepper *n*
filim (aflaam) film *n*; movie *n*
filke (filek) rotary, roundabout *n*
filter (felaatir, filteraat) filter *n*
findiq (fenaadiq) hotel *n*
firche (firech) brush *n*; **firchet asnaan** (firech asnaan) toothbrush *n*
firin oven *n*
firqe (fireq) squad, corps *n*; ~ **moseeqiyye** orchestra *n*
fishel (yifshel) fail *v*
fistaan (fesaateen) dress *n*
fitaH (yiftaH) open *v*
flaat apartment *n*
floos money *n*
fog above, on top of, over *prep*; upstairs *adv*
foolaadh steel *n*
franse France *n*
freezer (freezeraat) freezer *n*
frensi French *adj, n*
ftiqed (yiftiqed) VIII miss (a person) *v*
fuDHDHa silver *n*
fuDHeeHa (feDHaayiH) scandal *n*
fuj'eten suddenly *adv*
fukhudh (fkhaadhe) thigh *n*
furaat (il-furaat) Euphrates *n*
furSe (fureS) chance, opportunity *n*
fuSel (yifSul) fire, let go (job) *v*
fuToor major after-sunset meal during Ramadan *n*

g

gaa3 (gee3aan) floor *n*; land *n*; earth *n*
gaal (ygool) say *v*

gaam (ygoom) get up *v*
gaarsone waitress *n*
ga3ad (yig3ud) sit *v*
gabul ago *adv*; before *conj*
gabur (gboor) grave *n*
gahwe (gahaawi) *coll* coffee *n*; café *n*
gaHH (yguHH) cough *v*
gaHHa cough *n*
galbi my dearest (*lit.* my heart)
galub (gloob) heart *n*
gargoo3a (garaagee3) thunder *n*
gaSSaab butcher *n*
gbaal across, before, in front of *prep*
geraaj (geraajaat) garage *n*; ~ **is-seyyaaraat** parking lot *n*
geshsher (ygeshshir) II peel *v*
geSS (yguSS) cut *v*; ~ **sha3ar** haircut *n*
giddaam before, in front of *prep*
gider (yigder) can *v*; able *adj*
giwi hard, stiff *adj*
glaade (glaayid) necklace *n*
glaaS (glaaSaat) glass *n*
glob (globaat) light bulb *n*
gSeyyir (*f* gSeire *pl* gSaar) short *adj*
gubel ahead *adv*
gumer moon *n*
gumez (yugmuz) jump *v*
gumrug customs *n*
guTin cotton *n*

gh

ghaabe (ghaabaat) forest *n*
ghaali (*f* ghaalye) expensive *adj*
ghaare raid *n*
ghaaz gas *n*; ~ **museel lid-dimoo3** tear gas *n*
ghalaT incorrect *adj*
ghalTaan wrong *adj*
ghalTe (aghlaaT) mistake *n*
ghanna (yghanni) II sing *v*
gharaame fine *n*
gharb west *n*
gharbi occidental, western *adj*

ghareeb (*pl* ghurbe) alien *adj*; strange *adj*; stranger *n*
gharze stitch *n*
ghaseel melaabis laundry *n*
ghassaale kahrabaa'iyye washing machine *n*
ghaTTe (yghaTTi) II cover *v*
ghawwaaSe submarine *n*
ghazu invasion *n*
ghbaar dust *n*
ghede lunch *n*
gheiboobe coma *n*
ghereDH (aghraaDH) purpose *n*
gheyyer (ygheyyir) II change *v trans*
ghieme (ghyoom) cloud *n*
ghier qaanooni illegal *adj*
ghireg (yighreg) drown *v*
ghisel (yighsil) wash *v*
ghiTe cover *n*
ghize (yighzu) invade *v*
ghraam (ghraamaat) gram *n*
ghurfe (ghuref) room *n*; **ghurfet il-ma3eeshe** living room *n*; **ghurfet il-khuTTaar** guest room *n*; **ghurfet in-nom** bedroom *n*
ghuroob ish-shemis sunset *n*

h

haadhe (*f* haadhi) this *pron*
haadi' (*f* haad'e) calm, quiet *adj*
haarib (haarbeen) fugitive *n*
haay sh-aku? what's the matter?
habb (yhibb) blow (*wind*) *v*
haddam (yhaddim) II demolish *v*
hadef (ahdaaf) goal *n*
hadhole these *pron*
haishe (hawaayish) cow *n*
hard draiv hard drive *n*
hawe air *n*; wind *n*
hawiyye shekhSiyye (hawiyyaat shekhSiyye) identity card (ID) *n*
hedef (ahdaaf) target *n*
hedhaak that *pron*
hedheech *f* that *pron*
hedholaak those *pron*
hediyye (hedaaye) present (*gift*) *n*

heech such *adj*
hei'at it-tadrees faculty (*school*) *n*
heikel 3aDHmi (heyaakil 3aDHmiyye) skeleton *n*
hem also, too *adv*
hemmen, hemmien also, too *adv*
hendese engineering *n*
hesse already *adv.*; just *adv*; now *adv*
hezeeme defeat *n*
hijem (yihjim) attack *v*
hijoom attack *n*
hilikopter (hilikopteraat) helicopter *n*
hind (il-hind) India *n*
hindi (*pl* hnood) Indian *adj, n*
hiyye she *pron*
hlaal new moon, crescent *n*
hna here *adv*
hnak there *adv*
hol hall *n*
holende Netherlands *n*
holendi Dutch *adj, n*
hose noise *n*
hubooT iDHTiraari emergency landing *n*
hudne cease-fire *n*; truce *n*
huwwe he *pron*
hwaaye a lot of, plenty of, many, much, *adj*

H

Haadd (*f* Haadde) sharp *adj*
Haadith (Hawaadith) accident *n*
HaaDHir (*f* HaaDHre *pl* HaaDHreen) present, ready *adj*; OK
Haaffe (Hawaafi) edge *n*
Haaje need *n*
Haajiz (Hawaajiz) road block *n*
Haale condition, state *n*; **Haalet ij-jaww** weather forecast *n*
Haali (il-Haali) current *adj*
Haaliyyen currently *adv*
Haamil (Hawaamil) pregnant *adj*
HaamuDH acidic, sour *adj*
Haarr hot *adj*
Haasibe calculator *n*
Haasse (Hawaas) sense *n*

Haawel (yHaawil) III attempt *v*
Haawiye container *n*
HaayiT (HeeTaan) wall *n*
Haazim (*f* Haazme) firm *adj*
Habb (yHibb) like, love *v*
Habbe (Huboob) pill *n*; **Huboob munawwim** sleeping pill *n*
Habil (Hbaal) rope *n*
Hachi talk *n*
Hadd (*pl* Hidood) edge *n*; border *n;* ~ (yHidd) sharpen *v*
Hadeed iron *n*
Hadeeqe (Hadaayiq) garden *n*; park *n*; **Hadeeqet Haiwaanaat** zoo *n*
Hadeeth modern, recent, up-to-date *adj*
Hadeethen recently *adv*
Hadhdher (yHadhdhir) II warn *v*
Hadhir (*f* Hadhre *pl* Hadhreen) cautious *adj*
HaDHaare culture, civilization *n*
HaDHDHer (yHaDHDHir) II prepare *v*
HaDHeeret iT-Teyyaaraat hangar *n*
HaDHirtek you (*formal*) *pron*
HaDHirtich you *f* (*formal*) *pron*
Hafeed (aHfaad) grandson *n*
Hafeede granddaughter *n*
HaffaaDHe diaper *n*
Hafle party (*social event*) *n*
Haiwaan (Haiwaanaat) animal *n*
Hajim (aHjaam) size *n*
Hajiz reservation *n*
Hakk (yHukk) itch *v*
Hakke rash *n*
Halawiyyaat *coll* dessert *n*; sweets *n*
Haleeb *coll* milk *n*; ~ **aTfaal** formula (*infant*) *n*; ~ **kaamil id-desem** whole
    milk *n*
Haleef (Hulefaa') ally *n*
Halig (Hlooge) mouth *n*
Hall (Hilool) solution *n*
Hallaaq barber *n*; hairdresser (*for men and women*) *n*
Halqe wedding ring; circle *n*
Hamdu lillah (il-Hamdu lillah) thank God
Hamle campaign *n*
Hammaal porter *n*
Hammaam bathroom *n*
Haneen kind *adj*
Hanefiyye faucet *n*

Haqeeqe (Haqaayiq) fact *n*; reality *n*; truth *n*
Haqeeqi real, true *adj*
Haqil (Huqool) field *n*; ~ **alghaam** minefield *n*; ~ **nafuT** oilfield *n*
Haqq (Huqooq) right *n*; ~ **il-veeto** veto *n*; **il-Huqooq il-medeniyye** civil
     rights *n*
Haqqaani fair, just *adj*
Haqqaq (yHaqqiq) II achieve *v*
Haraam sin *n*
Haraami (*pl* Haraamiyye) thief, robber, burglar *n*
Haraare heat *n*
Hareer silk *n*
HareeS careful *adj*
Hareke movement *n*; **il-Hareke in-niswiyye** women's movement, feminism *n*
Harrer (yHarrir) II liberate *v*
Harub (Huroob) war *n*; **jareemet** ~ war crime *n*; **mujrim** ~ war criminal *n*;
     ~ **ahliyye** civil war *n*
Hasab according to *prep*
Hasheesh lawn *n*; grass *n*
Hashere bug, insect *n*
Hass (yHiss) feel *v*
Hassaas sensitive *adj*
Hassaasiyye min allergic to *adj (lit.* allergy from*)*
Hassen *(*yHassin) II improve *v*
HaSaad harvest *n*
HaSeere (HuSraan) mat *n*
HaSSel (yHaSSil) II earn, get, receive, attain, obtain *v*
Hatta walaw even if *prep*
Hatte in order to, so that *conj*
HaTT (yHuTT) put *v*; ~ **3alaame** mark *v*
Hawaali about, around, approximately *prep*
HawwaT (yHawwuT) II encircle *v*
Hawwel (yHawwil) II transfer *(money)* *v*
Hayaat life *n*
Hayaatek (w-Hayaatek il-baaqye) *response to condolences when speaking
     to a man*
Hayy (*pl* aHyaa') alive *adj*
Hayy faqeer (aHyaa' faqeere) slum *n*
Hazeen sad, unhappy *adj*
Hible (Hiblaat) pregnant *adj*
Hiche (yiHchi) speak, talk *v*
HiDHer (yiHDHer) attend *v*
HiDHoor attendance *n*
Hijez (yiHjiz) reserve *v*

Hilem (yiHlem) dream *v*
Hileq (yiHliq) shave *v*
Hilim (aHlaam) dream *n*
Hilu (*f* Hilwe *pl* Hilween) beautiful, pretty, sweet *adj*
Himaaye *coll* convoy *n*; protection *n*
Hime (yiHmi) protect *v;* heat (*liquids*) *v*
Hireg (yiHrig) burn *v*
HiSaar embargo *n*; siege *n*
Hiyaadi *n* neutral *adj*
Hizer (yiHzir) guess *v*
Hizib siyaasi (aHzaab siyaasiyye) political party *n*
Hizin mourning *n*
Hjaab (Hjaabaat) veil *n*
Hjaare (Hjaar) stone *n*; rock *n*
HoDH (HwaaDHe) sink *n*
Hosh (Hawaash) house *n*; central yard in traditionally built houses *n*
Hsaab bank account *n*; bill *n*
HSaan (HuSin) horse *n*
Htaaj (yiHtaaj) VIII need *v*
Htifel (yiHtifil) VIII celebrate *v*
Hubb love *n*
Huboob man3 il-Hamil birth-control pills *n pl*
HuDHoor presence *n*
Hufre (Hufer) hole *n*
Hukum (aHkaam) verdict, judgment *n*; rule *n*
Hukoome (Hukoomaat) government *n*
Humme fever *n*
HummuS *coll* chickpeas *n*
Hunjure (Hanaajir) throat *n*
HunTe wheat *n*
Huqooq il-insaan human rights *n*
Hurr (*pl* aHraar) free *adj*
Hurriyye freedom *n*
Hurriyyet il-kelaam freedom of speech *n*; ~ **iS-SaHaafe** freedom of the
      press *n*
Huzeiraan June *n*
Hzaam il-amaan (aHzimet il-amaan) seat belt *n*

i

i'tilaaf coalition *n*
i3daam (i3daamaat) execution *n*

i3joobe (3ajaayib) wonder *n*
i3laan notice; declaration *n*
i3timed (yi3timid) VIII rely on *v*
i3tine (yi3tini) VIII care *v*
i3tiref (yi3tirif) VIII admit *v*
i3tuber (yi3tubur) VIII consider *v*
ibaade besheriyye genocide *n*
ibbelaash free of charge *adj*
ibbidaal instead of *prep*
ib-buTu' slowly *adv*
ibhaam (ibhammaat) thumb *n*
ibin (abnaa', wilid) son *n*; ~ **3amm/3amme** cousin (*paternal*) *n m*;
    ~ **khaal/khaale** cousin (*maternal*) *n m;* ~ **akh/ukhut** nephew *n*
ibtisaame smile *n*
idaare administration *n*; management *n*
idha if *conj*
idhin (adhaan) ear *n*
idmaan addiction *n*
iDHaafe addition *n*
iDHaafi extra, additional *adj*
iDH-DHaahir apparently *adv*
iDHfir (aDHaafir) nail (*finger/toe*) *n*
iDHTihed (yiDHTihid) VIII persecute *v*
iflaas bankruptcy *n*
ightiSaab rape *n*
ightiyaal assassination *n*
ihtimaam interest *n*
iHne we *pron*
iHsaas (aHaasees) feeling *n*
iHSaa' (iHSaa'iyyaat) statistics *n*; census *n*
iHtejj (yiHtejj) VIII protest *v*
iHtell (yiHtell) VIII occupy *v*
iHtifaal celebration *n*
iHtijaaj (iHtijaajaat) protest *n*
iHtilaal (military) occupation *n*
iHtiraam respect *n*
iHtiyaaT reserves *n*
ijaaze license; permit *n*; **ijaazet siyaaqe** driver's license *n*
ije (yiji) come *v*
ijhaaDH (ijhaaDHaat) miscarriage; abortion *n*
ijraa' (ijraa'aat) procedure *n*
ijtimaa3 (ijtimaa3aat) meeting *n*
ijtimaa3i social *adj*

ijtima3 (yijtimi3) VIII meet *v*
ikhSaab fertilization *n*
ikhtibaar (ikhtibaaraat) test *n*
ikhtiraa3 (ikhtiraa3aat) invention *n*
ikhtiTaaf (ikhtiTafaat) kidnapping *n*; abduction *n*
ikhtiTaf (yikhtiTuf) VIII kidnap *v*
ikhtiyaar (ikhtiyaaraat) selection; choice *n*
ikhtiyaari voluntary *adj*
ikhwaan *way of addressing a group of male strangers* (*lit.* Brothers)
il- the *art*
ila akhirihi etc.(*et cetera*) *adv*
ilal-amaam! Forward! (*military command*)
ilghaa' cancellation *n*
ille rubu3 a quarter to... (*hour*) *adv*
iltihaab inflammation *n*
iltiHaq (yiltiHiq) VIII join *v*
iltiqe (yiltiqi) VIII meet *v*
imaam (a'imme) imam (*Islamic religious leader*) *n*
imma... aw either... or *conj*
imtiHaan (imtiHaanaat) examination, test *n*
imtiyaaz (imtiyaazaat) privilege *n*
inboob (anaabeeb) tube *n*
indaar (yindaar) VII turn around *v*
indhaar alarm *n*; ultimatum *n*; ~ **il-Hareeq** fire alarm *n*
infijaar (infijaaraat) blast, explosion *n*
infiraad isolation *n*
influwenze flu *n*
ingileezi (*pl* ingileez) English *adj*
ingiltere England *n*
inhaar (yinhaar) VII collapse *v*
inhizem (yinhizim) VII escape *v*
inj (injaat) inch *n*
injaaz achievement *n*
injeel Bible *n*
inkhuTbet (tinkhuTub) get engaged (*for women*) *v*
inkiser (yinkisir) VII break *v intrans*
inshaa' construction *n*
inshaalle God willing
insiHaab withdrawal *n*
insiHab (yinsiHib) VII withdraw *v*
intaaj production *n*
inte you (*informal*) *pron*
inti you *f* (*informal*) *pron*

intibaah attention *n*
intiDHer (yintiDHir) VIII wait *v*
intihaak (intihaakaat) violation *n*
intihe (yintihi) VIII end *v intrans*
intiHaar (intiHaaraat) suicide *n*
intikhaabaat elections *n*
intiSaar (intiSaaraat) victory *n*
intu you *pl (informal) pron*
inTeeni *imp* give me
iqleem (aqaaleem) province *n*
iqtiraaH (iqtiraaHaat) suggestion *n*
iqtiraH (yiqtiriH) VIII suggest *v*
iqtiSaad economy *n*
iqtiSaadi economic *adj*
irhaab terrorism *n*
irhaabi terrorist *adj, n*
irja3! come back!
irshaadaat directions (*road*) *n*
irtifaa3 height (*building, etc.*) *n*
is3aaf ambulance *n*
isboo3 (asaabee3) week *n*
isboo3i weekly *adj*
ish3aa3 radiation *n*
ish3aal ignition *n*
ish3aar notice *n*
ishaare (ishaaraat) sign *n*; ~ **khefeefe** (ishaaraat khefeefe) hint *n*
ish-sharq il-awSaT Middle East *n*
ishtiraaki socialist *adj, n*
isim (asmaa') name *n*
iskaan housing *n*
islaam Islam *n*
islaami Islamic *adj*
isloob style (*writing; way of talking*) *n*
israa'eel Israel *n*
israa'eeli Israeli *adj, n*
ista3jel (yista3jil) X hurry up *v*
isteeraad (isteeradaat) import *n*
istereeH have a seat (*polite way of asking someone to sit down*)
istifsaar (istifsaaraat) inquiry *n*
istiftaa' (istiftaa'aat) poll *n*; referendum *n*
istijaabe response *n*
istijwaab interrogation *n*
istikaan (istikaanaat) small tea glass *n*

istilaam delivery (*goods*) *n*
istimaare form (*paper*) *n*
istiqbaal reception *n*
istiqlaal independence *n*
istiraaHa rest *n*; **istiraaHat il-ghede** lunch break
istiraateeji strategic *adj*
istislaam surrender *n*
istithmaar (istithmaaraat) investment *n*
istithnaa' (istithnaa'aat) exception *n*
istithnaa'i exceptional, unusual *adj*
iSbi3 (aSaabi3) finger *n*; ~ **ir-rijil** toe *n*
it3ashshe (yit3ashshe) V have/eat dinner *v*
itjannab (yitjannab) V avoid *v*
ittihaam accusation *n*
ittihem (yittihim) VIII accuse *v*
ittiHaad unity *n*
ittijaah waaHid one-way street *n*
ittiSaal (ittiSaalaat) communication *n*; contact *n*; **ittiSaalaat silkiyye w-la silkiyye** telecommunications *n*
ittiSal (yittiSil) VIII contact *v*
iTaali Italian *adj, n*
iTaalye Italy *n*
iTaar (iTaaraat) frame *n*
iTfaa'iyye *coll* firefighter *n*; fire station *n*
izdiHaam il-muroor traffic jam *n*

j

jaa'ize (jewaa'iz) prize *n*
jaab (yjeeb) bring *v*
jaahil (*pl* jahaal) child *n*
jaahiz (*f* jaahze) ready *adj*
jaami3 (jawaami3) mosque *n*
jaami3a (jaami3aat) university *n*
jaanib (jawaanib) side *n*
jaar (jeeraan, jwaareen) neighbor *n*
jaasoos (jawaasees) spy *n*
jaaweb (yjaawub) III answer, reply *v*
jaay (ij-jaay) the following, the next *adj*
jadded (yjaddid) II renew *v*
jaHeem hell *n*
jamaa3a (jamaa3aat) group *n*; ~ **sirriyye** underground group *n*

jam3iyye association *n*; society *n*
janTe (juneT) bag *n*; briefcase *n*; suitcase *n*
jaraS (ajraaS) bell *n*
jarraare drawer *n*
jarreb (yjarrub) II try *v*
jaw atmosphere; weather *n*
jawaab (ajwibe) answer *n*
jawaaz (jawaazaat) passport *n*
jawhere (jawaahir) gem *n*
jawle tour *n*; ~ **siyaaHiyye** sightseeing *n*
jazaa'ir (ij-jazaa'ir) Algeria *n*
jazaa'iri Algerian *adj, n*
jebhe front (*military*) *n*
jedhir (jidhoor) root *n*
jedhri radical *adj*
jedwel (jedaawil) schedule *n*; stream *n*
jeel (ajyaal) generation *n*
jefaaf drought *n*
jehhez (yjehhiz) II provide, supply *v*
jeish army *n*
jelse session *n*
jem3iyye ta3aawiniyye cooperative *n*
jenned (yjennid) II recruit *v*
jereede (jeraayid) newspaper *n*
jereeme (jeraayim) murder, crime *n*
jeriH (jrooH) cut, wound, injury *n*
jerr (yjurr) pull *v*; ~ **khaTT** underline *v*
jerthoome (jeraatheem) germ *n*
jewaab (ajwibe) reply, answer *n*
jewwe below, beneath, under *prep*; down; indoors, inside *adv*; ~ **il-gaa3**
      underground *n*
jeyyid good *adj*
jezeere (juzur) island *n*
jibel (jibaal) mountain *n*
jibin cheese *n*
jidd grandfather *n*
jidde grandmother *n*; midwife *n*
jiddi serious, earnest *adj*; my grandfather *n*
jideed (*pl* jidded) new *adj*
jidir (jdoore) pot *n*
jieb (jyoob) pocket *n*; jeep *n*
jigaare (jigaayir) cigarette *n*
jihaaz il-haDHum digestive system *n*

jilid (*pl* jilood) leather *n*; skin *n*
jima3 (yijma3) collect *v*
jimel (jmaal) camel *n*
jinis (ajnaas) gender *n*
jinoob south *n*
jinoobi southern *adj*
jinsi sexual *adj*
jisim (ajsaam) body *n*
jisir (jsoore) bridge *n*
jismi physical *adj*
jizer *coll* carrot(s) *n*
jizu' (ajzaa') fraction *n*; part *n*
jnaaH (ajniHa, jinHaan) wing *n*
joo3aan hungry *adj*
joz *coll* walnut(s) *n*
jozi brown *adj*
jriedi (jrediyye) rat *n*
jughraafye geography *n*
juhud (juhood) effort *n*
jum3a (ij-jum3a) *f* Friday *n*
jumhoor public *n*
jumhooriyye republic *n*
jumjume (jamaajum) skull *n*
jumle (jumel) sentence *n*
junbud *coll* roses *n*
jundi (jnood) soldier, troops *n*
juneT *pl* baggage, luggage *n*
jur3a azyed min il-laazim overdose *n*
juruf river bank *n*
juththe (jutheth) corpse *n*
juzdaan (jazaadeen) wallet *n*
juzme (jizem) boot *n*
jwaareeb socks *n*

k

kaafi (*f* kaafye) sufficient, adequate, enough *adj, adv*
kaaghed *coll* paper *n*
kaamil (*f* kaamle) complete, full, perfect, whole *adj*
kaamire camera *n*
kaanoon il-awwel December *n*
kaanoon ith-thaani January *n*

kaarithe (kawaarith) catastrophe *n*
kaashifet il-alghaam mine detector *n*
kaatholeek Catholic *adj, n*
kaatib (*pl* kuttaab) writer *n*; clerk *n*; ~ **Taabi3a** typist *n*
kadhdhaabi false, fake
kahaf (kuhoof) cave *n*
kahrabaaʻ electricity *n*
kahrabaaʻi electric *adj*; electrician *n*
kahrabaaʻiyyaat electric appliances *n*
kalaam speech *n*; talk *n*
kareem generous *adj*
karton (kartonaat) carton *n*
kash cash *n*
kasiet (kasetaat) cassette *n*
kaslaan (*pl* kesaale) lazy *adj*
kawboi jeans *n*
kawkab seyyaar (kawaakib seyyaare) planet *n*
kebed liver *n*
keebord keyboard *n*
keemyaawi chemical *adj*; **asliHe keemyaawiyye** chemical weapons *n*
kefooʻ efficient *adj*; qualified *adj*
kelime word *n*
kellef (ykellif) II cost *v*
kemeen (kemaaʻin) trap *n*
kemmel (ykemmil) II complete *v*
kemmiyye quantity *n*
kenede Canada *n*
kenedi Canadian *adj, n*
keneese (kenaayis) church *n*
kereeh offensive (*smell*; *appearance*) *adj*
kerek shovel *n*
kerkook Kirkuk *n*
kerwe fare *n*
kesir (kisoor) fracture *n*
kesser (ykessir) II break *v trans*
kidhbe (kidhbaat) lie *n*
kidheb (yikdhib) lie (*not tell the truth*) *v*
kieloo (kieloowaat) kilogram *n*
kielumetir (kielumetraat) kilometer *n*
kifaaH struggle *n*
kilfe cost *n*
kimpyooter (kimpyooteraat) computer *n*
kireh (yikreh) hate *v*

kiser (yiksir) break *v trans;* turn (*direction*) *v*
kiteb (yiktib) write *v;* ~ **teqreer** report *v*
kitli (ketaali) kettle *n*
kleeneks tissue (*paper*) *n*
kome (akwaam) pile *n*
kongres (**il-kongres**) congress *n*
konkreet concrete *n*
koob (kwaabe) cup *n*
kosaj shark *n*
kredit kard credit card *n*
ktaab (kutub) book *n*
ktishef (yiktishif) VIII discover *v*
kuber (yikber) grow *v*
kull all, each, every *adj;* ~ **mekaan** everywhere *adv;* ~ **saa3a** hourly *adv;*
    ~ **shee** everything *pron;* ~ **shee tamaam** all set; ~ **shekhiS** everybody
    pron; ~ **waaHid** everyone *pron*
kulle (*f* kulhe) entire *adj*
kulli total *adj*
kullish very *adv*
kulliyye college *n;* faculty *n;* **kulliyet il-adaab** College of Arts *n;* **kulliyyet**
    iT-Tibb School of Medicine *n*
kurdi Kurdish *adj*
kure ball *n;* **kuret qedem** soccer *n*
kurraase leaflet *n*
kursi (karaasi) chair *n;* ~ **mitHarrik** (karaasi mitHarrike) wheelchair *n*
kuteyyib (kuteyyibaat) handbook, manual *n*
kutle (kutel) lump *n*
kwiet (**il-kwiet**) Kuwait *n*

kh

khaaber (ykhaabur) III call (*telephone*) *v*
khaaf (ykhaaf) fear, be afraid *v*
khaal uncle (*maternal*) *n*
khaale aunt (*maternal*) *n; respectful address to women older than the*
    speaker
khaali (*f* khaalye) deserted *adj;* **khaali min ir-riSaaS** lead-free *adj*
khaamis (*f* khaamse) fifth *adj*
khaanaat entries (*on a form*) *n pl*
khaariji exterior *adj*
khaashooge (khawaasheeg) spoon *n;* **khaashooget chai** small teaspoon *n;*
    ~ **koob** teaspoon *n;* ~ **akil** tablespoon *n*

khaaS special *adj*
khaaSS particular *adj*; private *adj*
khaaSSeten particularly *adv*
khaawli(yye) (khaawliyyaat) towel *n*
khaayif (*f* khaayfe *pl* khaayfeen) afraid *adj*
khaayin (khewene) traitor *n*
khabber (ykhabbur) II tell *v*
khabeer (khuberaaʻ) expert *n*; ~ **faHiS in-neDHer** optician *n*
khaleeT mixture *n*
khalfiyye background *n*
khall vinegar *n*
khalleS (ykhalliS) finish *v;* save *v*
khamees (il-khamees) Thursday *n*
khamis five (*with noun*) *adj*
khamismeet five hundred (*with noun*) *adj*; ~ **alif** five hundred thousand *adj*
khamismiyye five hundred (*standing alone*) *adj*
khamistalaaf five thousand *adj*
khamse five (*standing alone*) *adj*
khamseen fifty *adj*; ~ **alif** fifty thousand *adj*
khamur (khimoor) wine *n*
kharaab ruin *n*
kharbaan unconscious *adj*; out of order *adj*
khareef fall, autumn *n*
khareeTe (kharaayiT) map *n*
kharoof (khurfaan) lamb, sheep *n*
kharrab (ykharrub) II ruin *v*
khaTar danger *n*
khaTeer serious, grave *adj*
khaTiyye! poor thing! poor guy! (*m/f*)
khaTir hazardous, dangerous *adj*
khaTT (khTooT) line *n*; ~ **anaabeeb** (khuTooT anaabeeb) pipeline *n*
khaTTaT (ykhaTTiT) II plan *v*
khawaati my sisters; *way of addressing female strangers*
khazeene treasury *n*
khazzaan (khazzaanaat) tank (*storage*); reservoir *n*
khefeef light (*weight*) *adj*
khelfi rear *adj*
khelli let's…; ~ **nrooH** let's go
khenzeer (khenazeer) pig *n*
kherr (ykhurr) leak *v*
khesaare (khesaaʼir) loss *n*
khesheb wood *n*
kheshebi *adj* wooden

kheshim (khshoome) nose *n*
khess lettuce *n*
kheSir waist *n*
kheTeeb fiancé *n*
kheTeebe fiancée *n*
kheyaal imagination; shadow *n*
kheyyaaT tailor *n*
kheyyeT (ykheyyiT) II sew *v*
khidem (yikhdim) serve *v*
khidme (khadamaat) service *n*; **khidmet il-ghuref** room service *n*
khieme (khiyem) tent *n*
khieT (khyooT) string *n*; thread *n*
khilaal within (*time*) *prep*
khileq (yikhluq) create *v*
khisheb wood *n*; ~ **binaa'** timber *n*
khitem (yikhtim) seal *v*
khiTeb (yikhTub) deliver a speech *v*; get engaged (*for men*) *v*
khof fear *n*
khokh *coll* peach(es) *n*
khoodhe (khuwedh) helmet *n*
khosh good *adj*
khtaar (yikhtaar) VIII choose *v*
khtife (yikhtifi) VIII disappear *v*
khtineg (yikhtinig) VIII suffocate *v*
khtiTaf (yikhtiTuf) VIII abduct, hijack *v*
khubeT (yikhbuT) mix *v*
khubuz *coll* bread *n*
khuDHer *coll* herb(s), greens *n*
khuDHrewaat vegetables *n*
khumuSTa3ash fifteen *adj*
khurde change (*money*) *n*
khurooj exit *n*
khuSoobe fertility *n*
khuSooSen especially *adv*
khuTTaar *pl* guests *n*
khuTTe (khuTeT) plan *n*
khuTwe step *n*
khyaar *coll* cucumber(s) *n*

l

l- for, into, to *prep*
la no *adv*

la b-alle! you must be kidding! (*casual*)
laaf (yloof) turn, change direction *v*
laaHaDH (ylaaHiDH) III observe *v*
laaji' refugee *n*
laakh (*f* lukhkhe) other *adj*; another *adj*
laakin but *conj*
laayiq appropriate, suitable *adj*
laazim + *v* must *(aux)*
la3aabe doll *n*
lahaane *coll* cabbage *n*
laHam (luHoom) meat *n*; ~ **beqer** beef *n*; ~ **ghenem** mutton *n*; ~ **khenzeer**
    pork *n*
laH-DHe moment *n*
laHin (alHaan) melody *n*
lait (laitaat) flashlight *n*
lajne (lijaan) committee *n*
lammaa3 (*f* lammaa3a) shiny *adj*
lap tup laptop *n*
las3a sting *n*
la-silki wireless *adj*
lawHa blackboard *n*; **lawHat il-mafaateeH** keyboard (*computer*) *n*
leebi Libyan *adj, n*
leebye Libya *n*
leelwaaye (leelu) pearl *n*
leff (yliff) wrap *v*
leffaaf (leffaafaat) scarf *n*
leffe sandwich *n*; **leffet kabaab** kebab sandwich *n*
lehje dialect, accent *n*
leTeef nice *adj*
li- for, into, to *prep*
li-annahu because *conj*; due to *prep*
li3ab (yil3ab) play *v*
li3baan nefis nausea *n*
li3be (*pl* al3aab) game; (*pl* malaa3eeb) toy *n*
liben yogurt *n*
libes (yilbes) dress, put on, wear *v*
liel (leyaali) night *n*
liesh why *adv*
liezer laser *n*
lige (yilgi) find *v*
lighe (yilghi) cancel *v*
li-giddaam forward *adv*
li-haadha therefore *adv*

liHag (yilHag) follow *v;* catch up with *v*
liHye (liHa) beard *n*
lijoo' siyaasi political asylum *n*
lil- for, to *prep*; **~-abed** forever *adv*
lizem (yilzem) catch *v;* touch *v*
lo or *conj*
lon (alwaan) color *n*
lori (loriyyaat) truck *n*
loz *coll* almond(s) *n*
lsaan (lsaanaat) tongue *n*
ltifet (yiltifit) VIII turn one's face *v*
lubnaan Lebanon *n*
lubnaani Lebanese *adj, n*
lughe language *n*
lughum (alghaam) mine *n*

m

ma not *adv*
ma'loof common, familiar *adj*
ma ameen unsafe *adj*
ma daqeeq inaccurate *adj*
ma ftihem (ma yiftihim) VIII misunderstand *v*
ma hna not here *adv*
ma kaamil incomplete *adj*
ma laayiq inappropriate *adj*
ma ma3roof unknown *adj*
ma mirtaaH uncomfortable *adj*
ma mlaa'im (*f* ma mlaa'me) inconvenient *adj*; unsuitable *adj*
ma mu'aththeth unfurnished *adj*
ma mu'dhi harmless *adj*
ma qibel (ma yiqbel) refuse *v*
ma SaHeeH false, incorrect *adj*
ma SiHHi unhealthy *adj*
ma waaDHiH (*f* ma waaDH-Ha) unclear *adj*
ma yhimm it doesn't matter
ma yigder (*f* ma tigder *pl* ma yigderoon) *v* incapable, unable *adj*
ma yinshaaf *v* (*f* ma tinshaaf) invisible *adj*
ma zien bad *adj*
maa3oon (mawaa3een) dish, plate *n*
maadde (mawaadd) item *n*; ingredient *n*; material *n*

maaDHi past *n*

maal- belong to *v*

maali (maaliyye) financial, fiscal *adj*; ... belongs to me

maalik (*pl* mullaak) owner, landowner *n*

maashye (il-maashye) cattle *n*

maat (ymoot) die *v*

maaTorsikil (maaTorsiklaat) motorcycle *n*

maayoh (maayohaat) women's swimsuit *n*

ma3a il-asef I am sorry

ma3a innahu although *conj*

ma3a s-salaame good-bye *n*

ma3bad (ma3aabid) temple *n*

ma3den (ma3aadin) metal *n*

ma3had (ma3aahid) institute, institution *n*

ma3joon asnaan toothpaste *n*

ma3loomaat *pl* information *n*; knowledge *n*; data *n*

ma3mal (ma3aamil) factory *n*

ma3meel (ma3aameel) client, customer *n*

ma3ne (ma3aani) meaning *n*

ma3qool reasonable *adj*

ma3raDH (ma3aariDH) (trade) show, exhibition *n*

ma3reke (ma3aarik) battle, combat *n*

ma3roof well-known *adj*; favor *n*

ma3yoob defective *adj*

mabee3aat sales *n*

mablagh (mabaaligh) amount, sum *n*

mabrook! congratulations

mabyoog stolen *adj*

madfe'e fireplace *n*

madkhal entrance *n*

maDHakhkha (maDHakhkhaat) pump *n*; **maDHakhkhat baanzeen** gas
    pump *n*

maDHher (maDHaahir) appearance *n*

mafhoom concept *n*; understood *adj*

mafqood missing (*person*) *adj*

maghrib (il-maghrib) Morocco *n*

maghribi (*pl* maghaarbe) Moroccan *adj, n*

mahjoor (mahjoore) deserted *adj*

maHall (maHallaat) shop *n*; ~ **il-feeterchi** auto repair shop *n*

maHalle district, neighborhood *n*

maHalli domestic, local *adj*

maHaTTe (train) station *n*; **maHaTTet kahrabaa'** power plant *n*

maH-DHooDH lucky *adj*

maHHad nobody *pron*
maHjooz booked, reserved *adj*
maHkeme (maHaakim) court *n*
maHSool ziraa3i (**maHaaSeel ziraa3iyye**) produce, crops *n*
majhool unknown *adj*
majjaanen free of charge *adj*
majmoo3 total amount *n*
majmoo3a collection *n*
majrooH wounded *adj*
makhbez (makhaabuz) bakery *n*
makhToob engaged *adj*
makhTooTe manuscript *n*
makhzan (makhaazin) store, shop *n*
makkook faDHaa'i space shuttle *n*
maktoob (makateeb) letter *n*
maku there isn't/aren't; ~ **b-ei mekaan** nowhere to be found *adv*; ~ **shee**
    there is nothing *pron*
malaabis *coll* clothes *n*
mal3ab stadium *n*
malja' (malaaji') shelter *n*
malyaan full, filled *adj*
mamerr hallway *n*
mamnoo3 it-tadkheen no smoking
mamnoon you are welcome (*response to* shukran *"thanks"*)
manaa3a jismiyye immune system *n*
manaaDHir eyeglasses *n*; ~ **shemsiyye** sunglasses *n*
manaakh climate *n*
man3 il-Hamil contraception *n*
man3 it-tajawwul curfew *n*
manDHar (manaaDHir) scene, view *n*
maneSSe (maneSSaat) platform *n*
manhej (menaahij) program *n*
manTeqe (manaaTiq) area, region *n*
maq3ad (maqaa3id) seat *n*
maqbare (maqaabur) cemetery *n*
maqfool locked *adj*
maqhoor sad *adj*
maraaHeeDH toilet *n*
maraaseem *pl* ceremony *n*
mareDH (amraaDH) disease; sickness *n*
mareeDH ill, sick *adj*; patient, sick person *n*
margat baamye okra stew with lamb and tomato sauce *n*
marHabe hello

marHale (maraaHil) stage, phase *n*
marja3 (maraaji3) reference *n*
markez (maraakiz) center *n*; ~ **ra'eesi** headquarters *n;* ~ **shurTe** police
    station *n*
markezi central *adj*
marraat often, sometimes *adv*
mart il-3amm mother-in-law *n*
martien twice *adv*
mas'ool responsible, liable *adj*
mas'ooliyye responsibility *n*
masaafe distance *n*
masbaH (masaabiH) swimming pool *n*
masdood closed, shut (e.g. door) *adj*
maseeHi Christian *adj, n*
mashbooh suspect *n*
mashghool busy *adj*
mash-hoor famous, well-known *adj*
mashroo3 Sinaa3i business (*industrial*) *n*
mashroo3 tijaari business (*commercial*) *n*
mashroob (mashroobaat) drink *n*; **mashroobaat ghaaziyye** soft drinks *n*;
    mashroobaat kuHooliyye alcoholic drinks *n*
maskoon populated *adj*
masraH stage; theater *n*
masroor glad *adj*
maS3ad (maSaa3id) elevator *n*
maSallakh (*f* mSallikhe *pl* mSallikheen) naked *adj*
maSdar (maSaadir) source *n*
maSfe (maSaafi) refinery *n*
masHooq ghaseel detergent *n*
maSir Egypt *n*
maSlakh (maSaalikh) slaughterhouse *n*
maSna3 (maSaani3) factory *n*
maSri Egyptian *adj, n*
matHaf (mataaHif) museum *n*
maththal (ymeththil) II represent; act *v*
maTaar (maTaaraat) airport *n*
maT3am (maTaa3um) restaurant *n*
maTbakh (maTaabukh) kitchen *n*
maT-Hoon ground (*food*) *adj*
maTleb (maTaalub) requirement *n*
maw3id (mawaa3eed) appointment *n*; **aakhir** ~ deadline *n*
mawDHoo3 (mawaaDHee3) subject *n*
mawDHoo3i objective *adj*

mawje (amwaaj) wave *n*
mawjood available, existing *adj*
mawkib (mawaakib) convoy *n*
mawlood born *adj*; ~ **jideed** (mawaleed jidded) newborn *n*
mawqi3 (mawaaqi3) location *n*; position *n*; site *n*
mawqif (mawaaqif) attitude *n;* ~ **seyyaaraat** parking lot *n*
mawrid (mewaarid) revenue *n*
mazeej combination *n*
mazra3a (mazaari3) farm *n*
m3azzil closed (shop) *adj*
mbellel wet *adj*
mdarrej layered (*hair*) *adj*; graded *adj*
mdewwer (*f* mdewre) round *adj*
medeene (mudun) city, town *n*; **medeenet il-al3aab** amusement park *n*
medeni civilian *adj, n*; civil *adj*
medrej (medaarij) runway *n*
medrese (medaaris) school *n*; ~ **ibtidaa'iyye** elementary school *n*;
　　　~ **mutawassiTe** middle school *n*; ~ **thaanewiyye** high school *n*
meekaaneeki mechanical *adj*
meel (amyaal) mile *n*
meelaad birth *n*
meenaa' (mawaani') port, harbor *n*
meet hundred (with a noun) *adj*; ~ **alif** one hundred thousand *adj*
meetien two hundred *adj*; ~ **alif** two hundred thousand *adj*
meezaan (mawaazeen) scale (*weight*) *n*
meezaaniyye meter *n*; budget *n*
meeze (meezaat) advantage *n*
meftooH (*f* meftooHa) open *adj*
mehed cradle *n*
mei water *n*; **azmet** ~ water shortage *n*
meikhaalif agreed *adj*; never mind
mejlis council *n*; ~ **il-amin fi hei'at il-umem il-muttaHide** UN Security
　　　Council *n*; ~ **ish-shiyookh** senate *n*; ~ **tashree3i** congress *n*
mejnoon (*pl* mejaaneen) mad *adj*
mejzere (mejaazir) massacre *n*
mekaan (mekaanaat) place *n*
mekeene (mekaayin) engine, machine *n*; **mekeenet it-telifon** answering
　　　machine *n*
mekhfi hidden *adj*
meksoor broken *adj*
mekteb (mekaatib) office *n*; desk *n*; ~ **il-bareed** post office *n*
mektebe (mektebaat) bookstore *n*; library *n*
melaak (malaa'ike) angel *n*

melik (milook) king *n*
meni sperm *n*
mentooj (mentoojaat) product *n*
mere (niswaan, nisaa') woman *n*; wife *n*
mesaa' il-khier good evening
mesaa' in-noor good evening (*response to* mesaa' il-khier)
meseere march *n*
meshi on foot *adv*
meshlool paralyzed *adj*
meshroo3 (meshaaree3) project *n*
mesjoon (mesaajeen) prisoner *n*
mesraHiyye play (*theater*) *n*
methel (amthile) example *n*
mewaarid resources *n*; ~ **maaliyye** funds *n*
meytem (meyaatim) orphanage *n*
meyyez (ymeyyiz) II recognize *v*
meyyit (*f* meite *pl* meiteen) dead *adj*
mezheriyye vase *n*
mfattiH open (store) *adj*
mgaddi (*pl* mgaadi) beggar *n*
mghaTTe (*f* mghaTTaaye) covered *adj*
mgheyyim cloudy *adj*
mheffe fan (*manual*) *n*
mi3de stomach *n*; ~ **mkharbuTe** upset stomach *n*
mi3Tef (ma3aatif) coat *n*
mi3timid (*f* mi3temde *pl* mi3temdeen) dependent on *adj*
miDHelli paratrooper *n*
miez (myooze) table *n*
miftaaH (mafaateeH) key *n*; ~ **bTaale** bottle opener *n*
mihne (mihen) profession *n*; career *n*
miHbes (maHaabis) ring *n*
miHne ordeal *n*
miHraar (maHaarer) thermometer *n*
miHtirif (*f* miHterfe) professional *adj*
mijelle magazine *n*
mikrafon (mikrafonaat) microphone *n*
mikriskob (mikriskobaat) microscope *n*
mikrob (mikrobaat) bacteria *n*
miktifi (*f* miktefye *pl* miktifeen) satisfied, self-sufficient *adj*
mikyaaj make-up *n*
milaaHe navigation *n*
mile (pronounced mi-le) (yimli) fill *v*
milek (yimluk) own *v*

miliH salt *n*
milyon (melaayeen) million *n*
min from; since *prep*; than *conj*
min DHiminhum including *prep*
min esh from what *interr*
min feDHlek please (*request*) *adv*
min il-waaDHiH obviously *adv*
min ish-sharq il-awSaT Middle Eastern *adj*
min khilaal through *prep*
min weqit early *adv*
mina3 (yimna3) prevent *v*
minemmil (*f* mnemle) numb *adj*
minfuSil (*f* minfeSle) separate *adj*
minHa (minaH) grant *n*
minshaar (menaasheer) saw *n*
minu who *pron*
minzi3ij (*f* minza3je *pl* minza3jeen) upset *adj*
miqyaas ir-resim scale (*map*) *n*
misaH (yimsaH) erase, wipe *v*
mishe (yimshi) walk *v*; ~ **bil-meseere** (yimshi bil-meseere) march *v*
mishmish *coll* apricot(s) *n*
mista3jil in a hurry *adj*
mistilim receiver *n*
mistiwi (mistawye) ripe *adj*
mit'akhkhir delayed, late *adj*
mit'akkid certain, sure *adj*
mit'assif sorry *adj*
mit'azzim in a critical situation *adj*
mit3awwid to be used to *v*
mitberri3 (mitbarri3a) donor *n*
mithaali ideal *adj*
mitHarrir liberal *adj*
mitHaDHDHir civilized *adj*
mithil as *adv*; like *prep*; similar to *adj*
mitkabbur (*f* mitkabre *pl* mitkabbureen) haughty *adj*
mitkharmush scratched *adj*
mitmaddin urban *adj*; civilized *adj*
mitmarrid rebel *n*
mitnawwi3 (*f* mitnawwi3a) various *adj*
mitqaa3id (*f* mitqaa3de *pl* mitqa3deen) retired *adj*
mitsaawi (*f* mitsaawye) equal *adj*
mitshaabih (*f* mitshaabhe *pl* mitshaabheen) identical, alike *adj*
mitwaaDHi3 (*f* mitwaaDH3a *pl* mitwaaDH3een) modest *adj*

mitwaffur available *adj*

mitzawwij married *adj*

miTTarruf extreme *adj*; extremist *n* (*pl* miTTarrufeen)

miTTawwi3 (*f* miTTaw3a) volunteer *n*

miyaah ma3deniyye mineral water *n*

miyye hundred (*standing alone*) *adj*

mjawwaf (*f* mjawfe) hollow *adj*

mkhabbal (*f* mkhable *pl* mkhaabeel) mad *adj*

mkhadde (mekhaadeed) pillow *n*

mkhaDHDHar *coll* vegetables *n*

mlawwath (*f* mlawwithe) contaminated, polluted *adj*

mlawwen (*f* mlawwine) colored *adj*

mmien from where

mode fashion *n*

modim (modimaat) modem *n*

moodiel (moodielaat) style (*clothing, hair*) *n*

moos Hilaaqe (amwaas Hilaaqe) razor *n*

mooSil (**il-mooSil**) Mosul *n*

moseeqe music *n*

mot *coll* death *n*

moz *coll* bananas *n*

mraaye mirror *n*

mreyye (mreyyaat, niswaan, nisaa') woman *n*

msaTTaH (*f* msaTTiHa) flat *adj*

mshawwish confusing *adj*

mtaa3 (amti3a) luggage *n*

mTalleg (*f* mTalge) divorced *adj*

mu'aamele treatment *n*

mu'aamere conspiracy *n*

mu'addab civil, polite *adj*

mu'assese foundation, institution *n*

mu'aththeth furnished *adj*

mu'aththir effective *adj*

mu'dhi harmful *adj*

mu'tamar (mu'tamaraat) conference *n*; ~ **saHafi** (mu'tamaraat saHafiyye) press conference *n*

mu3aahede treaty, pact *n*; ~ **duweliyye** international treaty *n*

mu3aareDHe opposition *n*

mu3aaSir contemporary *adj*

mu3aawene aid, assistance *n*

mu3addel average *adj*

mu3allim teacher *n*

mu3aqqam sterile *adj*

mu3aqqed complex *adj*
mu3awweq disabled, handicapped *adj*
mu3di contagious *adj*
mubaareyaat match (*sports*) *n*
mubaashereten directly *adv*; immediately *adv*
mubaashir direct *adj*
mudarra3a armored car
mudarris teacher *n*
mudeer (*pl* muderaa') director *n*; manager, executive *n*; headmaster *n*
mudhakkaraat autobiography *n*
mudhnib guilty *adj*
mudiel (mudielaat) model *n*
muDHaa3af double *adj*
muDHaadd anti- *adj*
muDHaahere (muDHaaheraat) demonstration *n*
muDHeyyif flight attendant, steward *n*
mufaaje'e surprise *n*
mufaaweDHe negotiation *n*
mufaDHDHal preferable *adj*
mufaSSal detailed *adj*
mufeed useful *adj*
mufettish inspector *n*
muflis penniless, bankrupt *adj*
mugeSS (magaaSeeS) scissors *n*
mughaadere departure *n*
mughanni singer *n*
mughrub (mughrubiyyaat) evening *n*
muhaajir immigrant *n*
muhandis engineer *n*
muheen degrading *adj*; offensive (*language, conduct*) *adj*
muhimm important *adj*; considerable *adj*
muhimme task *n*
muHaafiDH governor *n*; mayor *n*
muHaakeme trial *n*
muHaami (muHaameen) lawyer, attorney *n*
muHaasib cashier *n*; accountant *n*
muHaawele attempt *n*
muHallifeen jury *n*
muHarram forbidden *adj*; first month of the Islamic calender *n*
muHarrir editor *n*
muHawwil (muHawwilaat) transformer *n*
muHeeT ocean *n*; **il-muHeeT il-hindi** Indian Ocean *n*; **il-muHeeT il-aTlasi** Atlantic Ocean *n*; **il-muHeeT il-haadi** Pacific Ocean *n*

muHteweyaat contents *n*
mujaadele argument *n*
mujamma3 compound *n*
mujelled (mujelledaat) volume (*book*) *n*
mujtama3 (mujtama3aat) community *n*; society *n*
mukebbir iS-Sot (mukebbiraat iS-Sot) loudspeaker *n*
mukeyyef air-conditioned *adj*
mukhaabare (mukhaabaraat) phone call *n*; **mukhaabaraat** secret service *n*
mukhaddaraat drugs (*narcotics*) *n*
mukheyyem (mkheyyemaat) camp *n*
mukhrij director (*film*) *n*
mukhtaTaf hijacked *adj*
mukhtaTif hijacker *n*
mukhteber (mukhteberaat) laboratory *n*
mukhteSer brief *adj*
muknaase kahrabaaʻiyye (mekaanis kahrabaaʻiyye) vacuum cleaner *n*
mulaaHaDHe note *n*
mulaaHiDH observer *n*
mulHaq attaché *n*; ~ **thaqaafi** cultural attaché *n*; ~ **3askari** military attaché *n*
muluk property *n*
mumarriDH nurse *n*
mumeet fatal *adj*
mumeththil (mumeththile) actor *n*; representative *n*
mumkin possible *adj*
mumtaaz excellent *adj*
munaafese competition *n*
munaaqeshe discussion *n*
munaasebe occasion *n*; event *n*
munaawere (munaaweraat) maneuver *n*
munebbih qelbi (munebbihaat qelbiyye) pacemaker *n*
muneDHDHeme (muneDHDHemaat) organization *n*
muntaDHam (*f* muntaDHame) regular *adj*
muntezeh (muntezehaat) park *n*
muqaabele (muqaabelaat) interview *n*
muqaaTa3a boycott *n*
muqaawele (muqaawelaat) contract *n*
muqaawil contractor *n*
muqaddas (*f* muqaddese) holy *adj*
muqaddime (muqaddimaat) introduction *n*
muqareneten b- compared to *adj*
muqaTa3a (muqata3aat) province in *n*
muqteraH (muqtereHaat) proposal *n*
muraafiq escort *n*; bodyguard *n*

muraahiq teenager *n*
muraaji3 patient; person who goes to a government office on business *n*
muraasil correspondent *n*; reporter *n*; messenger *n*
murabba3 (murabba3aat) square *adj, n*
mureeH (*f* mureeHa) comfortable *adj*
mureshshaH candidate *n*
murshid guide; **il- ~** guidebook *n*
musaa3ade aid, help, assistance *n*
musaafir passenger *n*
musallaH armed *adj*
museddes (museddesaat) gun *n*
musejjil vidyowaat video recorder *n*
musekkin (musekkinaat) painkiller *n*
muselsele TV series *n*
mushaahid audience *n*
mushaarik participant *n*
mus-hil laxative *n*
mushkile (meshaakil) problem, trouble *n*
muslim Muslim *adj, n*
musta3mare settlement (*land*) *n*
mustaHeel impossible *adj*
mustakhdam employee *n*
mustami3 listener *n*
mustaqbal future *n*
mustaqill independent *adj*
mustaqirr stable *adj*
mustathmir investor *n*
mustawa (mustawayaat) level *n*; **~ maqbool** standard *n*
mustawda3 (mustawda3aat) warehouse *n*; depot *n*
mustawTane (mustawTanaat) settlement (*land*) *n*
mustemirr constant *adj*
musteshfe (musteshfeyaat) hospital *n*
muSawwir photographer *n*
muSelliH meekaaneeki mechanic *n*
muSfi (maSaafi) filter, strainer *n*
mutahaddith bi-isim spokesperson for *n*
mutefejjiraat *pl* explosives *n*
muterjim interpreter, translator *n*
mutheer exciting *adj*
muthelleth triangle *n*
muttaHid united *adj*
muTer rain *n*

muTret (timTur) rain *v*
muwaafeqe (muwaafeqaat) agreement *n*; approval *n*
muwaaSelaat transportation *n*
muwaaTin citizen *n*
muwaDHDHaf istiqbaal receptionist *n*
muwallide (muwallidaat) generator *n*
muwaqqet temporary *adj*
muweDHDHef employee *n*
muz3ij inconvenient *adj*; annoying *adj*
muzeel il-3araq deodorant *n*
mwaafiq agreed *adv*
mzawwer (*f* mzawwire) fake, counterfeit *adj*
mzeyyin (mzaine, mzeineen) barber, hairdresser (*for men only*) *n*

n

naaʻib (nuwwaab) deputy *n*
naa3im (*f* naa3me) soft *adj*
naadi (nawaadi) club *n*
naaDHij (*f* naaDHje) mature, ripe *adj*
naafoore fountain *n*
naajiH (*f* naajHa *pl* naajHeen) successful *adj*
naam (ynaam) sleep *v*
naaqesh (ynaaqish) III discuss *v*
naaqiS minus *prep;* (*f* naaqSe) incomplete, lacking *adj*
naar fire *n*; hell *n*
naas people, persons *n*
naashif (*f* naashfe) dry *adj*
naaSi (*f* naaSye) low *adj*
na3am yes (*formal*) *adv*
na3eemen *courtesy expression after someone has had a haircut or taken a bath* (*lit.* May you enjoy)
nabaati vegetarian *n*
naDHaafe hygiene *n*; cleanliness *n*
naDHDHaf (ynaDHDHuf) II clean *v*
naDHeef clean *adj*
naDHer vision, eyesight *n*
nafnoof (nafaaneef) dress *n*
nafuT oil (*petroleum*) *n*
naghme tune *n*
nailon plastic *n*

najjaar (nijaajeer) carpenter *n*
namsaawi Austrian *adj, n*
namse (in-namse) Austria *n*
naqiDH (in-naqiDH) veto *n*
naqqaal (naqqaalaat) mobile phone *n*
naseej (mansoojaat) textile *n*
naSeeHa advice *n*
naSS (nuSooS) text *n*
naw3 sort *n*
naw3iyye (naw3iyyaat) quality *n*
nawbe qelbiyye heart attack *n*
naz3 is-silaaH disarmament *n*
nebi (anbiyaaʻ) prophet *n*
neDHeriyye theory *n*
nee (*f* niyye) raw *adj*
neeli navy blue *adj*
neesaan April *n*
nefaadh expiration *n*
nefeq (anfaaq) tunnel *n*
nefer (neferaat) person *n*; people (*when counting*) *n*
neferaat collective taxi *n*
nefis same *adj*
nefis-he herself *pron*
nefis-hum themselves *pron*
nefiskum yourselves *pron*
nefisne ourselves *pron*
nefse himself *pron*
nefsek *m* yourself *pron*
nefsi myself *pron*
nefsich *f* yourself *pron*
neher (anhaar) river *n*
nejme (nijoom) star *n*
nekhe flavor *n*
neqi pure *adj*
neqil transport *n*
nerweej (in-nerweej) Norway *n*
nerweeji Norwegian *adj*
neshaaT (neshaaTaat) activity *n*
nesheeT active *adj*
neshle cold (*sickness*) *n*
neshshaal pickpocket *n*
neSir victory *n*
neteeje (netaayij) result *n*; conclusion *n*

nhiebi plunderer *n*
ni3naa3 mint (*herb*) *n*
nibaH (yinbaH) bark *v*
niDHaam (anDHime) regime *n*; system *n*; order *n*
nihaaye end; conclusion *n*; **nihaayet il-isboo3** weekend *n*
niheb (yinheb) loot *v*
nime (yinmu) grow *v*
nimoodhaj (namaadhij) sample *n*
nimu growth *n*
niqaabe union *n*; **niqaabet il-3ummaal** trade union *n*
niqaabi unionist *n*
niqedh (yinqudh) rescue *v*
niqel (yinqul) transport *v*
nisbe mi'awiyye percent *n*
nisbiyyen relatively *adv*
nise (yinse) forget *v*
nishef (yinshef) dry *v*
nisher (yinshur) spread *v*
niSeb (yinSub) install *v*
niTe (yinTi) give *v*
niza3 (yinza3) take off, undress *v*
nizef (yinzif) bleed *v*
nizel (yinzil) get down; get off (*vehicle*) *v*; ~ **thelij** snow *v*
nizool check-in (*hotel*) *n*
no3 (anwaa3) kind, class, type *n*
noomi HaamuDH *coll* lemon *n*
nufeDH (yinfuDH) shake *v*
nuHaas copper *n*
nuqTe (nuqeT, niqaaT) dot, drop, point *n*; **nuqTet tafteesh** (nuqeT tafteesh) checkpoint *n*
nuskhe (nusekh) copy, photocopy *n*
nuSS half *n*; middle *n*; ~ **il-liel** midnight *n*
nuwaaye (nuwe) seed *n*

O

ogef! stop! *imp*
oksijeen oxygen *n*
ootiel (ootielaat) hotel *n*
orgin (orginaat) organ (*music*) *n*
oruppe Europe *n*
oruppi European *adj, n*

p

paatri (paatriyyaat) battery *n*
paawen (paawenaat) pound *n*
panTiroon (penaaTeer) pants *n*; ~ **gSeyyir** shorts *n*
pashkeer (pashaakeer) towel *n*
parawaane propeller *n*
pasport (pasportaat) passport *n*
paS (paSaat) bus *n*; **mawqif** ~ bus stop *n*
penke fan (*electric*) *n*
perde curtain *n*
pereshoot (pereshootaat) parachute *n*
perlemaan parliament *n*
pianu piano *n*
piTaaqe ticket *n*
plasteek plastic *n*
pump (pumpaat) pump *n*
purtuqaal *coll* orange (*fruit*) *n*
purtuqaali orange (*color*) *adj*
putiete *coll* potato(es) *n*

q

qaaʻid (quwwaad) leader *n*
qaaʻime (qawaaʻim) list *n*; **qaaʻimet il-akil** (qawaaʻim il-akil) menu *n*
qaa3ide jewwiyye (qawaa3id jewwiyye) air base *n*
qaa3idet il-beyaanaat database *n*
qaadim next *adj*
qaaDHi (quDHaat) judge *n*
qaahire (il-qaahire) Cairo *n*
qaamoos (qawaamees) dictionary *n*
qaaren (yqaarin) III compare *v*
qaarib nejaat (qawaarib nejaat) lifeboat *n*
qaarre continent *n*
qaas (yqees) measure *v*
qaaSir (*f* qaaSre) minor, underaged person *n*
qaatil fatal, mortal, lethal *adj*; killer *n*
qaaT (qooT) suit *n*
qabeeH ugly *adj*
qabile maʻdhoone midwife *n*
qabuDH capture; constipation *n*
qadder (yqaddir) II estimate *v*

qadeem old, ancient (*object*) *adj*
qaDHiyye (qaDHaaya) case (*court*) *n*; issue *n*
qafaS (aqfaaS) cage *n*
qaliq (*f* qalqe *pl* qalqeen) concerned, worried *adj*
qamar Sinaa3i satellite *n*
qameeS (qumSaan) shirt *n*
qannaaS (qannaaSe) sniper *n*
qanoon (qawaaneen) law; musical instrument *n*
qanooni legal *adj*
qappooT (qapaapeeT) coat *n*
qaraar (qaraaraat) decision *n*; resolution *n*
qareeb close, near *adj*
qareeben soon *adv*
qarrar (yqarrir) II decide *v*
qarye (qura) village *n*
qassam (yqassim) II divide *v*; ~ **bin-nuSS** II halve *v*
qaSir (quSoor) palace *n*
qatar Qatar *n*
qatil killing *n*
qaTTaa3 (qaTTaa3aat) zone *n*
qawi (*pl* aqwiyaa') powerful, strong *adj*
qawmi national *adv*
qawmiyye nationality *n*
qeddem (yqeddim) II apply; introduce; offer *v*
qedhaare dirt *n*
qeeme value *n*
qeleel few *adj*; little *n*
qelem (aqlaam, qlaam) pen *n*; ~ **jaff** (qlaam jaffe) ballpoint pen *n*; ~ **Hibir** ink pen *n*; ~ **riSaaS** pencil *n*
qellel (yqellil) II reduce *v*
qenaat (qenewaat) canal; channel *n*
qenefe (qenefaat) sofa *n*
qesem oath *n*
qess (qusus) priest *n*
qeswe cruelty *n*
qeSeede (qeSaayid) poem *n*
qibel (yiqbel) accept *v*
qileq (yiqleq) worry *v*
qire (yiqre) read *v*
qirin (quroon) century *n*
qisim (aqsaam) department *n*; section *n*
qiSed (yiqSud) mean *v*
qitel (yuqtul) kill *v*

qiTaar (qiTaaraat) train *n*; ~ **il-liel** night train *n*; ~ **in-nahaar** day train *n*
qiTa3 il-ittiSaal (yiqTa3 il-ittiSaal) disconnect *v*
qiyaade leadership *n*
qiyaadi leading *adj*
qiyaas (qiyaasaat) measurement *n*
qmaash (qmaashaat) fabric *n*
qoori teapot *n*
qooTiyye (qawaaTi) can *n*; **miftaaH qawaaTi** can opener *n*
qtireb (yiqtirib) VIII approach *v*
qubeDH (yiqbuDH) capture; receive *v*
qubTaan captain *n*
qudre ability *n*
quds (il-quds) Jerusalem *n*
quful (qfaale) lock *n*
qumme (qumem) summit *n*
qunbule (qanaabul) bomb *n*; ~ **dherriyye** atomic bomb *n*
qunderchi shoemaker *n*
qunSul consul *n*
qur'aan Koran *n*
qurS Salib hard drive *n*
quSSe (quSaS) story *n*
quT3a (quTa3) piece *n*
quTub (aqTaab) pole *n*
quwwe (quwwaat) force, power, strength *n*; **quwwaat musallaHa** armed
    forces *n*

r

ra'ees (ru'asaa') chief *n*; president *n*; ~ **il-lejne** chairman *n*; ~ **wuzeraa'**
    prime minister *n*
ra'eesi main *adj*; major *adj*
ra'sen directly *adv*; immediately *adv*
raabi3 (*f* raab3a) fourth *adj*
raad (yreed) require *v;* want *v*
raadyo (radyowaat) radio *n*
raaH (yrooH) go *v;* ~ **lil-biet** go home *v*
raakhi (*f* raakhye) loose *adj*
raakib (rukkaab) passenger (*vehicle*) *n*
raami maahir sharp shooter *n*
raaqab (yraaqib) III watch *v*

raas (roos) head *n*; ~ **is-sene** New Year *n*
raatib (rawaatib) salary *n*
ra3id thunder *n*
rabbaaT (rabbaaTaat) link *n*
rabbet biet (rabbaat byoot) housewife *n*
rabee3 spring *n*
rabTe scarf *n*
rachiete (rachietaat) prescription *n*
radaar radar *n*
radikaali radical *adj*
raff (rfoof) shelf *n*
rafuDH refusal *n*
rahham (yrahhum) II match *v*
raHle desk (*school*) *n*
rajaa'an please (*request*) *adv*
ramaDHaan Ramadan *n*; ~ **kareem** *courtesy exchanged at the beginning of Ramadan* (*lit.* Ramadan is generous.)
ramul sand *n*
ramz bareedi zip code *n*
raqam it-telifon phone number
raqeeq fine, delicate *adj*
raqmi digital *adj*
rasheeq slim *adj*
rashshaash spray *n*
rashshaashe machine gun, semi-automatic gun *n*
rasmi official *adj*
raSeef (raSaayif) sidewalk *n*
raTub (*f* raTbe) humid *adj*
rawDHe kindergarten *n*
rdaan (rdaanaat) sleeve *n*
re'i (araa') opinion *n*
redd fi3il (ridood af3aal) reaction *n*
reef countryside *n*
reefi rural *adj*
reeHa (rewaa'iH) odor, smell *n*; (*pl* riyaH) perfume *n*
reff (rfoof) rack, shelf *n*
reggi *coll* watermelon *n*
reheene (rehaa'in) hostage *n*
rei irrigation *n*
rejil (ryaajeel) husband *n*
rekheeS cheap *adj*

remiz (rumooz) symbol *n*
reshwe (reshaawi) bribe *n*
resim (risoomaat) drawing *n*; ~ **tawDHeeHi** illustration *n*
ribaaT (arbiTe) tie *n*
ribiH (arbaaH) gain, profit *n*
rigeS (yirguS) dance *v*
rigSe (rigSaat) dance *n*
rihem (yirhem) fit *v*
rija3 (yirja3) come back, get back, return *v*
rijil (rijlien, rijlienaat) foot *n*; leg *n*
rijjaal (ryaajeel) man *n*
rikeb (yirkeb) ride *v*
rikeDH (yirkuDH) run *v*
rime (yirmi) shoot *v*
riqaabe censorship *n*
risaale (resaa'il) message *n*
risem (yirsim) draw *v*
rishe (yirshi) bribe *v*
riSaaS lead (*metal*) *n*
riSaaSe (riSaaS) bullet *n*
riSaaSi gray *adj*
riwaaye novel *n*
riyaaDHe sports *n*
riyoog breakfast *n*
riyye lung *n*
rizem (yirzim) pack *v*
roobyaan *coll* shrimp *n*
rooH! (*f* rooHi!) go! *imp*
roosi (*pl* roos) Russian *adj, n*
roosye Russia *n*
rubaH (yirbaH) win *v*
rubeT (yirbuT) tie *v*
rubu3 quarter *n*
rufa3 (yirfa3) raise *v*
rugbe (rgaab) neck *n*
rukbe (rkaab) knee *n*
rukhSe license *n*; permission *n*
rumaadi gray *adj*
rummaan *coll* pomegranate
rummaane grenade *n*
rusugh wrist *n*

rutbe (ruteb) rank (*military*) *n*
ruToobe moisture *n*
ruzme (ruzem) package, parcel *n*

S

saa'iH (suwwaaH) tourist *n*
saa'il (sawaa'il) liquid *adj, n*
saa3a (sa3aat) clock, hour, watch *n*; o'clock *adv*
saa3ad (ysaa3id) III aid, help *v*
saabi3 (*f* saab3a) seventh *adj*
saabiq (*f* saabqe) former, previous *adj*
saadis (*f* saadse) sixth *adj*
saafer (ysaafir) III travel *v*
saaHa rotary, traffic circle *n*; playground (*school*) *n*
saaHibe ventilator *n*
saaHil (sawaaHil) beach, shore, coast *n*
saakin (sukkaan) inhabitant *n*; ~ **b-** living in *adj*
saakit (*f* saakte) silent *adj*
saam poisonous, toxic *adj*
saaq (ysooq) drive *v*
saatilait dish satellite dish *n*
saayiq (suwwaaq) chauffeur, driver *n*; ~ **teksi** taxi driver *n*
sa3eed happy *adj*
sab3a seven (standing alone) *adj*
sab3een seventy *adj*; ~ **alif** seventy thousand *adj*
sabboore (sabbooraat) blackboard *n*
sabi3 (sbaa3) lion *n*; brave *adj*
sabi3 seven (*with a noun*) *adj*
sabi3meet seven hundred (*with noun*) *adj*; ~ **alif** seven hundred thousand *adj*
sabi3miyye seven hundred (*standing alone*) *adj*
sabi3talaaf seven thousand *adj*
sabit (is-sabit) Saturday *n*
safaare embassy *n*
safeene shira3iyye (sufun shira3iyye) sailboat *n*
safeenet il-faDHaa' space shuttle *n*
safeer (suferaa') ambassador *n*
saguf (sgoofe) ceiling *n*
saHaafe press *n*
sakhkhaan furnace *n*
salaam peace *n*; **is-salaamu 3aleikum** may peace be upon you (*greeting*)
sandaweeche sandwich *n*

saree3 (*f* saree3a) express, fast, quick *adj*

sareer bed *n*; ~ **mal nefer waaHid** twin/single bed; ~ **mal neferien** queen/king bed

sarraH (ysarriH) II lay off *v*

saT-Hi shallow *adj*

saTiH (sTooH) rooftop; surface *n*

sbaTa3ash seventeen *adj*

sebbaabe index finger *n*

sebeb (asbaab) reason; cause *n*

sedd (ysidd) block; close, shut; turn off *v*; ~ **it-telifon** hang up *v*

sedde (sidood) dam *n*

see-dee (see-diyyaat) compact disc *n*

seeneme cinema, the movies *n*

sefer travel *n*

sefre trip, picnic *n*

sehem (as-hum) stock; arrow *n*

sehil (*f* sehle) easy *adj*

seiTer (yseiTir) control *v*

seiTere control *n*

sejjel (ysejjil) II enroll; record *v*

sekraan (*pl* skaare) drunk *adj*

sekte demaaghiyye stroke *n*; ~ **qelbiyye** cardiac arrest *n*

selle (slaal) basket *n*

sene (senewaat) year *n*

senewi annual *adj*

sereTaan cancer *n*

seriqe robbery, theft *n*

sewwe (ysewwi) do, make *v;* ~ **ma3roof** do someone a favor *v*

seyyaare (seyyaaraat) car *n*

seyyid (is-seyyid) Mr., Sir *n*

seyyide (is-seyyide) Mrs., lady, madam *n*

si'al (yis'al) ask *v*; ~ **wien iT-Tareeq** ask for directions *v*

si3a capacity *n*

si3al (yis3al) cough *v*

si3ir (as3aar) price; rate *n*; ~ **il-faa'ide** interest rate *n*

si3oodi Saudi *adj, n*

si3oodiyye (is-si3oodiyye) Saudi Arabia *n*

sibaH (yisbaH) swim *v*

sichcheene (sichaacheen) knife *n*

sief (syoofe) sword *n*

sijen (yisjin) imprison *v*

sijill (sijillaat) record *n*

sijin (sijoon) prison, jail *n*

sikirtier secretary *n*
sikket Hadeed (sikek Hadeed) railroad track *n*
silaaH (asliHa) weapon *n*
sileb (yislib) hold up; rob *v*
silk (aslaak) wire *n*
silsile (salaasil) chain *n*; series (*publications*) *n*; (muselselaat *pl*) TV series *n*
sima3 (yisma3) hear, listen *v*
simaH (yismaH) allow *v*
sime sky *n*
simech *coll* fish *n*
simeen (*pl* smaan) fat *adj*
simint concrete *n*
simmaa3a(at) headphones *n*
sinn (asnaan, snoon) tooth *n*
sinni (*pl* sinne) Sunni *adj, n*
sirdaab (saraadeeb) basement *n*
sire (siraawaat) row; line (*for writing*) *n*
sirr (asraar) secret *n*
sirri secret, undercover *adj*
sit six (*with noun*) *adj*; way of addressing women, especially female teachers
sitmeet six hundred (*with noun*) *adj*; ~ **alif** six hundred thousand *adj*
sitmiyye six hundred (*standing alone*) *adj*
sitre jacket *n*
sittalaaf six thousand *adj*
sitte six (*standing alone*) *adj*
sitteen sixty *adj*; ~ **alif** sixty thousand *adj*
siTTa3ash sixteen *adj*
siweed (is-siweed) Sweden *n*
siwiyye together *adv*
siyaaHa tourism *n*
siyaaj hedge; fence *n*
siyaase policy; politics *n*
siyaasi political *adj*; politician *n*
skhoone fever *n*
slaaH (asliHa) arm, weapon, firearm *n*
soo' fehim misunderstanding *n*
soog (swaage) bazaar, market *n*; ~ **il-borSe** stock market *n*
soori *m* Syrian *adj, n*
soorye Syria n
spaani Spanish *adj, n*
spaanye Spain *n*
sprei mal sha3ar hairspray *n*
srinje syringe *n*

sta3mal (yista3mil) X use *v*
staqaal (yistaqeel) X resign *v*
stawred *(*yistawrid*)* X import *v*
stemarr (yistemurr) X continue *v*
stensekh (yistensikh) X copy, photocopy *v*
steraaH (yistereeH) X rest *v*
sterkhe (yisterkhi) X relax *v*
stilem (yistilim) VIII receive *v*
su'aal (as'ile) question *n*
su3aal cough *n*
sufre daayme *courtesy at the dinner table* (*lit.* May your table be like this forever.)
suHoor small pre-sunrise meal during Ramadan
sukkaan people; population *n*; ~ **is-seyyaare** steering wheel *n*
sukkar diabetes *n*
sukoot silence *n*
sullem kahrabaa'i escalator *n*
sulTe (sulTaat) authority *n*; ~ **qaDHaa'iyye** jurisdiction *n*
sur3a speed *n*; **is-** ~ **il-quSwa** speed limit *n*
suwe together *adv*
sweech (sweechaat) switch *n*; ~ **is-seyyaare** ignition key *n*
sweedi Swedish *adj, n*
sweesre Switzerland *n*
sweesri Swiss *adj, n*

S

Saafi net; clear (*water*) *adj*
SaaHi (*f* SaaHye *pl* SaaHeen) sober; awake *adj*
SaaHib (*f* SaaHbe *pl* aS-Haab) owner *n*
Saalon (Hilaaqe) barbershop; hairdresser's shop *n*
Saam (ySoom) fast (*during the month of Ramadan*) *v*
Saan (ySoon) maintain *v*
Saar (ySeer) become; happen *v*; OK!
Saayigh (Siyyaagh) jeweler *n*
Sa3ub (*f* Sa3be) difficult, hard *adj*
SabaaH il-khier good morning
Saboon *coll* soap *n*
Sadaqe charity *n*
Saddag (ySaddig) II believe *v*
Sadder (ySaddir) II export *v*
Sadeeq (aSdiqaa') friend *n*

Sadir chest *n*

Sadme shock *n*

Saff (Sufoof) class, grade (*school*) *n*

SafHa (SafHaat) page; side *n*

Safqe (Safqaat) deal *n*

SaHafi journalist

SaHeeH (*f* SaHeeHa) correct, right *adj*; ~? is that right?

SaHib il-biet (aS-Haab il-biet/il-byoot) landlord *n*

SaHin faDHaa'i satellite dish *n*

SaHraa' desert *n*

Salib (*f* Salbe) solid *adj*

SallaH (ySalliH) II repair; correct *v*

Sammaam (Sammaamaat) valve *n*

Sammam (ySammim) II determine *v*

Sammoon *coll* bread *n*

Samugh glue *n*

Sandoog (Sanaadeeg) box; trunk (*car*) *n*; ~ **il-bareed** mailbox, letterbox *n*

SaqqeT (ySaqqiT) II overthrow (*government*) *v*

Sarookh (Sawaareekh) rocket *n*

Sarraaf teller (*bank*); money changer *n*

Sarref (ySarruf) II cash (*a check*), change (*money*) *v*

Sawwat (ySawwit) II vote *v*

Seboor patient *adj*

Seen (iS-Seen) China *n*

Seeni Chinese *adj*

Seeniyye (Swaani) tray *n*

Seideliyye pharmacy *n*

Sekk (Sukook) check *n*

Selaat prayer *n*

Selle (ySelli) II pray *v*

SeyyaH (ySeyyiH) II shout *v*

Sief summer *n*

Sifir zero *n*

SiHHa health *n*; ~ **3aqliyye** mental health *n*

SiHHi healthy; sanitary *adj*

Sinaa3a industry *n*

Sinaa3i industrial *adj*

Siref (yiSruf) spend *v*

Siyaane *n* maintenance

Soda soda drink

Soof wool *n*

Soore (Suwer) image; picture; painting; photo *n*

Sope heater *n*

SoS sauce *n*
SoSij sausage *n*
Sot (aSwaat) sound; voice; volume (*sound*) *n*
STuwaane cylinder; record (*vinyl*) *n*
Subegh (yiSbugh) paint *v*
Subugh paint *n*
SubuH morning *n*
Sudaa3 headache *n*
Sudug truth *n;* ~? really? *adv*
Sughra (iS-Sughra) the minimum *n*
Sukook il-musaafireen traveler's checks

sh

shaabb young man *n*
shaabbe young woman *n*
shaaf (yshoof) look; see *v*
shaahid (shihood) witness *n*; ~ **3ayaan** eyewitness *n*
shaaHib (*f* shaaHbe *pl* shaHbeen) pale *adj*
shaaHine semi-truck *n*
shaal (ysheel) carry; lift, pick up *v*
shaarek (yshaarik) III participate *v*
shaari3 (shawaari3) road, street *n*
shaayi3 (*f* shaay3a) popular; widespread *adj*
shaayib (*pl* shiyyaab) old (*man*) *adj*
sha3ab (shi3oob) people *n*
sha3abi (*f* sha3abiyye) public; popular *adj*
sha3ar hair *n*
sha3riyye noodles *n*
shabaab youth *n*
shafre razor blade
shahaade certificate, degree, diploma *n*
shaHam fat (*body*); ~ **it-tezyeet** lubricant (*car*) *n*
shakk (yshukk) doubt *v*
sham3a (shumoo3) candle *n*
shami3 wax *n*
shampu shampoo *n*
shareeHa (sharaayiH) slice *n*
shareeT (sharaayiT) ribbon; ~ **il-vidyo** video tape *n*; ~ **tasjeel** tape
    (*recording*) *n*
sharraH (ysharriH) II slice *v*
shaTT (shTooT) river *n*

shawwaaye grill *n*

shbaaT February *n*

shebeket 3amel (shebekaat a3maal) network *n*

shedeed strong, severe *adj*

shee (ashyaa') object, thing *n*

shee3i (shee3a) Shiite *adj, n*

shefqe hat *n*

sheggeg (ysheggig) II tear *v*

shegheb riot *n*

sheheed (shuhedaa') martyr *n*

sheher (ashhur) month *n*

shehim (shehmeen) gentlemanly, considerate, attentive *adj*

shehiyye appetite *n*

shehri monthly *adj*

shejere (ashjaar) tree *n*

sheker sugar *n*

shekhiS (ashkhaaS) person, people (*when counting*) *n*

shekhSi personal *adj*

shemis sun *n*

shemsiyye (shemsiyyaat) umbrella *n*

sheraab kuHooli liquor *n*

sherbet fruit syrup diluted in water, served with ice *n*

shereek (*pl* shurekaa') partner *n*

sheref honor *n*

sherike company; corporation *n*

sherq east *n*

sherqi eastern *adj*

sherr evil *n*

shewwesh (yshewwish) II disturb; confuse *v*

shged how much; ~ **yib3id/tib3id…?** how far is…?

shi3ar (yish3ur) feel *v*

shi3ir poetry *n*

shi3oor feeling *n*

shiba3 (yishba3) be full after eating *v*

shibbaach (shabaabeech) window *n*

shiffe (shfaayif) lips *n*

shihed (yishhed) testify *v*

shiker (yishkur) thank *v*

shikil (ashkaal) shape, form *n*

shimaal north *n*

shimaali northern *adj*

shineene yogurt drink *n*

shinoo what *pron*; ~ **il-qaDHiyye** what's the matter?

shiraH (yishraH) explain *v*
shireb (yishreb) drink *v*
shite winter *n*
shiyoo3i communist *adj, n*
shlon how *adv*
shorbe soup *n*
sh-Saar what's the matter?
shtemm (yishtemm) VIII smell *v*
shtighel (yishtughul) VIII work *v*
shtike (yishtiki) **min** VIII complain about…
shtire (yishtiri) VIII buy *v*
shu3aa3 ray *n*
shubuh jezeere peninsula *n*
shughul (ashghaal) profession; work *n*
shuHne cargo; charge (*electricity*) *n*
shukran thanks *n*; ~ **3ala** thanks for
shumer (yishmur) throw *v*
shuqqe (shuqeq) apartment *n*
shurooq ish-shemis sunrise *n*
shurTe police *n*
shurTi (shurTe) police officer; ~ **muroor** traffic officer *n*
shwaarub moustache *n*
shwei shwei slowly! (*step by step*) *adv*
shwekit when *adv*
shweyye bit, little *n*; slightly *adv*

t

t'ammel (yit'ammel) V hope *v*
t'awwah (yit'awwah) V moan *v*
ta'keed confirmation *n*; **bit-ta'keed** certainly *adv*
ta'kheer delay *n*
ta'meen insurance *n*
ta'sheere siyaaHiyye tourist visa
ta'sheeret dukhool (ta'sheeraat dukhool) entry visa
ta'theer (ta'theeraat) effect *n*
taanki (taankiyyaat) tank (*storage*) *n*
taareekh history; (*pl* tawaareekh) date; ~ **il-wilaade** date of birth
taareekhi *m* historical *adj*
taasi3 (*f* taas3a) ninth *adj*
taayer (taayeraat) tire *n*
taaze *m/f* fresh *adj*

ta3aal waraaye! follow me!
ta3aawin cooperation *n*
ta3baan *m* tired *adj*
ta3beer expression (*verbal*) *n*
ta3dheeb torture *n*
ta3leem education *n*
ta3leemaat instructions *n*
ta3leemi *m* educational *adj*
tabaadul (tabaadulaat) exchange *n*
tabdheer waste (squandering) *n*
tabigh (tuboogh) tobacco *n*
taboot (tawaabeet) coffin *n*
tadfi'e markeziyye central heating *n*
tadreeb training *n*
taDHaarub contradiction; clash *n*
tafteesh inspection *n*
tahdeed (tahdeedaat) threat *n*
taH-dheer warning
taH-DHeer (taH-DHeeraat) preparation *n*
taHiyyaat regards *n*
taHleel analysis *n*
taHqeeq (taHqeeqaat) investigation *n*
taHreer liberation *n*
taHweele detour; moving *n*
tajheezaat supplies *n*
takhreeb sabotage *n*
talqeeH (talqeeHaat) vaccination *n*
tamaamen completely, exactly *adv*
tammooz July *n*
tamur *coll* date (*fruit*) *n*
tanDHeef jaaff dry cleaner *n*
tanDHeem in-nesil birth control
tannoor clay oven *v*
tannoore skirt *n*
tanzeelaat sale *n*
taqdeer (taqdeeraat) estimate *n*
taqleed imitation; (taqaaleed) tradition *n*
taqleedi *m* traditional *adj*
taqreeben almost, approximately *adv*
taqreer account (*report*) *n*
taqseem division *n*
taqweem (taqaaweem) calendar *n*
taraaju3 withdrawal *n*

tarHeel deportation *n*
tashkheeS diagnose *n*
tasjeel ahdaaf score (*sports*) *n*
taSdeer (taSderaat) export *n*
taSfeeq applause *n*
taSleeH (taSleeHaat) repair *n*
taSmeem (taSaameem) design *n*
taSreeH (taSreeHaat) declaration, statement; announcement *n;*
    it-~ il-gumrugi customs declaration
taSweet vote *n*
taT3eem immunization *n*
taTweer development *n*
tawaazun balance *n*
tawjeehaat directives *n*
tawqee3 (tawaaqee3) signature *n*
tawSiye recommendation *n*
tawzee3 distribution *n*
t3aamel (yit3aamel) VI bargain, deal *v*
t3aaref (yit3aaref) VI get acquainted with
t3aarek (yit3aarek) VI fight *v*
t3allem (yit3allem) V learn *v*
tbenne (yitbenne) V adopt *v*
tdhekker (yitdhekker) V remember *v*
tDHammen (yitDHammen) V include *v*
te'theer influence *n*
tedreeji *m* gradual *adj*
tee shert (tee shertaat) T-shirt *n*
teen *coll* fig
teghdhiye nourishment *n*
teghyeer change (*modification*) *n*
tejammu3 (tejammu3aat) gathering *n*
tejrube (tajaarub) experience *n*
teknelojye technology *n*
teksi (teksiyyaat) cab, taxi *n*
tekyeef air conditioning *n*
telewwuth contamination, pollution *n*
telifon (telifonaat) telephone *n*
tell (tlaal) hill *n*
temerrud mutiny, rebellion *n*
temreeDH nursing *n*
temreen (tamareen) exercise *n*
temyeez discrimination *n;* ~ **3unSuri** racial discrimination
teqaa3ud pension *n*

teqaaTu3 (teqaaTu3aat) intersection *n*
teqaddum progress *n*
teqeni *m* technical *adj*
teqreer (teqaareer) report *n*
teraachi earrings *n*
teraaju3 retreat *n*
terjem (yterjim) translate *v*
teshweeh disfigurement *n*
teSaadum impact (*physical*), collision *n*
teSarruf(aat) behavior, conduct, manners *n*
tewettur stress, tension *n*
tezyeef forgery *n*
tfaaje' (yitfaaje') VI be surprised *v*
tfaDHDHal here it is (*response to a request*)
tgheyyer (yitgheyyer) V change *v intrans*
t-hejje (yit-hejje) V spell (*word*) *v*
tHaaresh (yitHaaresh) VI harass *v*
tHaDHDHer (yitHaDHDHer) V get ready *v*
tHarrek (yitHarrek) V move *v*
tHawwel (yitHawwel) move (*house*) *v*
tibin qish straw *n*
ti'mur very well (*lit.* your request is an order)
ti3laage hanger *n*
tijaare commerce, trade *n*
tijaari *m* commercial *adj*
tikit (tiktaat) ticket *n*; ~ **ghier murajja3** one-way ticket; ~ **murajja3** return ticket
tikraaren frequently *adv*
tilfizyon television *n*
tilmeedh (telaameedh) (*young*) student *n*
timmen rice *n*
tirek (yitruk) leave *v*
tis3a nine (*standing alone*) *adj*
tis3een ninety *adj*; ~ **alif** ninety thousand *adj*
tisaTa3ash nineteen *adj*
tishreen il-awwel October *n*
tishreen ith-thaani November *n*
tisi3 nine (*with a noun*) *adj*
tisi3meet nine hundred (*with a noun*) *adj*; ~ **alif** nine hundred thousand *adj*
tisi3miyye nine hundred (*standing alone*) *adj*
tisi3talaaf nine thousand *adj*
tislem that's very nice of you (*response to received favors*)
tiSbaH 3ala khier good night

tiSbaH 3ala noor good night (*response to* tiSbaH 3ala khier)
tkallam (yitkallam) V speak *v*
tkhaaber (yitkhaaber) VI talk on the phone *v*
tkharraj (yitkharraj) V graduate *v*
tkheSSes (yitkheSSes) V specialize in *v*
tkheyyel (yitkheyyel) V imagine *v*
tlaathe three *adj* (*standing alone*)
tlaatheen thirty *adj*; ~ **alif** thirty thousand *adj*
tlath three (*with a noun*) *adj*
tlatta3ash thirteen *adj*
tlattalaaf three thousand *adj*
tlethmeet three hundred (*with a noun*) *adj*; ~ **alif** three hundred thousand *adj*
tlethmiyye three hundred (*standing alone*) *adj*
tmenne (yitmenne) V wish *v*
tmeshshe (yitmeshshe) V go for a walk *v*
tneffes (yitneffes) V breathe *v*
tnekker (yitnekker) V disguise *v*
tom twins *n*
toonis Tunisia *n*
toonisi (*pl* twaanse) Tunisian *adj, n*
tqeyye' (yitqeyye') V vomit *v*
traaja3 (yitraaja3) VI withdraw, retreat VI
tsallaq (yitsallaq) V climb *v*
tshaarek (yitshaarek) VI share *v*
tsherrafne nice to meet you
tSaadeq (yitSaadeq) VI become friends
tSarraf (yitSarraf) V conduct, behave *v*
tSewwer (yitSewwer) V think (suppose) *v*
tuffaaH *coll* apples
turbe soil *n*
turki (*pl* atraak) Turkish *adj, n*
turkiye Turkey *n*
twaaliet toilet *n*
twaqqa3 (yitwaqqa3) V expect *v*
tweffe (yitweffe) II pass away *v*
twennes (yitwennes) V enjoy, have fun *v*
tzawwej (yitzawwej) V marry *v*

T

Taabi3 (Tawaabi3) stamp *n*
Taabiq (Tawaabiq) story (*building*) *n*; **iT-Taabiq ith-thaani** second floor, upstairs *adv*

Taaleb (yTaalub) III claim *v*
Taalib (*pl* Tullaab) student *n*
Taaqe energy *n*
Taar (yTeer) fly *v*
Taase bowl *n*
Taawe pan *n*
Ta33am (yTa33um) II feed *v*
Tab3an of course *adv*
Tabbaakh cook; stove *n*
Tabee3a nature *n*
Tabee3i *m* natural, normal *adj*
Tabeeb (aTibbaaʻ) doctor, physician *n*; ~ **3yoon** eye doctor,
    opthamologist *n*; ~ **asnaan** dentist *n*; ~ **beiTeri** veterinarian *n*;
    ~ **nefsaani** psychologist *n*; ~ **nisaaʻi** gynecologist *n*
Tal3a check-out (*hotel*) *n*
Talqa shot *n*
TamaaTa tomato *n*
Tann (aTnaan) ton *n*
Tareeq (*pl* Turuq) way, road *n*; ~ **khaariji** (Turuq khaarijiyye) highway *n*;
    ~ **mukhteSer** shortcut *n*
Tareeqe (Turuq) method *n*
Tawaariʻ *pl* emergency *n;* **makhraj iT-Tawaariʻ** emergency exit *n*
Taw3i *m* voluntary *adj*
Tawwar (yTawwir) II develop *v*
Tebeqe layer *n*
Teen mud *n*
Teffe (yTeffi) switch off; extinguish (*fire*) *v*
Teleb (Telebaat) application (*form*); claim; demand *n*
Teyyaar pilot *n*
Teyyaare airplane *n*
Teyyib fine (OK); delicious, tasty *adv*
Tibb medicine *n*; ~ **3adli/shar3i** forensics *n*
Tibbi medical *adj*
Tief (aTyaaf) apparition *n*
Tier (Tyoor) bird *n*
Tifil (aTfaal) (young) baby; child; ~ **raDHee3** infant *n*
TiHan (yiT-Han) grind *v*
TiHeen flour *n*; ~ **abyeDH** white flour; ~ **asmer** whole wheat
Tileb (yiTlub) demand, require; order (*at a restaurant or store*) *v*
Tili (Tilyaan) lamb, sheep *n*
Tired (yiTrud) expel; dismiss, send away *v*
Tobe (Tobaat) ball *n*
Tool height (*person*); length *n*

Toz dust *n*
Tuba3 (yiTba3) print; type *v*
Tubekh (yiTbukh) cook *v*
Tufoole childhood *n*
Turshi pickles *n*
Tweel (*pl* Twaal) tall; long *adj*

th

thaabit (*f* thaabte) stable *adj*
thaalith (*f* thaalthe) third *adj*
thaalithen thirdly *adv*
thaamin (*f* thaamne) eighth *adj*
thaanewi *m* minor, secondary *adj*
thaani second *adj*
thaaniye (thawaani) moment; second (*time unit*) *n*
thaaniyyen secondly *adv*
thaqaafe culture; education *n*
thaqaafi cultural *adj*
thawre (thawraat) revolution, uprising *n*
thelaathaa' (**ith-thelaathaa'**) Tuesday *n*
thelij snow; ice, ice cubes *n*
theyyel lawn *n*
thigeel heavy *adj*
thikheen thick *adj*
thilith third *n*
thillaaje refrigerator *n*
thinien (**ith-thinien**) Monday *n*
thiqe confidence, trust *n*
thmaaneen eighty *adj*; ~ **alif** eighty thousand *adj*
thmaanye eight (*standing alone*) *adj*
thmanmeet eight hundred (*with a noun*) *adj*; ~ **alif** eight hundred
    thousand *adj*
thmanmiyye eight hundred (*standing alone*) *adj*
thmantalaaf eight thousand *adj*
thmen eight (*with a noun*) *adj*
thmunTa3ash eighteen *adj*
thna3ash twelve *adj*
thnien (*f* thintien) two (*standing alone*) *adj*
thnienhum both *adj*
thoom *coll* garlic *n*
thulaathi *m* triple *adj*

u

ubre (uber) needle; injection *n*
ufuq horizon *n*
ughniye (aghaani) song *n*
ujre fare *n*
ukhti my sister; polite way of addressing a female stranger
ukhut (khawaat) sister *n*
umer (yu'mur) order (command) *v*
umm (ummahaat) mother
umme (umem) nation *n*; **il-umem il muttaHide** United Nations *n*
ummi *m* illiterate *adj*; my mother *n*
umniye wish *n*
ustaadh (*pl* asaatidhe) professor; Sir *n*
usturaali *m* Australian *adj, n*
usturaalye Australia *n*
uSooli *m* fundamentalist *adj*

v

vairos (vairosaat) virus *n*
veeze visa *n*
vidyo (vidyowaat) video *n*
voltiyye voltage *n*

w

w- and *conj*
wa and *conj;* as well as *adv*
wa illa otherwise *adv*
waa3i (*f* waa3ye *pl* waa3een) aware *adj*
waadi (widyaan) valley *n*
waaDHiH (*f* waaDH-Ha) clear *adj*
waafeq (ywaafuq) III agree *v*
waaHa oasis *n*
waaHid (*f* wiHde) one *adj*
waajib (waajibaat) assignment; duty; homework *n*
waajihe (waajihaat) façade *n*
waaldien parents *n*
waaqi3 reality *n*
waaqi3i *m* real; realistic; actual *adj*

waarid (waarde) valid *adj*
waarum (*f* waarme) swollen *adj*
waasi3 (*f* waas3a) vast *adj*
waayer (waayeraat) wire *n*
wabaa' (awbi'a) epidemic *n*
waDHeefe (waDHaayif) job; homework *n*
waDHi3 (awDHaa3) situation; status *n*
wafid mufawwaDH delegation *n*
wagfe halt *n*
wagga3 (ywaggi3) II drop *v*
waggaf is-seyyaare (ywagguf is-seyyaare) II park *v*
waHash (yoHish) miss (a person) *v*
waHde (*f* waHHad-he) alone *adj, adv*
waHeed *m* alone; lonely *adj, adv*; **il-~** the only one
wakhkhar (ywakhkhir) II remove *v*
wakkal (ywakkil) II feed *v*
walaw even *adv*; although *conj*
w-alle by God; **~?** is that so?
waqf iTlaaq in-naar ceasefire *n*
waqqa3 (ywaqqi3) II sign *v*
warde (awraad) flower *n*
wareed (awride) vein *n*
wareeth (*pl* werethe) successor; heir *n*
waSfe prescription *n*
waSikh (*f* waSkhe) dirty *adj*
waSil (wuSoolaat) receipt *n*
waSiyye will (*testament*) *n*
waSSe (ywaSSi) II recommend *v*
waSuf account; report; description *n*
watheeqe (wathaa'iq) document *n*
wejbe meal *n*
wej3aan illegal *adj*
wekaale agency *n*; **wekaalet il-ghawth** (wekaalaat il-ghawth) relief agency *n*
wela waaHid none *pron*
weled (awlaad, wilid) boy *n*
weqit time *n*; **~ ak-thar/azyad** more time *n*
werdi *m* pink *adj*
were after, behind, beyond *prep*
wereq *coll* paper *n*; **~ twaaliet** toilet paper *n*
wereqe (awraaq) leaf *n*; sheet of paper *n*
werid rose *n*
wershe workshop *n*
wesaa'il il-i3laam media *n*

weseele (wesaa'il) means *n*; **weseelet naqil** vehicle *n*
weSeT medium *adj*; middle *n*
weSSe (yweSSi) II order (*at a restaurant or store*) *v*
weTen (awTaan) home country *n*
weTeni *m* patriotic; national *adj*
wezeer (wuzeraa') minister *n*; ~ **il-khaarijiyye** Minister of Foreign Affairs *n*;
      ~ **id-daakhiliyye** Minister of Interior Affairs *n*
wezin rhythm; weight; poetry *n*
wi3ad (yo3id) promise *v*
widdi *m* friendly *adv*
wien where *adv*
wiga3 (yoga3) fall *v*
wiHde *f* one *adj*; unit *n*
wija3 raas headache *n*
wijih (wjooh) face *n*
wilaade birth, labor, delivery *n*
wilaaye (wilaayaat) state *n*; **il-wilaayaat il-muttaHide il-amreekiyye**
      United States *n*
winse fun *n*
wiraathi *m* genetic *adj*
wirik (awraak) hip *n*
wiSef (yoSif) describe *v*
witheq (yothiq) trust *v*
wiyye with *prep*
wizaare ministry *n*; **wizaaret it-terbiyye** Ministry of Education *n*
wugef (yogef) rise; stand; stop *v*; ~ **bis-sire** stand in line *v*
wuqood fuel *n*
wuSekh dirt *n*
wuSel (yoSel) arrive; reach *v*
wuSool arrival *n*

y

yaa which *interr*
yaabaan (il-yaabaan) Japan *n*
yaabaani *m* Japanese *adj, n*
yaabis (*f* yaabse) hard (*stiff*) *adj*
yaahoo which *pron*
yaarde yard (measurement) *n*
ya3ni that means
yawmi (*f* yomiyye) daily *adj*
ybeyyin *v* obviously, apparently *adv*

yedde handle *n*
yedewi *m* manual *adj*
yDHaHHik *v* (*f* tDHaHHik) funny *adj*
yelle! let's go!
yemeen right (*opposite of left*) *adj*
yemm beside *prep;* close to *adv*
yeteem (*pl* eitaam) orphan *n*
yewaash yewaash slowly *adv*
yhoodi (*pl* yhood) Jewish *adj, n*
yikhtilif (*f* tikhtilif *pl* yikhtelfoon) different *adj*
yimkin maybe, perhaps, probably *adv*
yimnaawi right-handed *adj*
yimne right (*opposite of left*) *adj*
yisraawi left-handed *adj*
yisre left *adj*
yom (ayyaam) day *n;* **il-yom** today *adv*
yomiyyen daily *adv*
yooranyom uranium *n*
yooro (yoorowaat) euro *n*
yshehhi *v* (*f* tshehhi) appetizing *adj*
yunaan (il-yunaan) Greece *n*
yunaani (*pl* yunaan) Greek *adj, n*

Z

zaa'id plus *conj*
zaa'ir (*pl* zuwwaar) visitor *n;* visiting *adj m*
zaa3 (yzoo3) vomit *v*
zaahi *m* bright *adj*
zaar (yzoor) visit *v*
zaawiyye angle *n*
zafir odor of greasy food *n*
zaHme crowd *n*
zalaaTe salad *n*
zamaan time *n*
zawaaj marriage *n*
zawj (azwaaj) husband *n*
zawje wife *n*
zei 3askari uniform (*military*) *n*
zei muwaHHad uniform *n*
zeitoon *coll* olive(s) *n*
zemeel *m* colleague *n*

zenboor (zenaabeer) bee *n*
zengeen (*pl* zenaageen) rich *adj*
zeri3 (mazroo3aat) plant *n*
zeyyed *(*yzeyyid) II increase *v*
zgheyyir (*f* zgheire *pl* zghaar) young; small *adj*; **kullish** ~ very small, tiny *adj*
zibid butter *n*
zibil (zbaale) garbage, trash, waste *n*
ziboon (zebaayin) client, customer *n*
zien fine, good *adj*; well, okay *adv*
zieniyye favor *n*
ziet oil (edible) *n*; ~ **iz-zeitoon** olive oil *n*
zilzaal (zelaazil) earthquake *n*
zira3 (yizra3) plant, sow *v*
zireq (yizruq) inject *v*
ziwiyye (zewaaye) corner *n*
ziyaade increase *n*
ziyaare visit *n*
zoj pair, couple *n*
zufer (yizfur) exhale *v*
zukaam cold (*sickness*) *n*
zooliyye (zwaali) carpet *n*
zuruf hole *n*
zyaan haircut (*for men only*) *n*

ENGLISH-IRAQI ARABIC
DICTIONARY

A

abduct *v* khtiTaf (yikhtiTuf) VIII
abduction *n* ikhtiTaaf
ability *n* qudre
able *adj*; **to be ~** *v* gider (yigder) (see also Unit 6)
abortion *n* ijhaaDH (ijhaaDHaat)
about 1. *adv* (*approximately*) Hawaali 2. *prep* (*concerning*) bkhuSooS
above *prep* fog
academic *adj* akadeemi
accent *n* lehje
accept *v* qibel (yiqbel)
accident *n* Haadith (Hawaadith)
according to *prep* Hasab
account *n* (*report*) taqreer, waSuf; **bank ~** Hsaab
accountant *n* muHaasib
accusation *n* ittihaam
accuse *v* ittihem (yittihim) VIII
achieve *v* Haqqaq (yHaqqiq) II
achievement *n* injaaz
acidic *adj* HaamuDH
acquainted, get ~ with t3aaref (yit3aaref) VI
across *prep* 3ibr, gbaal
act 1. *n* 3amel (a3maal) 2. *v* (*perform*) maththal (ymeththil)
action *n* fa33aaliyye (fa33aaliyyaat)
active *adj* nesheeT (*f* nesheeTe)
activity *n* neshaaT (neshaaTaat)
actor *n* mumeththil (mumeththileen)
actress *n* mumeththile (mumeththilaat)
actual *adj* fi3li, waaqi3i
actually *adv/conj* bil-waaqi3
add *v* DHaaf (yDHeef)
addiction *n* idmaan
addition *n* iDHaafe
additional *adj* iDHaafi

address *n* 3inwaan (3anaaween)
adequate *adj* kaafi
administration *n* idaare
admit *v* i3tiref (yi3tirif) VIII
adopt *v* tbenne (yitbenne) V
advantage *n* meeze (meezaat)
advice *n* naSeeHa
Afghan(s) *n* il-afghaan *coll*
Afghanistan *n* afghaanistaan
afraid 1. *adj m* khaayif (*f* khaayfe *pl* khaayfeen); 2. *v* **be ~** khaaf (ykhaaf)
Africa *n* afreeqye
African *adj* afreeqi (*f* afreeqiyye *pl* afaariqe)
after 1. *adv* **~ that** ba3dien 2. *prep* (*location*) were; (*time*) ba3ad
afternoon *n* 3aSir
again *adv* hemmen, hemmien
against *prep* DHidd
age *n* 3umur
agency *n* wekaale (wekaalaat)
aggression *n* 3idwaan
ago *adv* gabul
agree *v* waafeq (ywaafuq) III
agreed *adv* meikhaalif, mwaafiq
agreement *n* muwaafeqe (muwaafeqaat)
ahead *adv* gubel, li giddaam
aid 1. *n* musaa3ade, mu3aawene; 2. *v* saa3ad (ysaa3id) III, 3aawen
      (y3aawin) III
AIDS *n* eidz
air *n* hawe
air base *n* qaa3ide jewwiyye (qawaa3id jewwiyye)
air-conditioned *adj* mukeyyef (*f* mukeyyefe)
air conditioning *n* tekyeef
airplane *n* Teyyaare (Teyyaaraat)
airport *n* maTaar (maTaaraat)
alarm *n* indhaar
Algeria *n* ij-jazaa'ir
Algerian *adj/n* jazaa'iri (*f* jazaa'iriyye *pl* jazaa'iriyyeen)
alien *adj* ghareeb (*f* ghareebe *pl* ghurbe), ajnebi (*f* ajnebiyye *pl* ajaanib)
alike *adj* mitshaabih (*f* mitshaabhe)
alive *adj* Hayy (*f* Hayye *pl* aHyaa')
all *adj/adv* kull
allergy *n* **~ against** Hassaasiyye min
alley *n* darboone (daraabeen)
allow *v* simaH (yismaH)

ally Haleef (Hulefaa')
almond(s) *n* loz *coll*
almost *adv* taqreeben
alone *adj/adv* waHeed (*f* waHeede), waHde (*f* waHHad-he)
along *prep* **all ~** 3ala Tool
already *adv* hesse
also *adv* hemmen, hemmien, hem
although *conj* ma3a innahu, walaw
always *adv* daa'imen, 3ala Tool
ambassador *n* safeer (suferaa')
ambulance *n* is3aaf
America *n* amreeke
American *adj* amreeki (*f* amreekiyye *pl* amreekaan)
among *prep* bien
amount *n* mablegh (mabaaligh)
amusement park *n* medeenet il-al3aab
analysis *n* taHleel
ancient *adj* qadeem (*f* qadeeme)
and *conj* w-/wa
angel *n* melaak (malaa'ike)
angle *n* zaawiyye
animal *n* Haiwaan (Haiwaanaat)
announce *v* a3len (yi3lin) IV
announcement *n* taSreeH
annoying *adj* muz3ij (*f* muz3ije)
annual *adj* senewi
another *adj* laakh (*f* lukhkhe)
answer 1. *n* jawaab (ajwibe) 2. *v* jaaweb (yjaawub) III
answering machine *n* mekeenet it-telifon
anti- *adj* DHidd, muDHaadd (*pl* muDHaaddaat)
any *adj* ei
anyone *pron* ei waaHid
anything *pron* ei shee; **~ else** ba3ad shee laakh
apart *adv* 3ala SafHa
apartment *n* shuqqe (shuqeq), flaat
apparently *adv* iDH-DHaahir; ybeyyin (*it seems*) *v*
apparition *n* Tief (aTyaaf)
appear *v* beyyen (ybeyyin) II
appearance *n* maDHher (maDHaahir)
appetite *n* shehiyye
appetizing *adj* yshehhi *v* (*f* tshehhi)
applause *n* taSfeeq
apple(s) tuffaaH *coll*
application (form) *n* Teleb (Telebaat)

apply *v* qeddem (yqeddim) II
appoint *v* 3ayyen (y3ayyin) II
appointment *n* maw3id (mawaa3eed)
approach *v* qtireb (yiqtirib) VIII
appropriate *adj* laayiq (*f* laayqe)
approximately *adv* taqreeben
apricot(s) *n* mishmish *coll*
April *n* neesaan
Arab(ic) *adj* 3arebi (*f* arebiyye)
Arabs *n* 3arab *coll*
area *n* manTeqe (manaaTiq)
argument *n* mujaadele (mujaadelaat)
arm *n* (*body part*) eed (eedenaat); (*weapon*) slaaH (asliHa)
armed *adj* musallaH (*f* musallaHa *pl* musallaHeen); ~ **forces** quwwaat
   musallaHa
armored car *n* mudarra3a
army *n* jeish
around *prep* Hawaali
arrest 1. *n* mawqoof; **under** ~ mawqoof 2. *adj* **arrested** mawqoof 3. *v* alqa
   il-qabuDH (yilqi il-qabuDH)
arrival *n* wuSool
arrive *v* wuSel (yoSel)
arrow *n* sehem (as-hum)
art *n* fenn
artist *n* fennaan (fennaaneen)
as *adv* mithil; ~ **well** ~ wa
aside *adv* 3ala SafHa
ask *v* si'al (yis'al)
assassination *n* ightiyaal
assignment *n* waajib (waajibaat)
assistance *n* musaa3ade (musaa'adaat)
association *n* jam3iyye (jam3iyyaat)
asylum *n* (political) lijoo' siyaasi
at *prep* b-/bi-
atmosphere *n* jaw
atomic bomb *n* qunbule dherriyye
attaché *n* mulHaq; **cultural** ~ mulHaq thaqaafi; **military** ~ mulHaq 3askari
attack 1. *n* hijoom 2. *v* hijem (yihjim)
attain *v* HaSSel (yHaSSil) II
attempt *n* muHaawele (muHaawelaat) 2. *v* Haawel (yHaawil) III
attend *v* HiDHer (yiHDHer)
attendance *n* HiDHoor
attention *n* intibaah

attitude *n* mawqif (mawaaqif)
attorney *n* muHaami (muHaameen)
audience *n* mushaahid (mushaahideen)
August *n* aab
aunt *n* (parental) 3amme (3ammaat); (maternal) khaale (khaalaat)
Australia *n* usturaalye
Australian *adj/n* usturaali (*f* usturaaliyye *pl* usturaaliyyeen)
Austria *n* in-namse
Austrian *adj/n* namsaawi (*f* namsaawiyye *pl* naamsawiyyeen)
authority *n* sulTe (sulTaat)
autobiography *n* mudhakkaraat
available *adj* mitwaffur (*f* mitwaffure *pl* mitwaffureen); mawjood (*f* mawjoode *pl* mawjoodeen)
average *adj* mu3addel
avoid *v* itjannab (yitjannab) V
awake *adj* SaaHi (*f* SaaHye *pl* SaaHeen)
aware *adj* waa3i (*f* waa3ye *pl* waa3een)
away *adj/adv* **someone being ~** ma hna; **go ~!** rooH! *m* (*f* rooHi!)

B

baby *n* Tifil (aTfaal)
back 1. *n* DHeher 2. *v* **come ~** rija3 (yirja3); **go ~!** irja3! *m sg*
background *n* khalfiyye
bacteria *n* mikrob (mikrobaat)
bad *adj* ma zien (*f* ma ziene *pl* ma zieneen)
bag *n* janTe (juneT); **paper ~** chees wereq (chyaase wereq); **plastic ~** chees nailon (chyaase nailon)
baggage *n* juneT
Baghdad *n* baghdaad
Bahrain *n* il-baHrien
bakery *n* makhbez (makhaabuz)
balance *n* tawaazun
balcony *n* baalqon (baalqonaat)
ball *n* kure (kuraat), Tobe (Tobaat)
banana(s) *n* moz *coll*
bandage *n* DHammaade (DHammaadaat)
bank *n* beng (binoog)
bankrupt *adj* muflis (*f* muflise *pl* mfalees, mufliseen)
bankruptcy *n* iflaas
barbed wire *n* aslaak shaa'ike
barber *n* Hallaaq (Hallaqeen), mzeyyin (mzaine, mzeineen)

barbershop *n* Saalon Hilaaqe
bargain *v* t3aamel (yit3aamel) VI
bark *v* nibaH (yinbaH)
barrel *n* barmeel (baraameel)
basement *n* sirdaab (saraadeeb)
basic *adj* asaasi (*f* asaasiyye)
basket *n* selle (slaal)
Basra *n* il-baSre
bathroom *n* Hammaam (Hammaamaat)
bathtub *n* baanyo
battery *n* paatri (paatriyyaat)
battle *n* ma3reke (ma3aarik)
bazaar *n* soog (swaage)
be *v past tense* chaan (no *v* in the present tense, see Unit 2)
beach *n* saaHil (sawaaHil)
bean(s) *n* faSoolye *coll*
beard *n* liHye (liHa)
beat *v* DHireb (yiDHrub)
beautiful *adj* Hilu (*f* Hilwe *pl* Hilween)
because *conj* li-annahu, chief
become *v* Saar (ySeer)
bed *n* churpaaye (churpaayaat); **twin/single** ~ sareer/churpaaye mal nefer
    waaHid; **queen/king** ~ sareer/churpaaye mal neferien; ~**room** *n*
    ghurfet in-nom (ghuraf in-nom)
bee *n* zenboor (zenaabeer)
beef *n* laHam beqer
beer *n* beere *coll*
before 1. *conj* gabul 2. *prep* giddaam, gbaal
beggar *n* mgaddi (*pl* mgaadi)
begin *v* bide (yibdi)
beginning *n* bidaaye
behave *v* tSarraf (yitSarraf) V
behavior *n* teSarruf
behind *prep* were
beige *adj* biejee (*f* biejiyye)
Belgian *adj/n* beljeeki (*f* beljeekiyye *pl* beljeekiyyeen)
Belgium *n* beljeeke
believe *v* Saddag (ySaddig) II
bell *n* jaraS (ajraaS)
belong to *v* (ownership) maal- (see also Unit 4)
below *prep* jewwe
beneath *prep* jewwe
benefit *n* faa'ide (fawaa'id)

beside *prep* yemm
best *adj* aHsen
better than *adj* aHsen min
between *prep* bien
beyond *prep* ab3ad, were
Bible *n* injeel
bicycle *n* baisikil (baisiklaat)
big *adj* chibeer (*f* chibeere *pl* kbaar)
bigger than *adj* akbar min
bill *n* Hsaab
billboard *n* lawHat, il-i3laanaat
billion *n* bilyon (belaayeen)
biological *adj* byalogi (*f* byalojiyye)
bird *n* Tier (Tyoor)
birth *n* meelaad, wilaade; **date of** ~ taareekh il-wilaade; ~ **control** tanDHeem in-nesil; **~-control pills** Huboob man3 il-Hamil
birthday *n* 3eed meelaad (a3yaad meelaad)
bit *n* shweyye
black *adj* aswed (*f* sode)
blanket *n* baTTaaniyye (baTTaaniyyaat)
blast *n* infijaar (infijaaraat)
bleed *v* nizef (yinzif)
block 1. *n* **road** ~ Haajiz (Hawaajiz) 2. *v* sedd (ysidd)
blond *adj* ashger (*f* shegre *pl* shugur)
blood *n* demm; ~ **test** taHleel demm; ~ **transfusion** 3amaliyyet naqil id-demm
blouse *n* blooze (bloozaat)
blow *v* (wind) habb (yhibb); ~ **up** fejjer (yfejjir) II
blue *adj* azreg (*f* zarge)
board *n* **black**~ lawHa (lawHaat), sabboore (sabbooraat)
boat *n* belem (blaame)
body *n* jisim (ajsaam)
bodyguard *n* muraafiq (muraafiqeen)
bomb *n* qunbule (qanaabul)
bone *n* 3aDHum (3DHaam)
book *n* ktaab (kutub)
booked *adj* maHjooz (*f* maHjooze)
bookstore *n* mektebe (mektebaat)
boot *n* juzme (jizem)
border *n* Hadd (Hidood)
born *adj* mawlood (*f* mawloode *pl* mawloodeen)
both *adj* thnienhum
bottle *n* buTul (bTaale); ~ **opener** miftaaH bTaale

bottom *adj/n* cha3ab
bowl *n* Taase (Taasaat)
box *n* Sandoog (Sanaadeeg), 3ilbe (3ileb)
boy *n* weled (awlaad, wilid)
boycott *n* muqaaTa3e
brain *n* dmaagh
brake 1. *n* brek (brekaat) 2. *v* daas brek (ydoos brek)
branch *n* fari3 (froo3)
brave *adj* sabi3 (sbaa3)
bread *n* khubuz, Sammoon *coll*
break *v trans* kiser (yiksir), kesser (ykessir) II; *intrans* inkiser (yinkisir) VII
breakfast *n* riyoog
breathe *v* tneffes (yitneffes) V
bribe 1. *n* reshwe (reshaawi) 2. *v* rishe (yirshi)
bride *n* 3aroos(e)
bridge *n* jisir (jsoore)
brief *adj* mukhteSer (*f* mukhteSere)
briefcase *n* janTe (juneT)
bright *adj* zaahi (*f* zaahiyye)
bring *v* jaab (yjeeb)
British *adj* beriTaani (*f* beriTaaniyye *pl* beriTaaniyyeen)
broad *adj* 3areeDH (*f* 3areeDHe)
broken *adj* meksoor (*f* meksoore)
bronze *n* 1. brunz 2. *adj* brunzi (*f* brunziyye)
brother *n* akh (ikhwaan)
brown *adj* jozi (*f* joziyye)
brunette *adj* asmer (*f* samre *pl* sumur)
brush *n* firche (firech)
budget *n* meezaaniyye
bug *n* Hashere (Hasheraat), (*eavesdropping device*) ajhizet inSaat sirriyye
build *v* bine (yibni)
building *n* binaaye (binaayaat)
bullet *n* riSaaSe (riSaaS)
burglar *n* Haraami (*pl* Haraamiyye)
burn *v* Hireg (yiHrig)
bury *v* difen (yidfin)
bus *n* paS (paSaat); ~ **stop** mawqif paS
business *n* (*commercial*) mashroo3 tijaari; (*industrial*) mashroo3 Sinaa3i
busy *adj* mashghool (*f* mashghoole *pl* mashghooleen)
but *conj* laakin
butcher *n* gaSSaab (gaSSaabeen, giSaaSeeb)
butter *n* zibid
button *n* dugme (digam)

buy *v* shtire (yishtiri) VIII
by *prep* b-/bi-

C

cab *n* teksi (teksiyyaat)
cabbage *n* lahaane *coll*
cabinet *n* deelaab (dawaaleeb)
café *n* gahwe (gahaawi)
cage *n* qafaS (aqfaaS)
Cairo *n* il-qaahire
calculator *n* Haasibe (Haasibaat)
calendar *n* taqweem (taqaaweem)
call 1. *n* (telephone) mukhaabare (mukhaabaraat) 2. *v* khaaber (ykhaabur) III
calm *adj* haadi' (*f* haad'e)
camel *n* bi3eer (bi3raan), jimel (jmaal)
camera *n* kaamire (kaamiraat)
camp *n* mukheyyem (mkheyyemaat)
campaign *n* Hamle (Hamlaat); **election** ~ Hamlet intikhaabaat
can 1. *n* qooTiyye (qawaaTi); ~ **opener** miftaaH qawaaTi 2. *v* gider (yigder)
Canada *n* kenede
Canadian *adj/n* kenedi (*f* kenediyye *pl* kenediyyeen)
canal *n* qenaat (qenewaat)
cancel *v* lighe (yilghi)
cancellation *n* ilghaa'
cancer *n* sereTaan
candidate *n* mureshshaH (mureshshaHeen)
candle *n* sham3a (shumoo3)
capacity *n* si3a
capital *n* (*city*) 3aaSime (3awaaSim)
captain *n* qubTaan
capture 1. *n* qabuDH 2. *v* qubeDH (yiqbuDH)
car *n* seyyaare (seyyaaraat)
cardiac arrest *n* sekte qelbiyye
care 1. *n* 3inaaye 2. *v* i3tine (yi3tini) VIII
career *n* mihne
careful *adj* HareeS (*f* HareeSe *pl* HareeSeen)
cargo *n* shuHne
carpenter *n* najjaar (nijaajeer)
carpet *n* zooliyye (zwaali)
carrot(s) *n* jizer *coll*
carry *v* shaal (ysheel)

carton *n* karton (kartonaat)
case *n* (court) qaDHiyye (qaDHaaya)
cash 1. *n* kash; 2. *v* (a check) Sarref (ySarruf) II
cashier *n* muHaasib (muHaasibeen)
cassette *n* kasiet (kasetaat)
cat *n* bazzoon (bazaazeen); **tomcat** hirre (hroore)
catastrophe *n* kaarithe (kawaarith)
catch *v* lizem (yilzem); ~ **up with** liHag (yilHag)
Catholic *adj/n* kaatholeek (*f* kaatholeekiyye *pl* katholeekiyyeen)
cattle *n* il-maashye
cause *n* sebeb (asbaab)
cautious *adj* Hadhir (*f* Hadhre *pl* Hadhreen)
cave *n* kahaf (kuhoof)
cease-fire *n* waqf iTlaaq in-naar, hudne
ceiling *n* saguf (sgoofe)
celebrate *v* Htifel (yiHtifil) VIII
celebration *n* iHtifaal
cell phone *n* naqqaal
cemetery *n* maqbare (maqaabur)
censorship *n* riqaabe
census *n* iHSaaʻ
center *n* markez (maraakiz)
central *adj* markezi (*f* markeziyye)
century *n* qirin (quroon)
ceremony *n* maraaseem *pl*
certain *adj* mitʻakkid (*f* mitʻakkide)
certainly *adv* bit-taʻkeed
certificate *n* shahaade (shahaadaat)
chain *n* silsile (salaasil)
chair *n* kursi (karaasi)
chairman *n* raʻees il-lejne (*committee*); (*department*) raʻees il-qisim
chance *n* furSe (fureS)
change 1. *n* (*modification*) teghyeer; (*money*) khurde, baaqi 2. *v intrans* tgheyyer (yitgheyyer) V; *trans* gheyyer (ygheyyir) II, beddel (ybeddil) II; (*money*) Sarref (ySarruf) II
channel *n* qenaat (qenewaat)
chapter *n* faSil (fuSool)
charge *n* (*electricity*) shuHne; **free of** ~ ibbelaash, majjaanen
charity *n* Sadaqe
chauffeur *n* saayiq (suwwaaq)
cheap *adj* rekheeS (*f* rekheeSe)
cheaper than *adj* arkhaS min
check 1. *n* Sekk (Sukook); **traveler's checks** Sukook il-musaafireen. 2. *v* daqqaq (ydaqqiq) II

check-in *n* nizool
check-out *n* Tal3a
checkpoint *n* nuqTet tafteesh (nuqeT tafteesh)
check-up *n* (*medical*) faHiS
cheese *n* jibin
chemical *adj* keemyaawi (*f* keemyaawiyye); ~ **weapons** asliHe
    keemyaawiyye
chest *n* Sadir
chewing gum *n* 3ilich
chicken *n* dijaaj *coll*
chickpeas *n* HummuS *coll*
chief *n* ra'ees (ru'asaa')
child *n* (young) Tifil (aTfaal); awlaad (*pl* only); jaahil (*pl* jahaal)
childhood *n* Tufoole
China *n* iS-Seen
Chinese *adj* Seeni (*f* Seeniyye *pl* Seeniyyeen)
chocolate *n* nestele
choice *n* ikhtiyaar
choose *v* khtaar (yikhtaar) VIII
Christian *adj/n* maseeHi (*f* maseeHiyye *pl* maseeHiyyeen)
church *n* keneese (kenaayis)
cigarette *n* jigaare (jigaayir)
cinema *n* seeneme (seenemaat)
circle *n* daa'ire (dawaa'ir), Halqe
circuit *n* daa'ire kahrabaa'iyye
circular *adj* daa'iri (*f* daa'iriyye)
circumstance *n* DHaruf (DHuroof)
citizen *n* muwaaTin (muwaaTineen)
city *n* medeene (mudun)
civil *adj* mu'addab (*f* mu'addabe), medeni (*f* medeniyye); ~ **rights**
    il-Huqooq il-medeniyye; ~ **war** Harub ahliyye
civilian *adj/n* medeni (*f* medeniyye *pl* medeniyyeen)
civilization *n* HaDHaare
civilized *adj* mitmaddin, mitHaDHDHir
claim 1. *n* Teleb (Telebaat) 2. *v* Taaleb (yTaalub) III
clash *n* taDHaarub
class *n* (*school*) Saff (Sufoof); **first** ~ dereje oola; **economy** ~ dereje
    siyaaHiyye
clean 1. *adj* naDHeef (*f* naDHeefe) 2. *v* naDHDHaf (ynaDHDHuf) II
cleanliness *n* naDHaafe
clear *adj* waaDHiH (*f* waaDH-Ha); (water) Saafi
clerk *n* kaatib (kuttaab)
client *n* ma3meel (ma3aameel), ziboon (zebaayin)
climate *n* manaakh

climb *v* tsallaq (yitsallaq) V
clinic *n* 3iyaade (3iyaadaat)
clock *n* saa3a (sa3aat)
close 1. *adj* qareeb (*f* qareebe) 2. *adv* ~ **to** yemm 3. *v* sedd (ysidd)
closed *adj* (*door, drawer etc.*) masdood (*f* masdoode); (*shop*) m3azzil
      (*f* m3azzile)
closer than *adj* aqrab min
closet *n* deelaab (dawaaleeb)
clothes *n* malaabis *coll*
cloud *n* ghieme (ghyoom)
cloudy *adj* mgheyyim (*f* mgheyyime)
club *n* naadi (nawaadi)
coalition *n* i'tilaaf
coast *n* saaHil
coat *n* mi3Tef (ma3aatif), qappooT (qapaapeeT)
coffee *n* gahwe *coll*
coffin *n* taboot (tawaabeet)
cold 1. *adj* baarid (*f* baarde) 2. *n* berid; (*sickness*) zukaam, neshle
colder than *adj* abred min
collapse *v* inhaar (yinhaar) VII
colleague *n* zemeel (zemeele)
collect *v* jima3 (yijma3)
collection *n* majmoo3a
college *n* kulliyye (kulliyyaat); **C~ of arts** kulliyet il-adaab
collision *n* teSaadum
color *n* lon (alwaan)
colored *adj* mlawwen (*f* mlawwine)
column *n* 3aamood (a3mide)
coma *n* gheiboobe
combat *n* ma3reke
combination *n* mazeej
come *v* ije (yiji)
comfortable *adj* mureeH (*f* mureeHa)
command *n* 1. amur (awaamir) 2. *v* umer (yu'mur)
commander *n* (*army*) aamir
commerce *n* tijaare
commercial *adj* tijaari (*f* tijaariyye)
commission *n* 3umoole (3umoolaat)
committee *n* lajne (lijaan)
common *adj* ma'loof (*f* ma'loofe)
communication *n* ittiSaal (ittiSaalaat)
communist *adj/n* shiyoo3i (*f* shiyoo3iyye *pl* shiyoo3iyyeen)
community *n* mujtama3 (mujtama3aat)

compact disc *n* see-dee (see-diyyaat)
company *n* sherike (sherikaat)
compare *v* qaaren (yqaarin) III; **compared to** muqareneten b-
competition *n* munaafese
complain about shtike (yishtiki) min VIII
complete 1. *adj* kaamil (*f* kaamle) 2. *v* kemmel (ykemmil) II
completely *adv* tamaamen
complex *adj* mu3aqqed (*f* mu3aqqede)
component *n* 3unSur (3anaaSir)
compound *n* mujamma3
computer *n* kimpyooter (kimpyooteraat)
concept *n* mafhoom
concerned *adj* qaliq (*f* qalqe *pl* qalqeen)
concerning *prep* bkhuSooS
conclusion *n* neteeje, nihaaye
concrete *n* konkreet, simint
condition *n* Haale (Halaat)
condolences *n* il-beqiyye b-Hayaat-kum (see Unit 12)
conduct 1. *n* teSarruf 2. *v* tSarraf (yitSarraf) V
conference *n* mu'tamar (mu'tamaraat)
confidence *n* thiqa
confirmation *n* ta'keed
confuse *v* shewwesh (yshewwish) II
confusing *adj* mshawwish (*f* mshawwishe)
congratulations mabrook!
congress *n* mejlis tashree3i
connection *n* 3ilaaqe
consider *v* i3tuber (yi3tubur) VIII
considerable *adj* chibeer (*f* chibeere)
conspiracy *n* mu'aamere
constant *adj* daa'im (*f* daa'ime), mustemirr (*f* mustemirre)
constipation *n* qabuDH
constitution *n* distoor
construction *n* binaa', inshaa'
consul *n* qunSul
contact 1. *n* ittiSaal; ~ **lens** 3adasaat laaSiqe 2. *v* ittiSal (yittiSil) VIII
contagious *adj* mu3di (*f* mu3diyye)
container *n* Haawiye (Haawiyaat), 3ilbe (3ileb)
contaminated *adj* mlawwath (*f* mlawwithe)
contamination *n* telewwuth
contemporary *adj* mu3aaSir (*f* mu3aaSire)
contents *n* muHteweyaat
continent *n* qaarre (qaarraat)

continue *v* stemarr (yistemurr) X
contraception *n* man3 il-Hamil
contract *n* 3aqid (3uqood), muqaawele (muqaawelaat)
contractor *n* muqaawil (muqaawileen)
contradiction *n* taDHaarub
contrast *n* 3akis
control 1. *n* seiTere 2. *v* seiTer (yseiTir)
convoy *n* (*protection*) Himaaye *coll*, mawkib (mawaakib)
cook 1. *n* Tabbaakh (Tabbakheen) 2. *v* Tubekh (yiTbukh)
cookie *n* biskit (basaakit)
cool *adj* baarid (*f* baarde)
cooperation *n* ta3aawin
cooperative *n* jem3iyye ta3aawiniyye
copper *n* nuHaas
copy 1. *n* nuskhe (nusekh) 2. *v* stensekh (yistensikh) X
corn *n* dhure
corner *n* ziwiyye (zewaaye)
corporation *n* sherike (sherikaat), jam3iyye (jam3iyyaat)
corps *n* firqe; **diplomatic ~** silk diblomaasi
corpse *n* juththe (jutheth)
correct 1. *adj* SaHeeH (*f* SaHeeHa) 2. *v* SallaH (ySalliH) II
correspondent *n* muraasil (muraasileen)
cost 1. *n* kilfe 2. *v* kellef (ykellif) II
cotton *n* guTin
cough 1. *n* su3aal, gaHHa 2. *v* si3al (yis3al), gaHH (yguHH)
council *n* mejlis (majaalis)
count *v* 3add (y3idd)
counterfeit *adj* mzawwer (*f* mzawwire)
country *n* beled (buldaan); **home ~** weten (awTaan)
countryside *n* reef
couple *n* zoj
court *n* maHkeme (maHaakim)
cousin *n* (*paternal*) *m* ibin 3amm/3amme (wilid 3amm/3amme); *f* bit
    3amm/3amme (banaat 3amm/3amme); (*maternal*) *m* ibin khaal/ibin
    khaale (wilid khaal/khaale), *f* bit khaal/khaale (banaat khaal/khaale)
cover 1. *n* ghiTe 2. *v* ghaTTe (yghaTTi) II
covered *adj* mghaTTe (*f* mghaTTaaye)
cow *n* beqere (beqeraat), haishe (hawaayish)
cradle *n* mehed
create *v* khileq (yikhluq)
credit *n* dien; **~ card** kredit kard
crime *n* jereeme (jeraayim)
crisis *n* azme

critical *adj* (*in a ~ situation*) mit'azzim (*f* mit'azzime)
crops *n* maHsool ziraa3i (maHaaSeel ziraa3iyye)
cross *v* ~ **the street** 3uber (yu3bur) ish-shaari3
crowd *n* zaHme
cruelty *n* qeswe
cry 1. *n* bechi *coll* 2. *v* biche (yibchi)
cucumber(s) *n* khyaar *coll*
cultural *adj* thaqaafi (*f* thaqaafiyye)
culture *n* thaqaafe, HaDHaare
cup *n* koob (kwaabe)
curfew *n* man3 it-tajawwul
currency *n* 3umle (umlaat)
current *adj* il-Haali (*f* il-Haaliyye)
currently *adv* Haaliyyen
curtain *n* perde (perdaat)
customer *n* ma3meel (ma3aameel), ziboon (zebaayin)
customs *n* gumrug; ~ **declaration** it-taSreeH il-gumrugi
cut 1. *n* (*wound*) jeriH (jrooH); **hair~** geSS sha3ar; **short~** Tareeq
　　mukhteSer 2. *v* geSS (yguSS)
cylinder *n* STuwaane (STuwaanaat)

D

daily 1. *adj* yawmi (*f* yomiyye) 2. *adv* yomiyyen
dam *n* sedde (sidood)
damage *n* DHarer
Damascus *n* dimashq
dance 1. *n* rigSe (rigSaat) 2. *v* rigeS (yirguS)
danger *n* khaTar
dangerous *adj* khaTir (*f* kheTre)
Danish *adj* denimaarki (*f* denimaarkiyye *pl* denimaarkiyyeen)
dark *adj* aDHlam (*f* DHalme)
darkness *n* DHalme
data *n* ma3loomaat
database *n* qaa3idet il-beyaanaat, daate bies
date *n* (*time*) taareekh (tawaareekh); (*fruit*) tamur *coll*
daughter *n* bint (banaat); ~-**in-law** chenne (chenaayin)
dawn *n* fejir
day *n* yom (ayyaam); ~ **train** qiTaar in-nahaar
dead *adj* meyyit (*f* meite *pl* meiteen)
deadline *n* aakhir maw3id (mawaa3eed akheere)
deaf *adj* aTresh (*f* Tarshe *pl* Turshaan)

deal 1. *n* Safqe (Safqaat) 2. *v* t3aamel (yit3aamel) VI
dear *adj* 3azeez (*f* 3azeeze *pl* 3azeezeen)
death *n* mot *coll*
debt *n* dien (diyoon)
December *n* kaanoon il-awwel
decide *v* qarrar (yqarrir) II
decision *n* qaraar (qaraaraat)
declaration *n* taSreeH (taSreeHaat); i3laan
deep *adj* 3ameeq (*f* 3ameeqe)
defeat *n* hezeeme
defective *adj* ma3yoob (*f* ma3yoobe)
defense *n* difaa3
degree *n* (*diploma*) shahaade (shahaadaat)
delay *n* ta'kheer
delayed *adj* mit'akhkhir (*f* mit'akhkhire)
delegation *n* wafid mufawwaDH
delivery *n* (*goods*) istilaam; (*baby*) wilaade
demand 1. *n* Teleb (Telebaat) 2. *v* Tileb (yiTlub)
democracy *n* deemuqraaTiyye
democratic *adj* deemuqraaTi (*f* deemuqraaTiyye)
demolish *v* haddam (yhaddim) II
demonstration *n* muDHaahere (muDHaaheraat)
Denmark *n* id-denimaark
dentist *n* Tabeeb asnaan (aTibaa' asnaan)
deodorant *n* muzeel il-3araq
department *n* qisim (aqsaam)
departure *n* mughaadere
dependent on *adj* mi3timid (*f* mi3temde *pl* mi3temdeen)
deportation *n* tarHeel
depot *n* mustawda3 (mustawda3aat)
deputy *n* naa'ib (nuwwaab)
describe *v* wiSef (yoSif)
description *n* waSuf
desert *n* SaHraa'
deserted *adj* khaali (*f* khaalye), mahjoor (*f* mahjoore)
design *n* taSmeem (taSaameem)
desk *n* (*school*) raHle (raHlaat); (*office*) mekteb (mekaatib)
dessert *n* Halawiyyaat *coll*
destroy *v* dammar (ydammur) II
destruction *n* damaar
detailed *adj* mufaSSal (*f* mufaSSale)
detergent *n* masHooq ghaseel, taid
determine *v* Sammam (ySammim) II

detour *n* taHweele
develop *v* Tawwar (yTawwir) II
development *n* taTweer
diabetes *n* sukkar
diagnose *n* tashkheeS
dialect *n* lehje (lehjaat)
diaper *n* HaffaaDHe (HaffaaDHaat)
dictator *n* diktator (diktatoriyyeen)
dictionary *n* qaamoos (qawaamees)
die *v* maat (ymoot); (*pass away*) tweffe (yitweffe) II
diesel *n* deezil
difference *n* fariq
different *adj* yikhtilif *v* (*in Arabic*) (*f* tikhtilif *pl* yikhtelfoon)
difficult *adj* Sa3ub (*f* Sa3be)
digital *adj* raqmi (*f* raqmiyye), dijitel
dinar *n* (*Iraqi currency*) deenaar (denaaneer)
dinner *n* 3ashe; **have/eat** ~ it3ashshe (yit3ashshe) V
diplomat *n* diblomaasi (diblomaasiyyeen)
direct *adj* mubaashir (*f* mubaashire)
directions *n* (*road*) irshaadaat; **ask for** ~ si'al wien iT-Tareeq (yis'al wien
   iT-Tareeq)
directives *n* tawjeehaat
directly *adv* mubaashereten, ra'sen
director *n* (*manager*) mudeer (muderaa'); (*film*) mukhrij (mukhrijeen)
directory *n* deleel
dirt *n* wuSekh, qedhaare
dirty *adj* waSikh (*f* waSkhe)
disabled *adj* mu3awweq (*f* mu3awweqe *pl* mu3awweqeen)
disagree *v* 3aareDH (y3aariDH) III
disappear *v* khtife (yikhtifi) VIII
disarmament *n* naz3 is-silaaH
disconnect *v* qiTa3 il-ittiSaal (yiqTa3 il-ittiSaal)
discover *v* ktishef (yiktishif) VIII
discrimination *n* temyeez; **racial** ~ temyeez 3unSuri
discuss *v* naaqesh (ynaaqish) III
discussion *n* munaaqeshe (munaaqeshaat)
disease *n* mareDH (amraaDH)
disfigurement *n* teshweeh
disguise *v* tnekker (yitnekker) V
dish *n* maa3oon (mawaa3een); **satellite** ~ SaHin faDHaa'i, saatilait dish
distance *n* masaafe
distribution *n* tawzee3

district *n* maHalle (maHallaat)
disturb *v* az3aj (yiz3ij) IV, shewwesh (yshewwish) II
divide *v* qassam (yqassim) II
division *n* taqseem
divorced *adj* mTalleg (*f* mTalge)
do *v* sewwe (ysewwi)
doctor *n* Tabeeb (aTibbaa')
doctorate *n* diktoraa
document *n* watheeqe (wathaa'iq)
dog *n* chelib (chlaab)
doll *n* la3aabe (la3aabaat)
dollar *n* doolaar (doolaaraat)
domestic *adj* maHalli (*f* maHalliyye)
donor *n* mitberri3 (mitbarri3a)
door *n* baab (abwaab, beebaan)
doorman *n* bawwaab (bawwaabeen)
dot *n* nuqTe (nuqeT)
double *adj* muDHaa3af (*f* muDHaa3afe), debel
doubt *v* shakk (yshukk)
down *adv* jewwe
downstairs *adv* iT-Taabiq ij-jewwaani
dozen *n* derzen (deraazin)
dramatic *adj* dramateeki (*f* dramateekiyye)
draw *v* risem (yirsim)
drawer *n* jarraare (jarraaraat)
drawing *n* resim (risoomaat)
dream 1. *n* Hilim (aHlaam) 2. *v* Hilem (yiHlem)
dress 1. *n* nafnoof (nafaaneef), fistaan (fesaateen) 2. *v* libes (yilbes)
drink 1. *n* mashroob (mashroobaat) 2. *v* shireb (yishreb)
drive *v* saaq (ysooq)
driver *n* saayiq (suwwaaq)**; driver's license** ijaazet siyaaqe
drop 1. *n* (*liquid*) nuqTe (nuqeT) 2. *v* wagga3 (ywaggi3) II
drought *n* jefaaf
drown *v* ghireg (yighreg)
drug *n* (*medical*) duwe (adwiye); (*narcotics*) mukhaddaraat
drunk *adj* sekraan (*f* sekraane *pl* skaare)
dry 1. *adj* naashif (*f* naashfe) 2. *v* nishef (yinshef)
dry cleaner *n* tanDHeef jaaff
due to *prep* li-annahu
during *prep* athnaa'
dust *n* ghbaar, Toz
Dutch *adj/n* holendi (*f* holendiyye *pl* holendiyyeen)
duty *n* waajib (waajibaat); **on ~** bil-waajib

E

each *adj* kull
ear *n* idhin (adhaan)
earlier *adv* awket min
early *adv* min weqit/wekit
earn *v* HaSSel (yHaSSil) II
earphones *n* simmaa3aat
earrings *n* teraachi
earth *n* gaa3
earthquake *n* zilzaal (zelaazil)
easily *adv* b-suhoole
east *n* sherq
eastern *adj* sherqi (*f* sherqiyye)
easy *adj* sehil (*f* sehle)
eat *v* akal (yaakul)
ecological *adj* bee'i (*f* bee'iyye)
economic *adj* iqtiSaadi (*f* iqtiSaadiyye)
economy *n* iqtiSaad; ~ **class** dereje siyaaHiyye
edge *n* Haaffe (Hawaafi)
editor *n* muHarrir (muHarrireen)
education *n* ta3leem, thaqaafe; **Ministry of E~** wizaaret it-terbiyye
educational *adj* ta3leemi (*f* ta3leemiyye)
effect *n* ta'theer (ta'theeraat)
effective *adj* mu'aththir (*f* mu'aththire)
efficient *adj* kefoo' (*f* kefoo'e *pl* kefoo'een)
effort *n* juhud (juhood)
egg *n* bieDH *coll*
eggplant *n* betinjaan *coll*
Egypt *n* maSir
Egyptian *adj/n* maSri (*f* maSriyye *pl* maSriyyeen)
eight *adj* (*standing alone*) thmaanye; (*with a noun*) thmen
eight hundred *adj* thmanmiyye; (*with a noun*) thmanmeet
eight hundred thousand *adj* thmanmeet alif
eight thousand *adj* thmantalaaf
eighteen *adj* thmunTa3ash
eighth *adj* thaamin (*f* thaamne)
eighty *adj* thmaaneen
eighty thousand *adj* thmaaneen alif
either *conj* ~... **or** imma... aw
elbow *n* 3ikis (3koos)
elections *n* intikhaabaat
electric *adj* kahrabaa'i (*f* kahrabaa'iyye); ~ **appliances** kahrabaa'iyyaat

electrician *n* kahrabaa'i (kahrabaa'iyyeen)
electricity *n* kahrabaa'
electronic *adj* eliketroni (*f* eliketroniyye)
element *n* 3unSur (3anaaSir)
elementary school *n* medrese ibtidaa'iyye (medaaris ibtidaa'iyye)
elevator *n* maS3ad (maSaa3id)
eleven *adj* da3ash
e-mail *n* eemiel (eemelaat); **send an ~** *v* dezz (ydizz) eemiel
embargo *n* HiSaar
embassy *n* safaare (safaaraat)
emergency *n* Tawaari' *pl*, **~ exit** makhraj iT-Tawaari', **~ landing** hubooT
     iDHTiraari
employee *n* mustakhdam (*pl* mustakhdameen); muweDHDHef (*pl* muweD-
     HDHefeen)
empty *adj* faarigh (*f* faarghe)
encircle *v* HawwaT (yHawwuT) II
end 1. *n* nihaaye (nihaayaat); **~ of the month** aakhir ish-sheher 2. *v trans*
     anhe (yinhi) IV; *intrans* intihe (yintihi) VIII
enemy *n* 3adu (a3daa')
energy *n* Taaqe
engaged *adj* makhToob (*f* makhToobe *pl* makhToobeen); **get ~ (men)**
     khiTeb; **get ~ (women)** inkhuTbet
engine *n* mekeene (mekaayin)
engineer *n* muhandis (muhandiseen)
engineering *n* hendese
England *n* ingiltere
English *adj* ingileezi (*f* ingileeziyye *pl* ingileez)
enjoy *v* twennes (yitwennes) V
enough *adj/adv* kaafi
enroll *v* sejjel (ysejjil) II
enter *v* dikhel (yidkhul)
entire *adj* kulle (*f* kulhe)
entrance *n* madkhal
entries *n* (*on a form*) khaanaat
envelope *n* DHaruf (DHuroof)
environment *n* bee'e
epidemic *n* wabaa' (awbi'a)
equal *adj* mitsaawi (*f* mitsaawye)
equipment *n* ajhize
erase *v* misaH (yimsaH)
escalator *n* sullem kahrabaa'i (selaalim kahrabaa'iyye)
escape *v* inhizem (yinhizim) VII
escort *n* muraafiq

especially *adv* khuSooSen
essential *adj* DHaroori (*f* DHarooriyye)
establish *v* asses (y'assis) II
estimate 1. *n* taqdeer (taqdeeraat) 2. *v* qadder (yqaddir) II
etc. *adv* ila akhirihi
Euphrates *n* il-furaat
euro *n* yooro (yoorowaat)
Europe *n* oruppe
European *adj/n* oruppi (*f* oruppiyye *pl* oruppiyyeen)
evacuate *v* akhle (yikhli) IV
even 1. *adj* 3adil (*f* 3adle) 2. *adv* walaw
evening *n* mughrub (mughrubiyyaat); **good ~** mesaa' il-khier
event *n* munaasebe (munaasebaat)
ever *adv* abed
every *adj* kull
everybody *pron* kull waaHid, kull shekhiS
everything *pron* kull shee
everywhere *adv* kull mekaan
evidence *n* deleel
evil *n* sherr
exact *adj* deqeeq (*f* deqeeqe)
exactly *adv* tamaamen
examination *n* imtiHaan (imtiHaanaat)
example *n* methel (amthile)
excellent *adj* mumtaaz (*f* mumtaaze)
except *prep* 3ada; **~ for** ma 3ada
exception *n* istithnaa' (istithnaa'aat)
exceptional *adj* istithnaa'i (*f* istithnaa'iyye)
exchange 1. *n* tabaadul (tabaadulaat); **~ rate** farq il-3umle 2. *v* (*money*) Sarref (ySarruf)
exciting *adj* mutheer (*f* mutheere)
execute *v* 3idem (yi3dim)
execution *n* i3daam (i3daamaat)
executive *n* mudeer (muderaa')
exercise *n* temreen (tamareen)
exhibition *n* ma3raDH (ma3aariDH)
exist *v* 3aash (y3eesh)
existing *adj* mawjood (*f* mawjoode)
exit *n* khurooj
expect *v* twaqqa3 (yitwaqqa3) V
expel *v* Tired (yiTrud)
expensive *adj* ghaali (*f* ghaalye); **more ~ than** aghle min
experience *n* tejrube (tajaarub)

expert *n* khabeer (khuberaa')
expiration *n* nefaadh
explain *v* shiraH (yishraH)
explosion *n* infijaar (infijaaraat)
explosives *n* mutefejjiraat *pl*
export 1. *n* taSdeer (taSderaat) 2. *v* Sadder (ySaddir) II
express 1. *adj* saree3 (*f* saree3a) 2. *v* 3abber (y3abbur) II
expression *n* ta3beer
exterior *adj* khaariji (*f* khaarijiyye)
extinguish *v* Teffe (yTeffi)
extra *adj* iDHaafi (*f* iDHaafiyye)
extreme *adj* miTTarruf (*f* miTTarrufe)
extremist *n* miTTarruf (*pl* miTTarrufeen)
eye *n* 3ien (3yoon)
eyeglasses *n* maanaDHir
eyewitness *n* shaahid 3ayaan (shihood 3ayaan)

F

fabric *n* qmaash (qmaashaat)
façade *n* waajihe (waajihaat)
face *n* wijih (wjooh)
fact *n* Haqeeqe (Haqaayiq)
factor *n* 3aamil (3awaamil)
factory *n* maSna3 (maSaani3), ma3mal (ma3aamil)
faculty *n* (*school and college*) hei'at it-tadrees; (*college*) kulliyye
fail *v* fishel (yifshel)
failure *n* feshel
fair *adj* (*just*) Haqqaani (*f* Haqqaaniyye)
faith *n* eemaan
fake *adj* mzawwer (*f* mzawwire)
fall 1. *n* (*season*) khareef 2. *v* wiga3 (yoga3)
false *adj* (*fake*) kadhdhaabi (*f* kadhdhaabiyye; (*incorrect*) ma SaHeeH (*f* ma SaHeeHa)
familiar *adj* ma'loof (*f* ma'loofe)
family *n* 3aa'ile (3awaa'il)
famous *adj* mash-hoor (*f* mash-hoore *pl* mash-hooreen)
fan *n* (*electric*) penke (penkaat); (*manual*) mheffe (mheffaat)
far *adj* bi3eed (*f* bi3eede); **how ~ is...?** shged yib3id...? *m*, shged tib3id ...? *f*
fare *n* ujre, kerwe
farm *n* mazra3a (mazaari3)

farmer *n* fallaaH (filiH, falaaleeH)
farther *adj* ab3ad min
fashion *n* mode (modaat)
fast 1. *adj* saree3 (*f* saree3a) 2. *v* (*in the month of Ramadan*) Saam (ySoom)
faster than *adj* asra3 min
fat 1. *n* dihin, (*body*) shaHam 2. *adj* simeen (*f* simeene *pl* smaan)
fatal *adj* mumeet (*f* mumeete), qaatil (*f* qaatile)
father *n* ab (abaa'); ~-**in-law** 3amm
faucet *n* Hanefiyye (Hanefiyyaat)
favor *n* ma3roof, zeniyye; **do someone a** ~ sewwe ma3roof (ysewwi ma3roof)
fax *n* faks (faksaat); **send a** ~ *v* dezz (ydizz) faks
fear 1. *n* khof 2. *v* khaaf (ykhaaf)
February *n* shbaaT
feed *v* Ta33am (yTa33um) II, wakkal (ywakkil) II
feel *v* Hass (yHiss), shi3ar (yish3ur)
feeling *n* iHsaas (aHaasees), shi3oor
feminism *n* il-Hareke in-niswiyye
fence *n* siyaaj
ferry *n* 3abbaare (3abbaaraat)
fertility *n* khuSoobe
fertilization *n* ikhSaab
fever *n* skhoone, Humme
few *adj* qeleel
fiancé *n* kheTeeb
fiancée *n* kheTeebe
field *n* Haqil (Huqool)
fifteen *adj* khumuSTa3ash
fifth *adj* khaamis (*f* khaamse)
fifty *adj* khamseen
fifty thousand *adj* khamseen alif
fig teen *coll*
fight 1. *n* 3arke (3arkaat) 2. *v* t3aarek (yit3aarek) VI
fighting *n* 3raak
file *n* faayel (faayelaat)
fill *v* mile (*pronounced **mi-le***) (yimli)
film *n* filim (aflaam)
filter *n* filter (felaatir, filteraat), muSfi (maSaafi)
final *adj* akheer (*f* akheere)
finally *adv* akheeren
financial *adj* maali (*f* maaliyye)
find *v* lige (yilgi)

fine 1. *adj* (*good*) zien (*f* ziene); (*delicate*) raqeeq (*f* raqeeqe) 2. *adv* Teyyib
   3. *n* gharaame (gharaamaat)
finger *n* iSbi3 (aSaabi3)
finish *v* khalleS (ykhalliS) II
fire 1. *n* naar; ~ **alarm** indhaar il-Hareeq 2. *v* (*from a job*) fuSel (yifSul)
firearm *n* slaaH (asliHa)
firefighter *n* iTfaaʻiyye *coll*
firehouse *n* iTfaaʻiyye
fireplace *n* madfeʻe
firm *adj* Haazim (*f* Haazme)
first *adj* awwel (*f* oola)
fiscal *adj* maali (*f* maaliyye)
fish *n* simech *coll*
fit *v* rihem (yirhem)
five *adj* (*standing alone*) khamse; (*with a noun*) khamis
five hundred *adj* khamismiyye; (*with a noun*) khamismeet
five hundred thousand *adj* khamismeet alif
five thousand *adj* khamistalaaf
flag *n* 3alem (a3laam)
flashlight *n* lait (laitaat)
flat *adj* msaTTaH (*f* msaTTiHa), 3adil (3adle)
flavor *n* nekhe (nekhaat)
flaw *n* 3ieb (3yoob)
flight attendant *n* muDHeyyif (*f* muDHeyyife)
flood *n* feyeDHaan (feyeDHaanaat)
floor *n* (*ground*) gaa3 (gee3aan); (*story*) Taabiq (Tawaabiq); **second** ~
   iT-Taabiq ith-thaani
flour *n* TiHeen
flower *n* warde (awraad)
flu *n* influwenze
fly 1. *n* dhibbaane (dhibbaan) 2. *v* Taar (yTeer)
follow *v* liHag (yilHag); ~ **me** ta3aal *m sg* waraaye
following *adj* ij-jaay (*f* ij-jaayye)
food *n* akil *coll*
foot *n* rijil (rijlien); **on** ~ meshi
for *prep* l-, li-, lil- (see also Unit 5)
forbidden *adj* muHarram (*f* muHarrame), mamnoo3 (*f* mamnoo3a)
force *n* quwwe (quwwaat)
forecast (*weather*) *n* Haalet ij-jaww
foreign *adj* ajnebi (*f* ajnebiyye); **Minister of F~ Affairs** wezeer
   il-khaarijiyye
foreigner *n* ajnebi (ajaanib)
forensics *n* Tibb 3adli/shar3i

forest *n* ghaabe (ghaabaat)
forever *adv* lil-abed
forgery *n* tezyeef
forget *v* nise (yinse)
fork *n* cheTel (cheTelaat)
form *n* (*shape*) shikil (ashkaal); (*paper*) istimaare (istimaaraat)
former *adj* saabiq (*f* saabiqe)
formula (*infant*) *n* Haleeb aTfaal
forty *adj* arba3een
forty thousand *adj* arba3een alif
forward *adv* li giddaam; (*military command*) ilal-amaam!
foundation *n* mu'assese (mu'assesaat)
fountain *n* naafoore (naafooraat)
four *adj* (*standing alone*) arba3a; (*with a noun*) arba3
four hundred *adj* arba3miyye; (*with a noun*) arba3meet
four hundred thousand *adj* arba3meet alif
four thousand *adj* arba3talaaf
fourteen *adj* arbaTa3ash
fourth *adj* raabi3 (*f* raab3a)
fraction *n* jizu' (ajzaa')
fracture *n* kesir (kisoor)
frame *n* iTaar (iTaaraat)
France *n* franse
free *adj* Hurr (*f* Hurre *pl* aHraar)
freedom *n* Hurriyye; ~ **of speech** Hurriyyet il-kelaam; ~ **of the press**
        Hurriyyet iS-SaHaafe
freezer *n* freezer (freezeraat)
French *adj/n* frensi (*f* frensiyye *pl* frensiyyeen)
frequently *adv* daa'iman
fresh *adj* taaze *m/f*
Friday *n* ij-jum3a
friend *n* Sadeeq (*f* Sadeeqe *pl m* aSdiqaa'); **become ~s** tSaadeq
        (yitSaadeq) VI
friendly *adv* widdi (widdiye)
from *prep* min; ~ **where** mmien
front 1. *n* (*military*) jebhe (jebhaat) 2. *prep* **in ~ of** giddaam, gbaal
fruit *n* fawaakih *coll*
fuel *n* wuqood
fugitive *n* haarib (haarbeen)
full *adj* (*filled*) malyaan (*f* malyaane); (*complete*) kaamil (*f* kaamle);
        v (*after eating*) **be ~** shiba3 (yishba3)
full-time *adj* dawaam kaamil
fun *n* winse; **have ~** *v* twennes (yitwennes) V

function *n* 3amel (a3maal)
fundamentalist *adj* uSooli (*f* uSooliyye *pl* uSooliyyeen)
funds *n* mewaarid maaliyye
funny *adj* yDHaHHik *v* (*f* tDHaHHik)
furnace *n* sakhkhaan
furnished *adj* mu'aththeth (*f* mu'aththethe)
furniture *n* athaath
future *n* mustaqbal

G

gain *n* ribiH (arbaaH)
game *n* li3be (al3aab)
gang *n* 3iSaabe (3iSaabat)
gap *n* fejwe (fejwaat)
garage *n* geraaj (geraajaat)
garbage *n* zibil
garden *n* Hadeeqe (Hadaayiq)
garlic *n* thoom *coll*
gas *n* ghaaz; ~ **pump** maDHakhkhat baanzeen; ~ **station** *n* baanzeen khaane
     f (baanzeen khaanaat)
gasoline *n* baanzeen
gate *n* bawwaabe (bawwaabaat)
gathering *n* tejammu3 (tejammu3aat)
gear *n* (*equipment*) 3idde (3uded)
general *adj* 3aamm (*f* 3aamme)
generally *adv* b-Soore 3aamme
generation *n* jeel (ajyaal)
generator *n* muwallide (muwallidaat)
generous *adj* kareem (*f* kareeme *pl* kareemeen)
genetic *adj* wiraathi (*f* wiraathiyye)
genitals *n* a3dhaa' tanaasuliyye
genocide *n* ibaade besheriyye
gentleman *n* shehim (shehmeen)
geography *n* jughraafye
germ *n* jerthoome (jeraatheem)
German *adj/n* almaani (*f* almaaniyye *pl* almaan)
Germany *n* almaanye
get *v* (*receive*) HaSSel (yHaSSil) II; ~ **back** (*return*) rija3 (yirja3);
     ~ **off/down** (*vehicle*) nizel (yinzil); ~ **up** gaam (ygoom); ~ **ready**
     tHaDHDHer (yitHaDHDHer) V
gift *n* hediyye (hedaaye)

girl *n* bneyye (banaat)

give *v* niTe (yinTi); ~ **me!** *imp* inTeeni

glad *adj* masroor (*f* masroore *pl* masrooreen)

glass *n* glaaS (glaaSaat); **small tea** ~ istikaan (istikaanaat)

glasses *n* manaaDHir

glove *n* cheff (chfoof)

glue *n* Samugh

go *v* raaH (yrooH)

goal *n* hadef (ahdaaf)

God *n* alle, alla; **by** ~ w-alle; ~ **willing** inshaalle

gold *n* dheheb

golden *adj* dhehebi (*f* dhehebiyye)

good *adj* zien (*f* ziene), jeyyid (*f* jeyyide); khosh

good-bye *n* ma3a s-salaame, fee-maan-illa

goods *n* biDHaa3a (baDHaayi3)

government *n* Hikoome (Hikoomaat)

governor *n* muHaafiDH (muHaafiDHeen)

grade *n* dereje (derejaat); (*school*) Saff (Sufoof)

graded *adj* mdarrej

gradual *adj* tedreeji (*f* tedreejiyye)

graduate *v* tkharraj (yitkharraj) V

gram *n* ghraam (ghraamaat)

granddaughter *n* Hafeede (Hafeedaat)

grandfather *n* jidd

grandmother *n* jidde, beebee

grandson *n* Hafeed (aHfaad)

grant *n* minHa (minaH)

grapes *n* 3ineb *coll*

grass *n* Hasheesh

grave *n* gabur (gboor)

gray *adj* riSaaSi (*f* riSaaSiyye), rumaadi (*f* rumaadiyye)

grease 1. *n* dihin 2. *v* dehhen (ydehhin) II

greasy *adj* (*smell*) zafir

great *adj* 3aDHeem (*f* 3aDHeeme), felle

Great Britain *n* beriTaanye

greater than *adj* a3DHam min

greatest *adj* a3DHam

Greece *n* il-yunaan

Greek *adj/n* yunaani (*f* yunaaniyye *pl* yunaan, yunaaniyyeen)

green *adj* akhDHar (*f* khaDHre)

greens *n* khuDHer

grenade *n* rummaane (rummaanaat)

grill *n* shawwaaye

grind *v* TiHan (yiT-Han)
grocer *n* baggaal (bgageel)
groom *n* 3arees
ground 1. *adj* (foods) maT-Hoon (*f* maT-Hoone) 2. *n* **on the ~** 3al gaa3
group *n* jamaa3a (jamaa3aat)
grow *v* kuber (yikber), nime (yinmu)
growth *n* nimu
guarantee 1. *n* DHamaan 2. *v* DHumen (yiDHmun)
guess *v* Hizer (yiHzir)
guest *n* DHief (DHyoof), khuTTaar *pl only*; **~room** ghurfet il-khuTTaar
guide *n* murshid (murshideen)
guidebook *n* murshid, deleel
guilty *adj* mudhnib (*f* mudhnibe *pl* mudhnibeen)
gun *n* museddes (museddesaat); **machine ~** (*semi-automatic*) *n* rashshaashe (rashshaashaat)
gynecologist *n* Tabeeb nisaa'i (*f* Tabeebe nisaa'iyye)
hair *n* sha3ar
haircut *n* geSS sha3ar, zyaan (*for men only*)
hairdresser *n* (*for men and women*) Hallaaq (*f* Hallaaqe); (*for men only*) mzeyyin

H

half *n* nuSS
hall *n* hol
hallway *n* mamerr
halt *n* wagfe
halve *v* qassam bin-nuSS (yqassim bin-nuSS) II
hammer *n* chakooch (chewaakeech)
hand *n* eed (eedenaat)
handbook *n* kuteyyib (kuteyyibaat)
handicapped *adj* mu3awweq (*f* mu3awweqe *pl* mu3awweqeen)
handle *n* yedde (yeddaat)
hang up *v* (*telephone*) sedd it-telifon (ysidd it-telifon)
hangar *n* HaDHeeret iT-Teyyaaraat
hanger *n* ti3laage (ti3laagaat)
happen *v* Saar (ySeer)
happy *adj* farHaan (*f* farHaane *pl* farHaaneen); sa3eed (*f* sa3eede *pl* sa3eedeen)
harass *v* tHaaresh (yitHaaresh) VI
harbor *n* meenaa' (mawaani')
hard *adj* (*difficult*) Sa3ub (*f* Sa3be); (*stiff*) yaabis (*f* yaabse), giwi (*f* giwiyye)

hard drive *n* qurS Salib, hard draiv
hardware *n* 3idde (3uded)
harmful *adj* mu'dhi (*f* mu'dhiyye)
harmless *adj* ma mu'dhi (*f* ma mu'dhiyye)
harvest *n* HaSaad
hat *n* shefqe (shefqaat)
hate *v* kireh (yikreh)
haughty mitkabbur (*f* mitkabre *pl* mitkabbureen)
have 3ind *prep* + suffix (*see Unit 2*); *v* (*own*) milek (yimluk)
hazardous khaTir (*f* kheTre)
he *pron* huwwe
head *n* raas (roos)
headache *n* Sudaa3, wija3 raas
headline *n* 3inwaan baariz (3anaaween baarze)
headmaster *n* mudeer (muderaa')
headphones *n* simmaa3a
headquarters *n* markez ra'eesi
health *n* SiHHa
healthcare *n* 3inaaye SiHHiyye
healthy *adj* SiHHi (*f* SiHHiyye)
hear *v* sima3 (yisma3)
heart *n* galub (gloob); ~ **attack** nawbe qelbiyye
heat 1. *n* Haraare 2. *v* deffe (ydeffi); (*liquid*) Hime (yiHmi)
heater *n* Sope
heating *n* **central** ~ tadfi'e markeziyye
heavy *adj* thigeel (*f* thigeele)
hedge *n* siyaaj
heel *n* cha3ab (ch3oobe)
height *n* (*person*) Tool; (*building, etc.*) irtifaa3, 3ilu
heir *n* wareeth
helicopter *n* hilikopter (hilikopteraat)
hell *n* jaHeem, naar
hello marHabe; (*telephone only*) aloo
helmet *n* khoodhe (khuwedh)
help 1. *n* musaa3ade 2. *v* saa3ad (ysaa3id) III, 3aawen (y3aawin) III
herb(s) *n* khuDHer *coll*
here *adv* hna
hero *n* baTal (abTaal)
herself *pron* nefis-he
hidden *adj* mekhfi (mekhfiyye), **maDHmoom** (*f* maDHmoome)
hide *v* khitel (yikhtil)
high *adj* 3aali (*f* 3aalye)
high school *n* medrese thaanewiyye (medaaris thaanewiyye)
higher than *adj* a3le min

highest *adj* a3le
highway *n* Tareeq khaariji (Turuq khaarijiyye)
hijack *v* khtiTaf (yikhtiTuf) VIII
hijacked *adj* mukhtaTaf
hijacker *n* mukhtaTif (mukhtaTifeen)
hill *n* tell (tlaal)
himself *pron* nefse
hint *n* ishaare khefeefe (ishaaraat khefeefe)
hip *n* wirik (awraak)
historical *adj* taareekhi (*f* taareekhiyye)
history *n* taareekh
hit *v* DHireb (yiDHrub)
hold up *v* (*bank*) sileb (yislib)
hole *n* Hufre (Hufer), zuruf (zroof)
holiday *n* 3uTle (3uTel); (*religious*) 3eed
hollow *adj* mjawwaf (*f* mjawfe)
holy *adj* muqaddas (*f* muqaddese)
home *n* biet; ~ **country** weTen; **go** ~ raaH lil-biet (yrooH lil-biet)
homework *n* waajib (waajibaat), waDHeefe
honest *adj* ameen (*f* ameene *pl* ameeneen)
honey *n* 3asel
honor *n* sheref
hook *n* chillaab (chillaabaat)
hope 1. *n* amel 2. *v* t'ammel (yit'ammel) V
horizon *n* ufuq
horrible *adj* faDHee3 (*f* faDHee3a)
horse *n* HSaan (HuSin)
hospital *n* musteshfe (musteshfeyaat)
hostage *n* reheene (rehaa'in); **take** ~ akhadh reheene (yaakhudh reheene)
hostile (*conduct*) *adj* 3idwaani
hot *adj* Haarr (*f* Haarre)
hotel *n* ootiel (ootielaat), findiq (fenaadiq)
hotter than *adj* aHarr min
hour *n* saa3a (saa3aat); **working** ~ dawaam *m sg*
hourly *adv* kull saa3a
house *n* biet (byoot)
housewife *n* rabbet biet (rabbaat byoot)
housing *n* iskaan
how *adv* shlon; ~ **many** chem; ~ **much** shged
huge *adj* DHakhum (*f* DHakhme)
human rights *n* Huqooq il-insaan
humid *adj* raTub (*f* raTbe)
hundred *adj* miyye; (*with a noun*) meet
hundred thousand *adj* meet alif

hungry *adj* joo3aan (*f* joo3aane *pl* joo3aaneen)
hurry (~ **up**) *v* ista3jel (yista3jil) X (*order to hurry*) b-sur3a!, sta3jil!; **in a ~** mista3jil (*f* mista3jile) *adj*
husband *n* zawj (azwaaj), rejil (ryaajeel)
hygiene *n* naDHaafe

I

I *pron* aani
ice *n* thelij
ice cream *n* dondirme
ice cubes *n* thelij
idea *n* fikre (afkaar)
ideal *adj* mithaali (*f* mithaaliyye)
identical *adj* mitshaabih (*f* mitshaabhe *pl* mitshaabheen)
identity card (ID) *n* hawiyye shekhSiyye (hawiyyaat shekhSiyye)
if *conj* idha
ignition *n* ish3aal; ~ **key** sweech is-seyyaare
ill *adj* mareeDH (*f* mareeDHe *pl* mareeDHeen)
illegal *adj* ghier qaanooni (*f* ghier qaanooniyye), ghier shar3i, wej3aan
illiterate *adj* ummi (*f* ummiyye *pl* ummiyyeen)
illustration *n* resim tawDHeeHi (risoom tawDHeeHiyye)
image *n* Soore (Suwer)
imagination *n* kheyaal
imagine *v* tkheyyel (yitkheyyel) V
imam *n* imaam (a'imme)
imitation *n* taqleed
immediately *adv* mubaashereten, ra'sen
immigrant *n* muhaajir (*f* muhaajire *pl* muhaajireen)
immune system *n* manaa3a jismiyye
immunization *n* taT3eem, talqeeh
impact (*physical*) *n* teSaadum
impolite *adj* edeb siz
import 1. *n* isteeraad (isteeradaat) 2. *v* stawred (yistawrid) X
importance *n* ahemiyye
important *adj* muhimm (*f* muhimme *pl* muhimmeen)
impossible *adj* mustaHeel (*f* mustaHeele)
imprison *v* sijen (yisjin)
improve *v* Hassen (yHassin) II
in *prep* b-/bi-
inaccurate *adj* ma daqeeq (*f* ma daqeeqe)
inappropriate *adj* ma laayiq (*f* ma laayqe)

incapable *adj* (*v in Arabic*) ma yigder (*f* ma tigder *pl* ma yigderoon)
inch *n* inj (injaat)
include *v* tDHammen (yitDHammen) V
including *prep* min DHiminhum
income *n* dekhel
incomplete *adj* naaqiS (*f* naaqSe), ma kaamil (*f* ma kaamle)
inconvenient *adj* muz3ij (*f* muz3ije), ma mlaa'im (*f* ma mlaa'me)
incorrect *adj* ghalaT (*m & f*)
increase 1. *n* ziyaade 2. *v* zeyyed (yzeyyid) II
indeed *adv* bil-fi3il
independence *n* istiqlaal
independent *adj* mustaqill (*f* mustaqille *pl* mustaqilleen)
index (*finger*) *n* sebbaabe
India *n* il-hind
Indian *adj/n* hindi (*f* hindiyye *pl* hnood)
Indian Ocean *n* il-muHeeT il-hindi
indicate *v* beyyen (ybeyyin) II
indigestion *n* 3usur haDHum
individual 1. *adj* ferdi (*f* ferdiyye) 2. *n* ferd (afraad)
indoors *adv* jewwe
industrial *adj* Sinaa3i (*f* Sinaa3iyye)
industry *n* Sinaa3a (Sinaa3aat)
infant *n* Tifil raDHee3 (aTfaal ruDHDHa3)
infection *n* 3adwe
infertile *adj* 3aaqir (*f* 3aaqre), 3aqeem (*f* 3aqeeme)
inflammation *n* iltihaab
influence *n* te'theer
information *n* ma3loomaat *pl*
infrastructure *n* il-bunye it-taHtiyye
ingredient *n* maadde (mawaadd)
inhabitant *n* saakin (sukkaan)
inject *v* DHireb ubre (yiDHrub ubre), zireq (yizruq)
injection *n* ubre (uber)
injury *n* jeriH (jrooH)
innocent *adj* beree' (*f* beree'e *pl* abriyaa')
inquiry *n* istifsaar (istifsaaraat)
insect *n* Hashere (Hasheraat)
inside *adv* jewwe
insomnia *n* areq
inspection *n* tafteesh
inspector *n* mufettish (mufettisheen)
install *v* niSeb (yinSub)
instead of *prep* ibbidaal

institute *n* ma3had (ma3aahid)
institution *n* mu'assese (mu'assesaat), ma3had (ma3aahid)
instructions *n* ta3leemaat
instrument *n* aale (aalaat)
insurance *n* ta'meen
insurgency *n* 3iSyaan
intellectual *adj* fikri (*f* fikriyye)
intensive care *n* 3inaaye murekkeze
intercourse (*sexual*) *n* 3ilaaqe jinsiyye
interest *n* ihtimaam; ~ **rate** (si3ir il-) faa'ide
interior 1. *adj* daakhili (*f* daakhiliyye), **Minister of I~ Affairs** wezeer
  id-daakhiliyye 2. *n* daakhil
internal (*medical*) *adj* baaTini (*f* baaTiniyye)
international *adj* 3aalemi (*f* 3aalemiyye), duweli (*f* duweliyye)
interpreter *n* muterjim (*f* muterjime *pl* muterjimeen)
interrogation *n* istijwaab
intersection *n* teqaaTu3 (teqaaTu3aat)
interview *n* muqaabele (muqaabelaat)
into *prep* l-/li-
introduce *v* qeddem (yqeddim) II
introduction *n* muqaddime (muqaddimaat)
invade *v* ghize (yighzu)
invasion *n* ghazu
invention *n* ikhtiraa3 (ikhtiraa3aat)
investigation *n* taHqeeq (taHqeeqaat)
investment *n* istithmaar (istithmaaraat)
investor *n* mustathmir (mustathmireen)
invisible *adj* ma yinshaaf *v* (*f* ma tinshaaf)
invitation *n* da3we (da3waat)
invite *v* di3a (yid3u), 3izem (yi3zim)
Iran *n* eeraan
Iranian *adj/n* eeraani (*f* eeraaniyye *pl* eeraaniyyeen)
Iraq *n* il-3iraaq
Iraqi *adj/n* 3iraaqi (*f* 3iraaqiyye *pl* 3iraaqiyyeen)
Ireland *n* erlende
Irish *adj/n* erlendi (*f* erlendiyye *pl* erlendiyyeen)
iron 1. *n* Hadeed 2. *v* DHireb ooti (yiDHrub ooti)
irrigation *n* rei
Islam *n* islaam
Islamic *adj* islaami (*f* islaamiyye)
island *n* jezeere (juzur)
isolation *n* infiraad, 3azil

Israel *n* israaʻeel
Israeli *adj/n* israaʻeeli (*f* israaʻeeliyye *pl* israaʻeeliyyeen)
issue 1. *n* qaDHiyye 2. *v* aSder *(yiSdur)* IV
Italian *adj/n* iTaali (*f* iTaaliyye *pl* iTaaliyyeen)
Italy *n* iTaalye
itch *v* Hakk (yHukk)
item *n* maadde (mawaadd)

J

jacket *n* chakiete (chakietaat), sitre (siteraat)
jail *n* sijin (sijoon)
January *n* kaanoon ith-thaani
Japan *n* il-yaabaan
Japanese *adj/n* yaabaani (*f* yaabaaniyye *pl* yaabaaniyyeen)
jaw *n* fech
jeans *n* kawboi
jeep *n* jieb
Jerusalem *n* il-quds
Jew *n* yhoodi (*pl* yhood)
jeweler *n* Saayigh (Siyyaagh)
Jewish *adj* yhoodi (*f* yhoodiyye *pl* yhood)
job *n* waDHeefe (waDHaayif)
join *v* iltiHaq (yiltiHiq) VIII
Jordan *n* il-ardun
Jordanian *adj/n* arduni (*f* arduniyye *pl* arduniyyeen)
journalist *n* SaHafi (*f* SaHafiyye *pl* SaHafiyyeen)
judge *n* qaaDHi (quDHaat)
judgment *n* Hukum
juice *n* 3aSeer
July *n* tammooz
jump *v* gumez (yugmuz)
June *n* Huzeiraan
jurisdiction *n* sulTe qaDHaaʻiyye
jury *n* muHallifeen
just 1. *adj* 3aadil (*f* 3aadle) 2. *adv* bes, fed
justice *n* 3adaale

K

keep *v* baqqe (ybaqqi) II
kettle *n* kitli (ketaali)

key *n* miftaaH (mafaateeH)
keyboard *n* (*computer*) lawHat il-mafaateeH, keebord
kidding (**you must be ~!**) la b-alle! (*casual*)
kidnap *v* ikhtiTaf (yikhtiTuf) VIII
kidnapping *n* ikhtiTaaf (ikhtiTafaat)
kidney *n* chilwe (chelaawi), kilye (kile)
kill *v* qitel (yuqtul)
killer *n* qaatil
killing *n* qatil
kilogram *n* kieloo (kieloowaat)
kilometer *n* kielumetir (kielumetraat)
kind 1. *adj* Haneen (*f* Haneene *pl* Haneneen) 2. *n* (*class*) no3 (anwaa3)
kindergarten *n* rawDHe (rawDHaat)
king *n* melik (milook)
Kirkuk *n* kerkook
kiss 1. *n* bose (bosaat) 2. *v* baas (yboos)
kitchen *n* maTbakh (maTaabukh)
knee *n* rukbe (rkaab)
knife *n* sichcheene (sichaacheen)
know *v* 3iref (yu3ruf), dire (yidri)
knowledge *n* ma3loomaat
Koran *n* qur'aan
Kurds *n* akraad *coll*
Kurdish *adj* kurdi (*f* kurdiyye)
Kuwait *n* il-kwiet

L

labor *n* (*work*) shughul, 3amel; (*childbirth*) wilaade (wilaadaat)
laboratory *n* mukhteber (mukhteberaat)
laborer 3aamil (3ummaal)
lacking 1. *adj* naaqiS 2. *v* **be ~** 3aaz (y3ooz)
ladder *n* derej
ladle *n* chemche
lady *n* seyyide (seyyidaat)
lake *n* buHaire (buHairaat)
lamb *n* kharoof (khurfaan), Tili (Tilyaan)
lamp *n* DHuwe (aDHwiye)
land *n* gaa3 (gee3aan), ariDH (araaDHi); **by ~** barri
landlord *n* SaHib il-biet (aS-Haab il-biet/il-byoot)
landowner *n* maalik (mullaak)
language *n* lughe (lughaat)

laptop *n* lap tup
large *adj* chibeer (*f* chibeere)
laser *n* liezer
last *adj* (*ultimate*) akheer (*f* akheere *pl* akheereen); **the ~** (*most recent*)
      il-faat (*f* il-faatet)
late *adv* mit'akhkhir (*f* mit'akhkhire)
later *adv* ba3dien
laugh *v* DHiHak (yiDH-Hak)
laundry *n* ghaseel melaabis
law *n* qanoon (qawaaneen)
lawn *n* Hasheesh, theyyel
laxative *n* mus-hil
lay off *v* sarraH (ysarriH) II
layer *n* Tebeqe (Tebeqaat)
layered (*hair*) *adj* mdarrej
lazy *adj* kaslaan (*f* kaslaane *pl* kesaale)
lead 1. *n* (*metal*) riSaaS 2. *adj* **~-free** khaali min ir-riSaaS
leader *n* qaa'id (quwwaad)
leadership *n* qiyaade
leading *adj* qiyaadi (*f* qiyaadiyye)
leaf *n* wereqe (awraaq)
leaflet *n* kurraase (kurraasaat)
leak 1. *n* kherkhere 2. *v* kherr (ykhurr)
learn *v* t3allem (yit3allem) V
leather *n* jilid (jilood)
leave *v* tirek (yitruk), 3aaf (y3oof)
Lebanese *adj/n* lubnaani (*f* lubnaaniyye *pl* lubnaaniyyeen)
Lebanon *n* lubnaan
left *adj* yisre; **~-handed** yisraawi
leg *n* rijil (rijlien, rijlienaat)
legal *adj* qanooni (*f* qaanooniyye)
lemon *n* noomi HaamuDH *coll*
length *n* Tool
lens *n* 3adese (3adesaat)
less 1. *adv* (*to a smaller extent*) aqall min 2. *prep* (*minus*) anqaS min
lesson *n* deris (droos)
let *v* **let's go** khelli nrooH; yelle
lethal *adj* qaatil (*f* qaatle)
letter *n* maktoob (makateeb)
letterbox *n* Sandoog il-bareed (Sanadeeg il-bareed)
lettuce *n* khess
level 1. *adj* (*ground*) 3adil 2. *n* mustawa (mustawayaat)
liable *adj* mas'ool (*f* mas'oole)

liberal *adj* mitHarrir (*f* mitHarrire *pl* mitHarrireen)
liberate *v* Harrer (yHarrir) II
liberation *n* taHreer
library *n* mektebe (mektebaat)
Libya *n* leebye
Libyan *adj/n* leebi (*f* leebiyye *pl* leebiyyeen)
license *n* ijaaze, rukhSe
lie 1. *n* kidhbe (kidhbaat) 2. *v* kidheb (yikdhib)
life *n* Hayaat
lifeboat *n* qaarib nejaat (qawaarib nejaat)
lift *v* shaal (ysheel)
light 1. *adj* (*weight*) khefeef (*f* khefeefe); (*color*) faatiH (*f* faatHa) 2. *n* (*artificial*) DHuwe (aDHwiye); (*daylight*) DHuwe in-nahaar 3. *v* (*fire*) 3ileg (yi3lig)
light bulb *n* glob (globaat)
lighter *adj* akhaff min
like 1. *prep* mithil 2. *v* Habb (yHibb); 3ijeb (yi3jib) + *personal suffix*
line *n* khaTT (khTooT); **stand in ~** wugef bis-sire (yogef bis-sire)
link *n* rabbaaT (rabbaaTaat)
lion *n* esed (isoode), sabi3 (sbaa3)
lips *n* shiffe (shfaayif)
liquid 1. *adj* saa'il (*f* saa'ile) 2. *n* saa'il (sawaa'il)
liquor *n* sheraab kuHooli
list *n* qaa'ime (qawaa'im)
listen *v* sima3 (yisma3)
listener *n* mustami3 (mustami3een)
literary *adj* edebi (*f* edebiyye)
literature *n* edeb
little *n* shweyye, qeleel
live *v* 3aash (y3eesh)
liver *n* kebed, chibde; (*food*) mi3laag
living in saakin b-
living room *n* ghurfet il-ma3eeshe
local *adj* maHalli (*f* maHalliyye)
location *n* mawqi3 (mawaaqi3)
lock *n* quful (qfaale)
locked *adj* maqfool (*f* maqfoole)
long *adj* Tweel (*f* Tweele)
longer *adj* aTwel min
look *v* baawe3 (ybaawi3) III, shaaf (yshoof)
loose *adj* raakhi (*f* raakhye)
loot *v* niheb (yinheb)
lose *v* DHeyya3(yDHeyyi3) II
loss *n* khesaare (khesaa'ir)

lost *adj* DHaayi3 (*f* DHaay3a *pl* DHaay3een)
lot *n* **a ~** hwaaye
loud *adj* 3aali (*f* 3aalye)
loudspeaker *n* mukebbir iS-Sot (mukebbiraat iS-Sot)
love 1. *n* Hubb 2. *v* Habb (yHibb)
low *adj* naaSi (*f* naaSye)
lower *adj* anSe min
lubricant *n* (*car*) shaHam it-tezyeet
lucky *adj* maH-DHooDH (*f* maH-DHooDHe *pl* maH-DHooDHeen)
luggage *n* mtaa3 (amti3a), juneT
lump *n* kutle (kutel)
lunch *n* ghede; **~ break** istiraaHat il-ghede
lung *n* riyye (riyyaat)

M

machine *n* mekeene (mekaayin)
mad *adj* mejnoon (*f* mejnoone *pl* mejaaneen), mkhabbal (*f* mkhable
     pl mkhaabeel)
madame *n* seyyide (seyyidaat)
magazine *n* mijelle (mijellaat)
mail *n* bareed
mailbox *n* Sandoog il-bareed (Sanaadeeg il-bareed)
mailing address *n* 3inwaan bareedi
main *adj* ra'eesi (*f* ra'eesiyye)
mainly *adv* b-Soore ra'eesiyye, 3al ak-thar
maintain *v* Saan (ySoon)
maintenance *n* Siyaane
major *adj* ra'eesi (*f* ra'eesiyye)
majority *n* aghlebiyye, il-ak-thariyye
make *v* sewwe (ysewwi)
make-up *n* mikyaaj
male *n* dheker, (*animal*) faHel
man *n* rijjaal (ryaajeel)
management *n* idaare
manager *n* mudeer (*f* mudeere *pl* muderaa')
maneuver *n* munaawere (munaaweraat)
manners *n* teSerrufaat; **good ~** edeb
manual 1. *adj* yedewi (*f* yedewiyye) 2. *n* kuteyyib (kuteyyibaat)
manuscript *n* makhTooTe (makhTooTaat)
many *adj* hwaaye
map *n* khareeTe (kharaayiT)

March *n* adhaar
march 1. *n* meseere (meseeraat) 2. *v* mishe bil-meseere (yimshi bil-meseere)
marine *n* baHriyye
mark 1. *n* 3alaame (3alaamaat) 2. *v* HaTT 3alaame (yHuTT 3alaame)
market *n* soog (swaage)
marriage *n* zawaaj
married *adj* mitzawwij (*f* mitzawwije *pl* mitzawwijeen)
marry *v* tzawwej (yitzawwej) V
martyr *n* sheheed (shuhedaaʻ)
massacre *n* mejzere (mejaazir)
mat *n* HaSeere (HuSraan)
match 1. *n* (*wooden*) 3oodet shikhkhaaT (3uwed shikhkhaaT); (*sports*)
    mubaareyaat 2. *v* rahham (yrahhum) II
material *n* maadde (mawaadd)
matter 1. *n* **what's the ~** sh-Saar, haay sh-aku; shinoo il-qaDHiyye 2. *v* **it**
    doesn't ~ ma yhimm
mattress *n* dosheg (dwaashig)
mature *adj* naaDHij (*f* naaDHje)
maximum *n* il-Hadd il-a3la
May *n* eyyaar
maybe *adv* yimkin
mayor *n* muHaafiDH (muHaafiDHeen)
meal *n* wejbe (wejbaat)
mean *v* qiSed (yiqSud); **that means** ya3ni
meaning *n* ma3ne (ma3aani)
means *n* weseele (wesaaʻil)
measure *v* qaas (yqees)
measurement *n* qiyaas (qiyaasaat)
meat *n* laHam (luHoom)
mechanic *n* muSelliH meekaaneeki (muSelliHeen meekaaneekiyyeen)
mechanical *adj* meekaaneeki (*f* meekaaneekiyye)
media *n* wesaaʻil il-i3laam
medical *adj* Tibbi (*f* Tibbiyye)
medication *n* 3ilaaj, duwe (adwiye)
medicine *n* Tibb
Mediterranean Sea *n* il-baHr il-abyeDH il-mutewaSSiT
medium *adj* weSeT
meet *v* iltiqe (yiltiqi) VIII, ijtima3 (yijtimi3) VIII
meeting *n* ijtimaa3 (ijtimaa3aat)
melody *n* laHin (alHaan)
melon *n* **musk ~** baTTeekh *coll*; **water~** reggi *coll*
melt *v* dhaab (ydhoob)
member *n* 3uDHu (a3DHaaʻ)

memory *n* (*ability*) dhaakire; (*remembrance*) dhikra (dhikreyaat)
menstruation *n* il-3aade (ish-shahriyye)
mental health *n* SiHHa 3aqliyye
mentality *n* 3aqliyye (3aqliyyaat)
mention *v* dhiker (yidhkur)
menu *n* qaa'imet il-akil (qawaa'im il-akil)
message *n* risaale (resaa'il)
messenger *n* muraasil (muraasileen)
metal *n* ma3den (ma3aadin)
meter *n* meezaaniyye (meezaaniyyaat)
method *n* Tareeqe (Turuq)
microphone *n* mikrafon (mikrafonaat)
microscope *n* mikriskob (mikriskobaat)
Middle East *n* ish-sharq il-awSaT
Middle Eastern *adj* min ish-sharq il-awSaT
middle *n* nuSS, weSeT; ~ **school** medrese mutawassiTe
midnight *n* nuSS il-liel
midwife *n* qabile ma'dhoone (qabilaat ma'dhoonaat), jidde (jiddaat)
mile *n* meel (amyaal)
military *n* 3askeri
milk *n* Haleeb *coll*
million *n* milyon (melaayeen)
mind 1. *n* 3aqil 2. *v* **never** ~ meikhaalif
mine *n* lughum (alghaam); ~ **detector** kaashifet il-alghaam
minefield *n* Haqil alghaam (Huqool alghaam)
mineral water *n* miyaah ma3deniyye
minimum *n* iS-Sughra
minister *n* wezeer (wuzeraa')
minor *adj* thaanewi (*f* thaanewiyye); *n* (*underage*) qaaSir (*f* qaaSre)
mint *n* (*herb*) ni3naa3
minus *prep* naaqiS
minute *n* deqeeqe (deqaayiq)
mirror *n* mraaye (mraayaat)
miscarriage *n* ijhaaDH (ijhaaDHaat)
Miss *n* aanise (aanisaat)
miss *v* (*an airplane, etc.*) fewwet (yfewwit) II; (*a person*) ftiqed (yiftiqed)
    VIII, waHash (yoHish)
missing (*person*) mafqood (*f* mafqoode *pl* mafqoodeen)
mistake *n* ghalTe (aghlaaT)
misunderstand *v* ftihem ghalaT (yiftihim ghalaT) VIII
misunderstanding *n* soo' fehim
mix *v* khubeT (yikhbuT)
mixture *n* khaleeT

moan *v* t'awwah (yit'awwah) V
mobile phone *n* naqqaal (naqqaalaat)
model *n* mudiel (mudielaat)
modem *n* modim (modimaat)
modern *adj* Hadeeth (*f* Hadeethe)
modest *adj* mitwaaDHi3 (*f* mitwaaDH3a *pl* mitwaaDH3een)
moisture *n* ruToobe
moment *n* laH-DHe (laH-DHaat), thaaniye (thawaani)
Monday *n* ith-thinien
money *n* floos
month *n* sheher (ashhur)
monthly *adj* shehri (*f* shehriyye)
moon *n* gumer; (*full*) bedir; (*new, crescent*) hlaal
more *adj* ba3ad; ~ **time** weqit azyad, weqit ak-thar; *adv* azyad min
morning *n* SubuH; **good** ~ SabaaH il-khier
Moroccan *adj/n* maghribi (*f* maghribiyye *pl* maghaarbe)
Morocco *n* il-maghrib
mortal *adj* qaatil (*f* qaatile)
mosque *n* jaami3 (jawaami3)
mosquito *n* begge (beggaat), ba3ooDHe (ba3ooDH)
most *adj* (*majority*) (il-)ak-thar
Mosul *n* il-mooSil
mother *n* umm (ummahaat); ~**-in-law** mart il-3amm
motorcycle *n* maaTorsikil (maaTorsiklaat)
mountain *n* jibel (jibaal)
mourning *n* Hizin
mouse *n* faare (feeraan)
mouth *n* Halig (Hlooge)
move *v* tHarrek (yitHarrek) V; (*house*) tHawwel (yitHawwel) V
movement *n* Hareke (Harekaat)
movie *n* filim (aflaam); ~ **theater** seeneme
moving *n* taHweele
Mr. *n* is-seyyid
Mrs. *n* is-seyyide
much *adj* (*large quantity*) hwaaye
mud *n* Teen
municipal *adj* beledi (*f* belediyye)
murder *n* jereeme (jeraayim)
muscle *n* 3aDHele (3aDHelaat)
museum *n* matHaf (mataaHif)
music *n* moseeqe
Muslim *adj/n* muslim (*f* muslime *pl* muslimeen)
must *v* laazim (*form doesn't change*) + *v*

mustache *n* shwaarub
mutiny *n* temerrud
mutton *n* laHam ghenem
myself *pron* nefsi

N

nail *n* (*metal*) bismaar (besaameer); (*finger/toe*) iDHfir (aDHaafir)
naked *adj* maSallakh (*f* mSallikhe *pl* mSallikheen, maSaaleekh)
name *n* isim (asmaa')
narrow *adj* DHeyyig (*f* DHeyge)
nation *n* umme (umem), weTen (awTaan)
national *adj* qawmi (*f* qawmiyye); weTeni (*f* weTeniyye)
nationality *n* qawmiyye (qawmiyyaat)
natural *adj* Tabee3i (*f* Tabee3iyye)
nature *n* Tabee3a
nausea *n* li3baan nefis
navigation *n* milaaHe
navy 1. *adj* ~ **blue** neeli (*f* neeliyye) 2. *n* baHriyye
near 1. *adj* (*nearby*) qareeb (*f* qareebe) 2. *adv* (*close to*) yemm
necessary *adj* DHaroori
neck *n* rugbe (rgaab)
necklace *n* glaade (glaayid)
need 1. *n* Haaje (Hajaat) 2. *v* Htaaj (yiHtaaj) VIII
needle *n* ubre (uber)
negotiation *n* mufaaweDHe (mufaaweDHaat)
neighbor *n* jaar (jeeraan, jwaareen)
neighborhood *n* maHalle (maHallaat)
nephew *n* (*son of brother*) ibin akh (wilid akh); (*son of sister*) ibin ukhut
(wilid ukhut)
nervous *adj* 3aSebi (*f* 3aSebiyye *pl* 3aSebiyyeen); ~ **system** ii-jihaaz
il-3aSebi
net *adj* Saafi
Netherlands *n* holende
network *n* shebeket 3amel (shebekaat a3maal)
neutral *adj* Hiyaadi (*f* Hiyaadiyye *pl* Hiyaadiyyeen)
never *adv* abeden
new *adj* jideed (*f* jideede *pl* jidded)
New Year *n* raas is-sene
newborn *n* mawlood jideed (mawaleed jidded)
newer than *adj* ajded min
news *n* akhbaar
newspaper *n* jereede (jeraayid)

next *adj* ij-jaay (*f* ij-jaayye), il-qaadim (*f* il-qaadime)

nice *adj* leTeef (*f* leTeefe *pl* leTeefeen); ~ **to meet you** tsherrafne

niece *n* (*daughter of brother*) bit akh (banaat akh), (*daughter of sister*) bit ukhut (banaat ukhut)

night *n* liel (leyaali); ~ **train** qiTaar il-liel; **good** ~ tiSbaH 3ala khier (*see also Unit 6*)

nine *adj* (*standing alone*) tis3a; (*with a noun*) tisi3

nine hundred *adj* tisi3miyye; (*with a noun*) tisi3meet

nine hundred thousand *adj* tisi3meet alif

nine thousand *adj* tisi3talaaf

nineteen *adj* tisaTa3ash

ninety *adj* tis3een

ninety thousand *adj* tis3een alif

ninth *adj* taasi3 (*f* taas3a)

no *adv* la

nobody *pron* maHHad

noise *n* hose, DHajeej

none *pron* wela waaHid

non-stop *adv* bidoon tawaqquf/inqiTaa3

noodles *n* sha3riyye

noon *n* DHuhur

normal *adj* (regular) 3aadi (*f* 3aadiyye); (natural) Tabee3i (*f* Tabee3iyye)

north *n* shimaal

northern *adj* shimaali (*f* shimaaliyye)

Norway *n* in-nerweej

Norwegian *adj* nerweeji (*f* nerweejiyye *pl* nerweejiyyeen)

nose *n* kheshim (khshoome)

not *adv* ma

note *n* mulaaHaDHe (mulaaHaDHaat)

notebook *n* defter (defaatir)

nothing *pron* maku shee

notice *n* ish3aar, i3laan

nourishment *n* teghdhiye

novel *n* riwaaye (riwaayaat)

November *n* tishreen ith-thaani

now *adv* hesse

nowhere *adv* maku b-ei mekaan

nuclear *adj* dherri (*f* dherriyye); ~ **weapons** asliHa dherriyye

numb *adj* minemmil (*f* mnemle)

number *n* 3aded (a3daad); **telephone** ~ raqam it-telifon

nurse *n* mumarriDH (*f* mumarriDHe *m pl* mumarriDHeen, *f pl* mumarriDHaat)

nursing *n* temreeDH

O

oasis *n* waaHa (waaHaat)
oath *n* qesem
object *n* shee (ashyaa')
objective *adj* mawDHoo3i (*f* mawDHoo3iyye)
observe *v* laaHaDH (ylaaHiDH) III
observer *n* mulaaHiDH (mulaaHiDHeen)
obstacle *n* 3aqebe (3aqebaat)
obtain *v* HaSSel (yHaSSil) II
obviously *adv* min il-waaDHiH, ybeyyin *v*
occasion *n* munaasebe (munaasebaat)
occidental *adj* gharbi (*f* gharbiyye)
occupation *n* (*military*) iHtilaal
occupy *v* iHtell (yiHtell) VIII
ocean *n* muHeeT
o'clock *adv* saa3a
October *n* tishreen il-awwel
odd *adj* (*number*) ferdi
odor *n* reeHa (rewaa'iH)
of course *adv* Tab3an
offensive *adj* (*conduct*) 3idwaani; (*language or conduct*) muheen; (*odor, appearance*) kereeh
offer *v* qeddem (yqeddim) II
office *n* mekteb (mekaatib); **doctor's ~** 3iyaade; **government ~** daa'ire
officer *n* (*police*) shurTi (shurTe); (*military*) DHaabuT (DHubbaaT); (*traffic*) shurTi muroor (shurTet muroor)
official *adj* rasmi (*f* rasmiyye)
often *adv* marraat
oil *n* (*edible*) ziet; (*petroleum*) nafuT
oilfield *n* Haqil nafuT (hiqool nafuT)
okay zien, HaaDHir, Saar
old *adj* (*object*) 3ateeg (*f* 3ateege), qadeem (*f* qadeeme); **~ man** shaayib (*pl* shiyyaab); **~ woman** 3ajooze (*pl* 3ajaayiz)
older than *adj* (*age*) akbar min; (*object*) aqdem min, a3teg min
olive(s) *n* zeitoon *coll*; **~ oil** ziet iz-zeitoon
Oman *n* 3umaan
on *prep* (*location*) 3ala; (*about*) 3an
once *adv* fed marre
one *adj* waaHid (*f* wiHde)
one-way street *n* ittijaah waaHid
one-way ticket *n* tikit ghier murajja3
only *adv* bes, fed; **the ~ one** il-waHeed

open 1. *adj* meftooH (*f* meftooHa); mfattiH (*f* mfattiHa); 2. *v* fitaH (yiftaH)
opening *n* fetHe
operation *n* 3amaliyye
operator *n* 3aamil beddaale
opinion *n* re'i (araa')
opportunity *n* furSe (fureS)
opposite *n* 3akis
opposition *n* mu3aareDHe
optician *n* khabeer faHiS in-neDHer
or *conj* aw, lo (see also Unit 5); **either...** ~ imma... aw
orange 1. *adj* (*color*) purtuqaali (*f* purtuqaaliyye) 2. *n* purtuqaal *coll*
orchard *n* bistaan (besaateen)
orchestra *n* firqe moseeqiyye (fireq moseeqiyye)
ordeal *n* 3adhaab, miHne
order 1. *n* (*command*) amur (awaamir) 2. *v* (*command*) umer (yu'mur); (*at a restaurant or store*) Tileb (yiTlub), weSSe (yweSSi) II
ordinary *adj* 3aadi (3aadiyye)
organ *n* (*body*) 3uDHu (a3DHaa'); (*music*) orgin (orginaat)
organization *n* muneDHDHeme (muneDHDHemaat)
original *adj* aSli (*f* aSliyye)
orphan *n* yeteem (*f* yeteeme *pl* eitaam)
orphanage *n* meytem (meyaatim)
other *adj* laakh (*f* lukhkhe)
otherwise *adv* wa illa
ourselves *pron* nefisne
out *prep* ~ **of order** 3aaTil (*f* 3aaTle), kharbaan; ~ **of work** baTTaal (*f* baTTaale *pl* baTTaaleen)
outer space *n* faDHaa' khaariji
outside *adv* berre
oven *n* firin; **clay** ~ tannoor
over *prep* (*location*) 3ala, fog
overdose *n* jur3a azyed min il-laazim
overthrow *v* (*government*) SaqqeT (ySaqqiT) II
own *v* milek (yimluk)
owner *n* maalik (*f* maalike *pl* mullaak), SaaHib (*f* SaaHbe *pl* aS-Haab)
oxygen *n* oksijeen

P

pacemaker *n* munebbih qelbi (munebbihaat qelbiyye)
pack *v* rizem (yirzim)
package *n* ruzme (ruzem)

pact *n* mu3aahede duweliyye (mu3aahedaat duweliyye)
page *n* SafHa (SafHaat)
pain *n* alem
painkiller *n* musekkin (musekkinaat)
paint 1. *n* Subugh 2. *v* Subegh (yiSbugh)
painting *n* lawHa (lawHaat)
pair *n* zoj
pajamas *n* bejaame (bejaamaat)
palace *n* qaSir (quSoor)
pale *adj* shaaHib (*f* shaaHbe *pl* shaHbeen)
Palestine *n* felesTeen
Palestinian *adj/n* felesTeeni (*f* felesTeeniyye *pl* felesTeeniyyeen)
pan *n* Taawe (Taawaat)
pants *n* panTiroon (penaaTeer)
paper *n* kaaghed, wereq *coll*; (*sheet*) wereqe (awraaq)
parachute *n* pereshoot (pereshootaat)
paragraph *n* feqere (feqeraat)
paralyzed *adj* meshlool (*f* meshloole *pl* meshlooleen)
paratrooper *n* miDHelli (miDHelliyyeen)
parcel *n* ruzme (ruzem)
pardon *v* ~ **me** il-3afu
parents *n* waaldien, umm w-ab
park 1. *n* Hadeeqe (Hadaayiq), muntezeh (muntezehaat) 2. *v* waggaf
    is-seyyaare (ywagguf is-seyyaare) II
parking lot *n* mawqif seyyaaraat (mawaaqif seyyaaraat), geraaj
    is-seyyaaraat (garaajaat is-seyyaaraat)
parliament *n* perlemaan
part *n* jizu' (ajzaa'); **spare parts** edewaat iHtiyaaTiyye
participant *n* mushaarik (mushaarikeen)
participate *v* shaarek (yshaarik) III
particular *adj* khaaSS (*f* khaaSSe)
particularly *adv* khaaSSeten
partner *n* shereek (*pl* shurekaa')
party *n* (*political*) Hizib siyaasi (aHzaab siyaasiyye); (*social event*) Hafle
    (Haflaat)
pass *v* 3uber (yu3bur)
passenger *n* (*traveler*) musaafir (musaafireen); (*in a vehicle*) raakib
    (rukkaab)
passport *n* jawaaz (jawaazaat), pasport (pasportaat)
past *n* maaDHi
patient 1. *adj* Seboor (*f* Seboore *pl* Sebooreen) 2. *n* (*medical*) mareeDH
    (*f* mareeDHe *pl* marDHa), muraaji3 (*f* muraaji3a *pl* muraaji3een)
patriotic *adj* weTeni (*f* weTeniyye *pl* weTeniyyeen)

pay *v* difa3 (yidfa3); **get paid** *v* qubeDH (yiqbuDH)
peace *n* salaam
peach(es) *n* khokh *coll*
pear(s) *n* 3armooT *coll*
pearl *n* leelwaaye (leelu)
peel *v* geshsher (ygeshshir) II
pen *n* qelem (aqlaam, qlaam); **ballpoint** ~ qelem jaff (qlaam jaffe)
penalty *n* 3uqoobe (3uqoobaat)
pencil *n* qelem riSaaS (qlaam riSaaS)
peninsula *n* shubuh jezeere
penniless *adj* muflis (*f* muflise *pl* mfalees, mufliseen)
pension *n* teqaa3ud
people *n* (*persons*) naas; (*population*) sukkaan; (*when counting*) nefer, shekhiS
pepper *n* filfil *coll*
percent *n* nisbe mi'awiyye
perfect *adj* kaamil (*f* kaamle)
performance *n* edaa'
perfume *n* reeHa (riyaH), 3uTur (3uToor)
perhaps *adv* yimkin
period *n* (time) fetre (fetraat)
permanent *adj* daa'imi (*f* daa'imiyye)
permission *n* rukhSe
permit *n* ijaaze
persecute *v* iDHTihed (yiDHTihid) VIII
person *n* shekhiS (ashkhaaS), nefer (neferaat)
personal *adj* shekhSi (*f* shekhSiyye)
personnel *n* il-afraad
perspiration *n* 3areg
petition *n* 3areeDHe (3araayiDH)
pharmacy *n* Seideliyye (Seideliyyaat)
photocopy 1. *n* nuskhe (nusekh) 2. *v* stensekh (yistensikh) X
photograph *n* Soore (Suwer)
photographer *n* muSawwir (muSawwireen)
physical *adj* jismi (*f* jismiyye)
physician *n* Tabeeb (aTibbaa')
piano *n* pianu
pick up *v* shaal (ysheel)
pickles *n* Turshi
picnic *n* sefre
pickpocket *n* neshshaal (neshshaaleen)
picture *n* Soore (Suwer)
piece *n* quT3a (quTa3)

pig *n* khenzeer (khenazeer)
pile *n* kome (akwaam)
pill *n* Habbe (Huboob)
pillow *n* mkhadde (mekhaadeed)
pilot *n* Teyyaar (Teyyaareen)
pin *n* denboos (denaabees)
pink *adj* werdi (*f* werdiyye)
pipeline *n* khaTT anaabeeb (khuTooT anaabeeb)
place *n* mekaan (mekaanaat)
plain *adj* (*simple*) 3aadi (3aadiyye)
plan 1. *n* khuTTe (khuTeT) 2. *v* khaTTaT (ykhaTTiT) II
planet *n* kawkab seyyaar (kawaakib seyyaare)
plant 1. *n* zeri3 (mazroo3aat) 2. *v* zira3 (yizra3)
plastic *n* plasteek, nailon
plate *n* maa3oon (mawaa3een)
platform *n* maneSSe (maneSSaat)
play 1. *n* (*theater*) mesraHiyye (mesraHiyyaat); 2. *v* li3ab (yil3ab)
playground *n* (*school*) saaHa
please (*in a request*) rajaa'an, min feDHlek *m sg* (*see also Unit 5*);
  (*response to a request*) tfaDHDHal *m sg* (*see also Unit 4*)
plenty *adv* hwaaye
pliers *n* chillaabtien
plum(s) *n* 3injaaS *coll*
plumber *n* abul-booriyyaat
plunderer *n* nhiebi (nhiebiyye)
plus *conj* zaa'id
pneumonia *n* dhaat ir-ri'e
pocket *n* jieb (jyoob)
poem *n* qeSeede (qeSaayid)
poetry *n* shi3ir, wezin
point *n* nuqTe (nuqeT, niqaaT)
poisonous *adj* saam (*f* saamme)
pole *n* quTub (aqTaab)
police *n* shurTe
police station *n* markez shurTe (maraakiz shurTe)
policeman *n* shurTi (shurTe)
policy *n* siyaase
political *adj* siyaasi (*f* siyaasiyye)
politician siyaasi (siyaasiyyeen)
politics *n* siyaase
poll *n* istiftaa' (istiftaa'aat)
polluted *adj* mlawwath (*f* mlawwithe)
pollution *n* telewwuth

pomegranate rummaan *coll*
pool *n* masbaH (masaabiH)
poor *adj* faqeer (*f* faqeere *pl* fuqeraa')
popular *adj* shaayi3 (*f* shaay3a), sha3bi (sha3biyye)
populated *adj* maskoon (*f* maskoone)
population *n* sukkaan
pork *n* laHam khenzeer
port *n* meenaa' (mewaani')
porter *n* Hammaal (Hammaaleen, Hmameel)
position *n* mawqi3 (mawaaqi3)
positive *adj* eejaabi (*f* eejaabiyye)
possible *adj* mumkin
post office *n* mekteb il-bareed (mekaatib il-bareed)
postman *n* boSTechi, abul-bareed
pot *n* jidir (jdoore)
potato(es) putiete *coll*
pottery *n* fikhaariyyaat
poultry *n* dewaajin *coll*
pound *n* paawen (paawenaat)
POW *n* aseer Harub (asra Harub)
power *n* quwwe
power plant *n* maHaTTet kahrabaa' (maHaTTaat kahrabaa')
powerful *adj* qawi (*f* qawiyye *pl* aqwiyaa')
practical *adj* 3amali (*f* 3amaliyye)
pray *v* Selle (ySelli) II
prayer *n* Selaat
precisely *adv* bi-DH-DHabuT
preferable *adj* mufaDHDHal (*f* mufaDHDHale)
pregnant *adj* Haamil (Hawaamil), Hible (Hiblaat)
preparation *n* taH-DHeer (taH-DHheeraat)
prepare *v* HaDHDHer (yHaDHDHir) II
prescription *n* rachiete (rachietaat), waSfe (waSfaat)
presence *n* HuDHoor
present 1. *adj* HaaDHir (*f* HaaDHre *pl* HaaDHreen) 2. *n* (*gift*) hediyye (hedaaye)
president *n* ra'ees (ru'asaa')
press conference *n* mu'tamar saHafi (mu'tamaraat saHafiyye)
press *n* saHaafe
pressure *n* DHaghiT
pretty *adj* Hilu (*f* Hilwe)
prevent *v* mina3 (yimna3)
previous *adj* saabiq (*f* saabqe), faat (*f* faayte)
price *n* si3ir (as3aar)

priest *n* qess (qusus)
prime minister *n* ra'ees wuzeraa' (ru'asaa' wuzeraa')
print *v* Tuba3 (yiTba3)
prison *n* sijin (sijoon)
prisoner *n* mesjoon (mesaajeen)
private *adj* khaaSS (*f* khaaSSe)
privilege *n* imtiyaaz (imtiyaazaat)
prize *n* jaa'ize (jewaa'iz)
probably *adv* yimkin (*lit.* it is possible)
problem *n* mushkile (meshaakil)
procedure *n* ijraa' (ijraa'aat)
produce 1. *n* maHaaSeel ziraa3iyye 2. *v* antej (yintij) IV
product *n* mentooj (mentoojaat)
production *n* intaaj
profession *n* (*occupation*) shughul (ashghaal), mihne (mihen)
professional *adj* miHtirif (*f* miHterfe)
professor ustaadh (*f* ustaadhe *pl* asaatidhe)
profit *n* ribiH (arbaaH)
program *n* manhej (menaahij)
progress *n* teqaddum
project *n* meshroo3 (meshaaree3)
promise *v* wi3ad (yo3id)
proof *n* burhaan (beraaheen)
propeller *n* parawaane (parawaanaat)
property *n* muluk
prophet *n* nebi (anbiyaa')
proposal *n* muqteraH (muqtereHaat)
prostitute *n* 3aahre (3aahraat)
protect *v* Hime (yiHmi)
protection *n* Himaaye
protest 1. *n* iHtijaaj (iHtijaajaat) 2. *v* iHtejj (yiHtejj) VIII
proud *adj* fakhoor (*f* fakhoore)
provide *v* jehhez (yjehhiz) II
province *n* iqleem (aqaaleem), muqaTa3a (muqaTa3aat)
psychologist *n* Tabeeb nefsaani
public 1. *adj* 3aamm (*f* 3aamme) 2. *n* jumhoor, sha3ab
publishing house *n* daar neshir (door neshir)
pull *v* jerr (yjurr)
pump *n* pump (pumpaat), maDHakhkha (maDHakhkhaat)
punctual *adj* daqeeq bil-mawaa3eed (*f* daqeeqe... *pl* daqeeqeen...)
punishment *n* 3uqoobe (3uqoobaat)
pure *adj* neqi (*f* neqiyye)
purple *adj* benefseji (*f* benefsejiyye)

purpose *n* ghereDH (aghraaDH)
push *v* difa3 (yidfa3)
put *v* (*place*) HaTT (yHuTT); ~ **on** (*clothing*) libes (yilbes)

Q

Qatar *n* qatar
qualified *adj* kefoo' (*f* kefoo'e *pl* kefoo'een)
quality *n* naw3iyye (naw3iyyaat)
quantity *n* kemmiyye (kemmiyyaat)
quarter *n* rubu3; **a ~ to five** (*o'clock*) khamse ille rubu3
question *n* su'aal (as'ile)
quick *adj* saree3 (*f* saree3a)
quickly *adv* b-sur3a
quiet *adj* haadi' (*f* haad'e)

R

racial *adj* 3unSuri (*f* 3unSuriyye)
racism *n* 3unSuriyye
rack *n* reff (rfoof)
radar *n* radaar
radiation *n* ish3aa3
radical *adj* jedhri (*f* jedhriyye), radikaali (*f* radikaaliyye *pl* radikaaliyyeen)
radio *n* raadyo (radyowaat)
raid *n* ghaare (ghaaraat)
railroad *n* sikket Hadeed (sikek Hadeed)
rain 1. *n* muTer 2. *v* muTret *f sg* (timTur)
raise *v* rufa3 (yirfa3), shaal (ysheel)
Ramadan *n* ramaDHaan
rank *n* (*military*) rutbe (ruteb)
rape *n* ightiSaab
rapidly *adv* b-sur3a
rash *n* Hakke
rat *n* jriedi (jrediyye)
rate *n* si3ir; **at any ~** 3ala kull Haal
raw *adj* nee (*f* niyye)
ray *n* shu3aa3
razor *n* moos Hilaaqe (amwaas Hilaaqe); ~ **blade** shafre (shafraat)
reach *v* wuSel (yoSel)
reaction *n* redd fi3il (ridood af3aal)

read *v* qire (yiqre)
ready *adj* HaaDHir (*f* HaaDHre *pl* HaaDHreen); jaahiz (*f* jaahze)
real *adj* Haqeeqi (*f* Haqeeqiyye), waaqi3i (*f* waaqi3iyye)
reality *n* Haqeeqe, waaqi3
really *adv* Sudug
realtor *n* dellaal (dellaale)
rear *adj* khelfi (*f* khelfiyye)
reason *n* sebeb (asbaab)
reasonable *adj* ma3qool (*f* ma3qoole)
rebel *n* mitmarrid (mitmarrideen), 3aSi (3usaat)
rebellion *n* temerrud, 3iSyaan
receipt *n* waSil (wuSoolaat)
receive *v* stilem (yistilim) VIII, qubeDH (yiqbuDH)
receiver *n* mistilim
recent *adj* Hadeeth (*f* Hadeethe)
recently *adv* Hadeethen
reception *n* istiqbaal
receptionist *n* muwaDHDHaf istiqbaal
recognize *v* meyyez (ymeyyiz) II
recommend *v* waSSe (ywaSSi) II
recommendation *n* tawSiye (tawSiyaat)
record 1. *n* sijill (sijillaat); (*vinyl*) STuwaane 2. *v* sejjel (ysejjil) II
recruit *v* jenned (yjennid) II
red *adj* aHmer (*f* Hamre)
Red Sea *n* il-baHr il-aHmer
reduce *v* qellel (yqellil) II
reference *n* marja3 (maraaji3)
referendum *n* istiftaaʻ (istiftaaʻaat)
refinery *n* maSfe (maSaafi)
refrigerator *n* thillaaje (thillaajaat)
refugee *n* laajiʻ (*f* laajiʻe *pl* laajiʻeen)
refusal *n* rafuDH
refuse *v* ma qibel (ma yiqbel)
regards *n* taHiyyaat
regime *n* niDHaam (anDHime)
region *n* manTeqe (manaaTiq)
regular *adj* (*customary*) 3aadi (*f* 3aadiyye); (*at regular intervals*)
          muntaDHam (*f* muntaDHame)
regularly *adv* b-intiDHaam
relationship *n* 3ilaaqe (3ilaaqaat)
relatively *adv* nisbiyyen
relax *v* sterkhe (yisterkhi) X
relief agency *n* wekaalet il-ghawth (wekaalaat il-ghawth)

religion *n* deen (diyaanaat)
religious *adj* deeni (*f* deeniyye)
rely on *v* i3timed (yi3timid) VIII
remain *v* buqe (yubqe)
remember *v* tdhekker (yitdhekker) V
remove *v* wakhkhar (ywakhkhir) II
renew *v* jadded (yjaddid) II
rent 1. *n* eejaar 2. *v* ajjer (y'ajjir) II
repair 1. *n* taSleeH (taSleeHaat); **auto ~ shop** maHall il-feeterchi
    2. *v* SallaH (ySalliH) II
repeat *v* 3aad (y3eed)
reply 1. *n* jewaab (ajwibe) 2. *v* jaaweb (yjaawub) III
report 1. *n* teqreer (teqaareer) 2. *v* kiteb teqreer (yiktib teqreer)
reporter *n* muraasil (muraasileen)
represent *v* maththal (ymeththil) II
representative *n* mumeththil (mumeththileen)
republic *n* jumhooriyye
require *v* raad (yreed), Tileb (yiTlub)
requirement *n* maTleb (maTaalub)
rescue *v* niqedh (yinqudh)
research *n* baHith (biHooth)
reservation *n* Hajiz
reserve *v* Hijez (yiHjiz)
reserved *adj* maHjooz (*f* maHjooze)
reserves *n* (*army*) iHtiyaaT
reservoir *n* khazzaan
resign *v* staqaal (yistaqeel) X
resolution *n* qaraar (qaraaraat)
resources *n* mewaarid
respect *n* iHtiraam
response *n* istijaabe (istijaabaat)
responsibility *n* mas'ooliyye (mas'ooliyyaat)
responsible *adj* mas'ool (*f* mas'oole *pl* mas'ooleen)
rest 1. *n* istiraaHa 2. *v* steraaH (yistereeH) X
restaurant *n* maT3am (maTaa3um)
result *n* neteeje (netaayij)
retired *adj* mitqaa3id (*f* mitqaa3de *pl* mitqa3deen)
retreat 1. *n* teraaju3 2. *v* traaja3 (yitraaja3) VI
return *v* rija3 (yirja3)
return ticket *n* tikit murajja3 (tiktaat murajja3a)
revenue *n* mawrid (mewaarid)
review *n* (*book, film*) 3ariDH (3urooDH)
revolution *n* thawre (thawraat)
rhythm *n* eeqaa3, wezin

ribbon *n* shareeT (sharaayiT)
rice *n* timmen
rich *adj* zengeen (*f* zengeene *pl* zenaageen)
ride *v* rikeb (yirkeb)
rifle *n* bundiqiyye (benaadiq)
right 1. *adj* (*correct*) SaHeeH (*f* SaHeeHa); (*opposite of left*) yemeen,
　　yimne; **to the ~ of** 3ala yemeen; **~-handed** yimnaawi
　　(*f* yimnaawiyye); 2. *n* Haqq (Huqooq)
ring *n* miHbes (maHaabis)
riot *n* shegheb
ripe *adj* naaDHij (*f* naaDHje), mistiwi (*f* mistawye)
rise *v* wugef (yogef)
river *n* shaTT (shTooT); neher (anhaar); **~ bank** juruf
road *n* derub (deraabeen), Tareeq (Turuq); **~ signs** alaamaat iT-Tareeq;
　　~block Haajiz (Hawaajiz)
rob *v* sileb (yislib), baag (yboog)
robber *n* bawwaag (bawwaageen), Haraami (*pl* Haraamiyye)
robbery *n* boge (bogaat), seriqe (seriqaat)
rock *n* Hjaare (Hjaaraat)
rocket *n* Sarookh (Sawaareekh)
role *n* dor (adwaar)
rooftop n saTiH (sTooH)
room *n* ghurfe (ghuref); **~ service** (*hotel*) khidmet il-ghuref
root *n* jedhir (jidhoor)
rope *n* Habil (Hbaal)
rose *n* junbud, werid *coll*
round 1. *adj* mdewwer (*f* mdewre); 2. *n* duwwiere (duwwieraat)
rotary (*traffic circle*) *n* saaHa (saaHaat), filke (filek)
row *n* sire (siraawaat)
rug *n* bSaaT (buSuT)
ruin 1. *n* kharaab; 2. *v* kharrab (ykharrub) II
rule *n* Hukum
run *v* rikeDH (yirkuDH)
runway *n* medrej (medaarij)
rural *adj* reefi (*f* reefiyye)
Russia *n* roosye
Russian *adj/n* roosi (*f* roosiyye *pl* roos)

S

sabotage *n* takhreeb
sad *adj* Hazeen (*f* Hazeene *pl* Hazeeneen), maqhoor (*f* maqhoore
　　pl maqhooreen)

safe *adj* ameen (*f* ameene)
safety *n* amaan
sailboat *n* safeene shira3iyye (sufun shira3iyye)
salad *n* zalaaTe (zalaaTaat)
salary *n* raatib (rawaatib)
sale *n* tanzeelaat
sales *n* mabee3aat
salt *n* miliH
same *adj* nefis
sample *n* 3ayyine, nimoodhaj (namaadhij)
sanction *n* 3uqoobe (3uqubaat)
sand *n* ramul
sandwich *n* sandaweeche (sandaweechaat), leffe (leffaat)
sanitary *adj* SiHHi (*f* SiHHiyye)
satellite *n* qamar Sinaa'3i
satisfied *adj* miktifi (*f* miktefye *pl* miktifeen)
Saturday *n* is-sabit
sauce *n* SoS
Saudi *adj/n* s3oodi (*f* s3udiyye *pl* s3udiyyeen)
Saudi Arabia *n* is-si3oodiyye
sausage *n* SoSij
save *v* anqedh (yinqudh) IV, khalleS (ykhalliS) II
saw *n* minshaar (menaasheer)
say *v* gaal (ygool)
scale *n* (*weight*) meezaan (*pl* mawaazeen); (*on a map*) miqyaas ir-resim
scandal *n* fuDHeeHa (feDHaayiH)
scar *n* ather jeriH (athaar jrooH)
scarf *n* leffaaf (leffaafaat), rabTe (rabTaat)
scene *n* (*view*) manDHer (menaaDHir)
schedule *n* jedwel (jedaawil)
school *n* medrese (medaaris); ~ **of medicine** kulliyyet iT-Tibb
science *n* 3ilim (3iloom)
scientific *adj* 3ilmi (*f* 3ilmiyye)
scientist *n* 3aalim (*pl* ulemaa')
scissors *n* mugeSS (magaaSeeS)
score *n* tasjeel ahdaaf
scratched *adj* mitkharmush (*f* mitkharmushe)
screwdriver *n* dernefees (dernefeesaat)
sea *n* baHar (buHoor)
seal *v* khitem (yikhtim)
search *v* fettesh (yfettish) II, dewwer (ydewwir) II
season *n* faSil (fuSool)
seat *n* maq3ad (maqaa3id)

seat belt *n* Hzaam il-amaan (aHzimet il-amaan)

second 1. *adj* thaani (*f* thaaniye) 2. (*time*) *n* thaaniye (thawaani)

secondly *adv* thaaniyyen

secret *adj* sirri (*f* sirriyye); ~ **service** mukhaabaraat 2. *n* sirr (asraar)

secretary *n* sikirtier (*f* sikirtiere)

section *n* qisim (aqsaam)

security *n* amaan, amin; **UN Security Council** mejlis il-amin fi hei'at il-umem il-muttaHide

see *v* shaaf (yshoof)

seed *n* nuwaaye (nuwe)

seem *v* beyyen (ybeyyin) II

selection *n* ikhtiyaar (ikhtiyaaraat)

selfish *adj* anaani (*f* anaaniyye *pl* anaaniyyeen)

sell *v* baa3 (ybee3)

senate *n* mejlis ish-shiyookh

send *v* dezz (ydizz)

sense *n* Haasse (Hawaas)

sensitive *adj* Hassaas (*f* Hassaase *pl* Hassaaseen)

sentence *n* jumle (jumel)

separate *adj* minfuSil (*f* minfeSle)

September *n* eilool

septic tank *n* balloo3a (balaalee3)

series *n* (*TV*) silsile (muselselaat)

serious *adj* (*significant*) khaTeer (*f* khateere); (*earnest*) jiddi (*f* jiddiyye)

serve *v* khidem (yikhdim)

service *n* khidme (khadamaat)

session *n* jelse (jelsaat)

set *v* you're all ~ kull shee tamaam

settlement *n* (*land*) musta3mare (musta3maraat), mustawTane (mustawTanaat)

seven *adj* (*standing alone*) sab3a; (*with a noun*) sabi3

seven hundred *adj* sabi3miyye; (*with a noun*) sabi3meet

seven hundred thousand *adj* sabi3meet alif

seven thousand *adj* sabi3talaaf

seventeen *adj* sbaTa3ash

seventh *adj* saabi3 (*f* saab3a)

seventy *adj* sab3een

seventy thousand *adj* sab3een alif

several *adj* chem

sew *v* kheyyeT (ykheyyiT) II

sex *n* (*gender*) jinis (ajnaas)

sexual *adj* jinsi (*f* jinsiyye)

shade *n* fei, DHil

shadow *n* kheyaal
shake *v* nufeDH (yinfuDH)
shallow *adj* saT-Hi (*f* saT-Hiyye)
shame *n* 3aar
shampoo *n* shampu
shape *n* shikil (ashkaal)
share *v* tshaarek (yitshaarek) VI
shark *n* kosaj
sharp *adj* Haadd (*f* Haadde); **~shooter** raami maahir
sharpen *v* Hadd (yHidd)
shave *v* Hileq (yiHliq)
she *pron* hiyye
sheep *n* kharoof (khurfaan), Tili (Tilyaan)
sheet *n* (*bed*) cherchef (cheraachif); (*paper*) wereqe (awraaq)
shelf *n* raff (rfoof)
shelter *n* malja' (malaaji')
Shiite *adj/n* shee3i (*f* shee3iyye *pl* shee3a)
shiny *adj* lammaa3 (*f* lammaa3a)
ship *n* baakhire (bawaakhir)
shirt *n* qameeS (qumSaan)
shock *n* Sadme
shoe *n* fardat Hidhaa' (aHdhiye)
shoemaker *n* qunderchi, raggaa3
shoot *v* rime (yirmi)
shop *n* dukkaan (dakaakeen), makhzen (makhaazin), maHall (maHallaat);
    ~keeper *n* baggaal (bgageel)
shore *n* saaHil (sawaaHil)
short *adj* gSeyyir (*f* gSeire *pl* gSaar)
shorts *n* panTiroon gSeyyir
shot *n* Talqa (Talqaat)
shoulder *n* chitif (chtoof)
shout *v* SeyyaH (ySeyyiH) II
shovel *n* kerek
show 1. *n* (*theater*) 3ariDH (3urooDH); (*trade*) ma3raDH (ma3aariDH)
    2. *v* 3iraDH (yi3ruDH)
shower *n* doosh; **take a ~** akhadh doosh (yaakhudh doosh), akhadh
    Hammaam (yaakhudh Hammaam)
shrimp *n* roobyaan *coll*
shut 1. *adj* masdood (*f* masdoode) 2. *v* sedd (ysidd)
sick *adj* mareeDH (*f* mareeDHe *pl* marDHa)
side *n* jaanib (jawaanib), SafHa
sidewalk *n* raSeef (raSaayif)
siege *n* HiSaar

sightseeing *n* jawle siyaaHiyye
sign 1. *n* 3alaame (3alaamaat), ishaare (ishaaraat) 2. *v* waqqa3 (ywaqqi3) II
signature *n* tawqee3 (tawaaqee3)
silence *n* sukoot
silent *adj* saakit (*f* saakte)
silk *n* Hareer
silver *n* fuDHDHa
similar to *adj* mithil
simple *adj* baseeT (*f* baseeTe)
sin *n* Haraam
since *prep* min
sing *v* ghanna (yghanni) II
singer *n* mughanni (mughanniye)
single *adj* (*not married*) 3aazib (*f* 3aazbe *pl* 3uzzaab)
sink *n* HoDH (HwaaDHe)
sir *n* seyyid, ustaadh
sister *n* ukhut (khawaat)
sit *v* ga3ad (yig3ud)
site *n* mawqi3 (mawaaqi3)
situation *n* waDHi3 (awDHaa3)
six *adj* (*standing alone*) sitte; (*with a noun*) sit
six hundred *adj* sitmiyye; (*with a noun*) sitmeet
six hundred thousand *adj* sitmeet alif
six thousand *adj* sittalaaf
sixteen *adj* siTTa3ash
sixth *adj* saadis (*f* saadse)
sixty *adj* sitteen
sixty thousand *adj* sitteen alif
size *n* Hajim (aHjaam)
skeleton *n* heikel 3aDHmi (heyaakil 3aDHmiyye)
skin *n* jilid
skirt *n* tannoore
skull *n* jumjume (jamaajum)
sky *n* sime
slaughterhouse *n* maSlakh (maSaalikh)
slavery *n* 3uboodiyye
sleep *v* naam (ynaam)
sleeping bag *n* chees mal nom (chyaase mal nom)
sleeping pill *n* Habbat munawwim (Huboob munawwim)
sleeve *n* rdaan (rdaanaat)
slice 1. *n* shareeHa (sharaayiH) 2. *v* sharraH (ysharriH) II
slightly *adv* shweyye
slim *adj* rasheeq (*f* rasheeqe *pl* rasheeqeen)

slow *adj* baTee' (*f* baTee'e)
slower than *adj* abTa' min
slowly *adv* ib-buTu'; yewaash yewaash; (*step by step*) shwei shwei!
slum *n* Hayy faqeer (aHyaa' faqeere)
small *adj* zgheyyir (*f* zgheire *pl* zghaar)
smaller than *adj* azghar min
smell 1. *n* reeHa (rewaayiH) 2. *v* shtemm (yishtemm) VIII
smile 1. *n* ibtisaame (ibtisaamaat) 2. *v* btisem (yibtisim) VIII
smoke 1. *n* dukhkhaan 2. *v* dakhkhen (ydakhkhin) II
smoking *n* no ~ mamnoo3 it-tadkheen
sneeze *v* 3iTes (yi3Tus)
sniper *n* qannaaS (qannaaSe)
snow 1. *n* thelij 2. *v* nizel thelij (yinzil thelij)
so that *conj* Hatte
soap *n* Saboon *coll*
sober *adj* SaaHi (*f* SaaHye *pl* SaaHeen)
soccer *n* kuret qedem
social *adj* ijtimaa3i (*f* ijtimaa3iyye)
socialist *adj/n* ishtiraaki (*f* ishtiraakiyye *pl* ishtiraakiyyeen)
society *n* mujtama3; (organization) jam3iyye
socks *n* jwaareeb
sofa *n* qenefe (qenefaat)
soft *adj* naa3im (*f* naa3me); ~ **drink** Soda, baarid (bawaarid), mashroobaat
    ghaaziyye
soil *n* turbe
soldier *n* jundi (jnood)
solid *adj* Salib (*f* Salbe)
solution *n* Hall (Hilool)
some *adj/pron* chem
someone *pron* fed waaHid
something *pron* fed shee
sometimes *adv* marraat
son *n* ibin (abnaa', wilid); ~**-in-law** niseeb (nsaabe)
song *n* ughniye (aghaani)
soon *adv* qareeben
sorry *adj* mit'assif (*f* mit'assife); il-3afu; ma3a il-asef
sort *n* naw3
sound *n* Sot (aSwaat)
soup *n* shorbe (shorbaat)
source *n* maSdar (maSaadir)
south *n* jinoob
southern *adj* jinoobi (*f* jinoobiyye)
sow *v* zira3 (yizra3)

space *n* faDHaa'; **~ shuttle** safeenet il-faDHaa', makkook faDHaa'i

Spain *n* spaanye

Spanish *adj/n* spaani (*f* spaaniyye *pl* spaaniyyeen)

speak *v* Hiche (yiHchi), tkallam (yitkallam) V

special *adj* khaaS (*f* khaaSSe)

specialize in *v* tkheSSes (yitkheSSes) V

speech *n* khiTaab, kalaam; **deliver a ~** *v* khiTeb (yikhTub)

speed *n* sur3a; **~ limit** is-sur3a il-quSwa

spell *v* t-hejje (yit-hejje) (*word*) V

spend *v* Siref (yiSruf)

sperm *n* meni

spices *n* bahaaraat

spicy *adj* bee hwaaye bahaaraat (*f* beehe hwaaye bahaaraat)

spine *n* 3amood faqari

spokesperson *n* (*for*) mutaHaddith bi-isim

spoon *n* khaashooge (khawaasheeg); **small tea~** khaashooget chai

sports *n* riyaaDHe

spot *n* (*dirt*) buq3a (buqa3)

spray *n* rashshaash; **hair~** sprei mal sha3ar

spread *v* nisher (yinshur)

spring *n* (*season*) rabee3

spy *n* jaasoos (jawaasees)

squad *n* firqe (fireq)

square *adj/n* murabba3 (murabba3aat)

squeeze *v* 3iSer (yi3Sur)

stable *adj* mustaqirr (*f* mustaqirre), thaabit (*f* thaabte)

stadium *n* mal3ab

stage *n* (*phase*) marHale (maraaHil)

stain *n* buq3a (buqa3)

staircase *n* derej

stamp *n* Taabi3 (Tawaabi3)

stand *v* wugef (yogef)

standard *n* mustawa maqbool; (*Arabic language*) faSeeH

star *n* nejme (nijoom)

start 1. *n* bidaaye 2. *v* bide (yibdi)

state *n* (*country*) wilaaye (wilaayaat)

statement *n* (*announcement*) taSreeH

station *n* (*train*) maHaTTe (maHaTTaat)

statistics *n* iHSaa' (iHSaa'iyyaat)

status *n* waDHi3, Haale

stay *v* buqe (yubqe)

steal *v* baag (yboog)

steam *n* bukhaar

steel *n* foolaadh
steering wheel *n* sukkaan is-seyyaare
step *n* khuTwe (khuTwaat)
sterile *adj* mu3aqqam (*f* mu3aqqame); (*infertile*) 3aaqir (3aaqre)
steward *n* muDHeyyif
stewardess *n* muDHeyyife
stick *n* 3aSaaye (3iSi)
still *adv* ba3de *m* (*f* ba3ad-he)
sting *n* las3a (las3aat)
stitch *n* gharze (gharzaat)
stock *n* sehem (as-hum); ~ **market** soog il-borSe
stolen *adj* mabyoog (*f* mabyooge)
stomach *n* mi3de
stone *n* Hjaare (Hjaar); **precious** ~ jawhere (jawaahir)
stop *v* wugef (yogef); *imp* ogef!
store *n* makhzan (makhaazin), dukkaan (dakaakeen)
storm *n* 3aaSife (3awaaSif)
story *n* quSSe (quSaS)
stove *n* Tabbaakh
straight *adj* 3adil (*f* 3adle)
strainer *n* muSfi
strange *adj* ghareeb (*f* ghareebe)
stranger *n* ghareeb (*pl* ghurbe)
strategic *adj* istiraateeji (*f* istiraateejiyye)
straw *n* tibin qish
stream *n* jedwel (jedaawil)
street *n* shaari3 (shawaari3)
strength *n* quwwe
stress *n* tewettur
strike 1. *n* dharbe 2. *v* dhireb (yidhrub)
string *n* khieT (khyooT)
stroke *n* sekte demaaghiyye
strong *adj* (*powerful*) qawi (*f* qawiyye); (*severe*) shedeed (*f* shedeede)
struggle *n* kifaaH
student *n* (*older*) Taalib (*f* Taalibe *pl* Tullaab)
study *v* dires (yidrus)
style *n* (*clothing, hair*) moodiel (moodielaat); (*writing*) isloob
subject *n* mawDHoo3 (mawaaDHee3)
submarine *n* ghawwaaSe (ghawwaaSaat)
suburbs *n* DHaaHiye (DHawaaHi)
successful *adj* naajiH (*f* naajHa *pl* naajHeen)
successor *n* wareeth (*f* wareethe *pl* werethe)
such *adj* heech

suddenly *adv* 3ala ghafle, fuj'eten
sufficient *adj* kaafi (*f* kaafye); **self-~** miktifi (*f* miktefye *pl* miktifeen)
suffocate *v* khtineg (yikhtinig) VIII
sugar *n* sheker
suggest *v* iqtiraH (yiqtiriH) VIII
suggestion *n* iqtiraaH (iqtiraaHaat)
suicide *n* intiHaar (intiHaaraat)
suit *n* qaaT (qooT)
suitcase *n* janTe (juneT)
sum *n* mablagh (mabaaligh)
summer *n* Sief
summit *n* qumme (qumem)
sun *n* shemis
Sunday *n* il-aHHad
sunglasses *n* manaaDHir shemsiyye
Sunni *adj/n* sinni (*f* sinniyye *pl* sinne)
sunrise *n* shurooq ish-shemis
sunset *n* ghuroob ish-shemis
supermarket *n* aswaaq
supplies 1. *n* tajheezaat 2. *v* jehhez (yjehhiz) II
support 1. *n* da3im 2. *v* da3am (yid3im)
sure *adj* mit'akkid (*f* mit'akkide *pl* mit'akkideen)
surface *n* saTiH
surgery *n* 3amaliyye (3amaliyyaat)
surprise 1. *n* mufaaje'e (mufaaje'aat) 2. *v* ~ **someone** faaja' (yfaaji') III;
    be ~d *v* tfaaje' (yitfaaje') VI
surrender *n* istislaam
suspect *n* mashbooh (mashbooheen)
sweat *n* 3areg
sweater *n* blooze Soof (bloozaat Soof)
Sweden *n* is-siweed
Swedish *adj/n* sweedi (*f* sweediyye *pl* is-siweediyyeen)
sweet *adj* Hilu (*f* Hilwe)
sweets *n* Halawiyyaat
swim *v* sibaH (yisbaH)
swimming pool *n* masbaH (masaabiH)
swimsuit *n* (*for women*) maayoh (maayohaat); (*for men*) chiswe (chiswaat)
Swiss *adj/n* sweesri (*f* sweesriyye *pl* sweesriyyeen)
switch 1. *n* sweech (sweechaat) 2. *v* ~ **on** 3ileg (yi3lig) ~ **off** Teffe (yTeffi)
Switzerland *n* sweesre
swollen *adj* waarum (*f* waarme)
sword *n* sief (syoofe)
symbol *n* remiz (rumooz)

symptoms a3raaDH *pl*
Syria n soorye
Syrian *adj/n* soori (*f* sooriyye *pl* sooriyeen)
syringe *n* srinje (srinjaat)
system *n* (*order*) niDHaam (anDHime); **digestive** ~ jihaaz il-haDHum

T

table *n* miez (myooze); **~spoon** khaashooget akil
tail *n* dhiel (dhyoole)
tailor *n* kheyyaaT (*f* kheyyaaTe *pl* kheyyaaTeen)
take *v* akhadh (yaakhudh); ~ **off** (*clothes*) niza3 (yinza3)
talk *v* Hiche (yiHchi)
tall *adj* Tweel (*f* Tweele *pl* Twaal)
tank *n* (*vehicle*) dabbaabe (dabbaabaat); (*storage*) taanki (taankiyyaat),
       khazzaan (khazzaanaat)
tape (*recording*) *n* shareeT tasjeel (sharaayiT tasjeel)
target *n* hedef (ahdaaf)
task *n* muhimme (muhimmaat)
taste 1. *n* dhawq (adhwaaq) 2. *v* DHaag (yDHoog)
tasty *adj* Teyyib
tax *n* DHareebe (DHaraayib)
taxi *n* teksi (teksiyyaat)
taxi driver *n* saayiq teksi (suwwaaq teksi)
tea *n* chai; **~pot** qoori; ~ **glass** istikaan (istikaanaat)
teach *v* darras (ydarris) II
teacher *n* (*elementary school*) mu3allim (mu3allimeen), (*middle school
       and up*) mudarris (mudarriseen)
team *n* fareeq (fireq)
tear 1. *n* dam3a (dmoo3); ~ **gas** ghaaz museel lid-dimoo3 2. *v* sheggeg
       (ysheggig) II
teaspoon *n* khaashooget koob (khawaasheeg koob); **small** ~ khaashooget
       chai (khawaasheeg chai)
technical *adj* teqeni (*f* teqeniyye)
technician *n* 3aamil fenni (3ummaal fenniyyeen)
technology *n* teknelojye
teenager *n* muraahiq (muraahiqeen)
telecommunications *n* ittiSaalaat silkiyye w-la silkiyye
telephone *n* telifon (telifonaat); ~ **number** raqam it-telifon
television *n* tilfizyon
tell *v* khabber (ykhabbur) II
teller *n* (bank) Sarraaf (Sarrafeen)

temperature *n* derejet il-Haraare (derejaat il-Haraare)
temple *n* ma3bad (ma3aabid)
temporary *adj* muwaqqet (*f* muwaqqete)
ten *adj* (*standing alone*) 3ashre; (*with a noun*) 3ashir
ten thousand *adj* 3ashirtalaaf
tension *n* tewettur
tent *n* khieme (khiyem)
tenth *adj* 3aashir (*f* 3aashre)
terrible *adj* faDHee3 (*f* faDHee3a)
terrorism *n* irhaab
terrorist *adj/n* irhaabi (irhaabiyyeen)
test *n* ikhtibaar (ikhtibaaraat), imtiHaan (imiHaanaat)
testify *v* shihed (yishhed)
text *n* naSS (nuSooS)
textile *n* naseej (mansoojaat)
than *conj* min
thank *v* shiker (yishkur); ~ **God** il-Hamdu lillah
thanks *n* shukran; ~ **for** shukran 3ala
that *pron* dhak (*f* dheech); hedhaak (*f* hedheech)
the *art* il-
theater *n* masraH (masaariH)
theft *n* seriqe (seriqaat)
themselves *pron* nefis-hum
then *adv* ba3dien
theory *n* neDHeriyye (neDHeriyyaat)
therapy *n* 3ilaaj
there *adv* hnak; ~ **is/are** aku; ~ **isn't/aren't** maku
therefore *adv* li-haadha
thermometer *n* miHraar (maHaarer)
these *pron* hadhole
they *pron* humme
thick *adj* thikheen (*f* thikheene)
thief *n* Haraami (*pl* Haraamiyye)
thigh *n* fukhudh (fkhaadhe)
thin *adj* (*person*) DHi3eef (*f* DHi3eefe *pl* DH3aaf)
thing *n* shee (ashyaa')
think *v* fekker (yfekkir) II; (*suppose*) tSewwer (yitSewwer) V
third 1. *adj* thaalith (*f* thaalthe) 2. *n* thilith
thirdly *adv* thaalithen
thirsty *adj* 3aTshaan (*f* 3aTshaane *pl* 3aTshaaneen)
thirteen *adj* tlatta3ash
thirty *adj* tlaatheen
thirty thousand *adj* tlaatheen alif

this *pron* haadhe (*f* haadhi)
those *pron* hedholaak
thought *n* fikre (afkaar)
thousand *adj* alif (alaaf)
thread *n* khieT (khyooT)
threat *n* tahdeed (tahdeedaat)
three *adj* (*standing alone*) tlaathe; (*with a noun*) tlath
three hundred *adj* tlethmiyye; (*with a noun*) tlethmeet
three hundred thousand *adj* tlethmeet alif
three thousand *adj* tlattalaaf
throat *n* Hunjure (Hanaajir)
through *prep* min khilaal
throw *v* shumer (yishmur)
thumb *n* ibhaam (ibhaammaat)
thunder *n* gargoo3a (garaagee3), ra3id
Thursday *n* il-khamees
ticket *n* tikit (tiktaat), piTaaqe (paTaayiq, piTaaqaat); **return ~** tikit murajja3 (tiktaat murajja3a)
tie 1. *n* ribaaT (arbiTe) 2. *v* rubeT (yirbuT)
Tigris *n* dijle
timber *n* khisheb binaa'
time *n* weqit, zamaan; **on ~** bil-weqit il-muhadded
tiny *adj* kullish zgheyyir (*f* kullish zgheire)
tip *n* bakhsheesh
tire *n* taayer (taayeraat)
tired *adj* ta3baan (*f* ta3baane *pl* ta3baaneen)
tissue *n* (*paper*) kleeneks
title *n* 3inwaan (3anaaween)
to *prep* l-, li-, lil- (*see also Unit 5*); **in order ~** Hatte
tobacco *n* tabigh (tuboogh)
today *adv* il-yom
toe *n* iSbi3 ir-rijil
together *adv* siwiyye, suwe
toilet *n* twaaliet, maraaHeeDH; **~ paper** wereq twaaliet
tomato *n* TamaaTa
tomorrow *adv* baachir; **day after ~** ba3ad baachir
ton *n* Tann (aTnaan)
tongue *n* lsaan (lsaanaat)
too *adv* hemmen, hemmien, hem
tools *n* edewaat *pl*
tooth *n* sinn (asnaan, snoon)
toothbrush *n* firchet asnaan (firech asnaan)
toothpaste *n* ma3joon asnaan

top *prep* **on ~ of** fog, 3ala; **at the ~** bil-qimme
torture 1. *n* ta3dheeb 2. *v* 3adhdhab (y3adhdhib) II
total 1. *adj* kulli (*f* kulliyye) 2. *n* majmoo3
touch *v* lizem (yilzem)
tour *n* jawle (jawlaat)
tourism *n* siyaaHa
tourist *n* saa'iH (suwwaaH)
towards *prep* bit-tijaaH
towel *n* khaawli, khaawliyye (khaawliyyaat), pashkeer (pashaakeer)
tower *n* burij (abraaj)
town *n* medeene (mudun)
toxic *adj* saam (*f* saamme)
toy *n* li3be (malaa3eeb)
track (railroad) *n* sikket Hadeed (sikek Hadeed)
trade *n* tijaare; **~ union** niqaabet il-3ummaal (niqaabaat il-3ummaal)
tradition *n* taqleed (taqaaleed)
traditional *adj* taqleedi (*f* taqleediyye)
traffic *n* muroor; **~ jam** *n* izdiHaam il-muroor; **~ lights** aDHwiyet il-muroor
train *n* qiTaar (qiTaaraat); **night ~** qiTaar il-liel; **day ~** qiTaar in-nahaar
training *n* tadreeb
traitor *n* khaayin (khewene)
transfer *v* (money) Hawwel (yHawwil) II
transformer *n* muHawwil (muHawwilaat)
transfusion (*blood*) *n* 3amaliyyet naqil id-demm (3amaliyyaat naqil id-demm)
transit *n* 3uboor
translate *v* terjem (yterjim)
translator *n* muterjim (*f* muterjime *pl* muterjimeen)
transport 1. *n* naqil 2. *v* niqel (yinqul)
transportation *n* muwaaSelaat
trap *n* fekh (afkhaakh), kemeen (kemaa'in)
trash *n* zibil (zbaale)
travel 1. *n* sefer 2. *v* saafer (ysaafir) III
traveler *n* musaafir (musaafireen); **~'s checks** Sukook il-musaafireen
tray *n* Seeniyye (Swaani)
treasury *n* khazeene
treatment *n* mu'aamele
treaty *n* mu3aahede (mu3aahedaat)
tree *n* shejere (ashjaar)
trial *n* muHaakeme (muHaakemaat)
triangle *n* muthelleth
trip *n* sefre (sefraat)
triple *adj* thulaathi (*f* thulaathiyye)

troops *n* jundi (jnood)
trouble *n* mushkile (meshaakil)
truce *n* hudne
truck *n* lori (loriyyaat); **semi-~** shaaHine (shaaHinaat)
true *adj* Haqeeqi (*f* Haqeeqiyye)
trunk (*car*) *n* Sandoog
trust 1. *n* thiqe 2. *v* witheq (yothiq)
truth *n* Haqeeqe
try *v* jarreb (yjarrub) II
T-shirt *n* tee shert (tee shertaat), faaneele (faaneelaat)
tube *n* inboob (anaabeeb)
Tuesday *n* ith-thelaathaaʹ
tune *n* naghme (naghmaat, anghaam)
Tunisia *n* toonis
Tunisian *adj/n* toonisi (*f* toonisiyye *pl* twaanse)
tunnel *n* nefeq (anfaaq)
Turkey *n* turkiye
Turkish *adj/n* turki (*f* turkiyye *pl* atraak)
turn *v* (*change direction*) laaf (yloof), kiser (yiksir); **~ around** indaar
　　(yindaar) VII; **~ off** sedd (ysidd); **~ one's face** ltifet (yiltifit) VIII
twelve *adj* thna3ash
twenty *adj* 3ishreen
twenty thousand *adj* 3ishreen alif
twice *adv* martien
twins *n* tom
two *adj* (*standing alone*) thnien (*f* thintien)
two hundred *adj* meetien
two hundred thousand *adj* meetien alif
type 1. *n* no3 (anwaa3) 2. *v* Tuba3 (yiTba3)
typist *n* kaatib Taabi3a (*f* kaatibet Taabi3a *pl* kuttaab Taabi3a)

U

ugly *adj* qabeeH (*f* qabeeHa *pl* qabeeHeen)
ultimatum *n* indhaar
umbrella *n* shemsiyye (shemsiyyaat)
unable *adj* ma yigder (*aux* in Arabic) (*f* ma tigder *pl* ma yigderoon)
unanimous *adj* bil-ijmaa3
unbelievable *adj* 3ajeeb ghareeb (*f* 3ajeebe ghareebe)
uncle *n* (*paternal*) 3amm; (*maternal*) khaal
unclear *adj* ma waaDHiH (*f* ma waaDH-Ha)
uncomfortable *adj* ma mirtaaH (*f* ma mirtaaHa)

unconscious *adj* kharbaan (*f* kharbaane *pl* kharbaaneen)
under *prep* jewwe
undercover *adj* sirri (*f* sirriyye)
underground *n* jewwe il-gaa3; ~ **group** jamaa3a sirriyye
underline (*text*) *v* jerr khaTT (yjurr khaTT)
undershirt *n* faaneele
understand *v* fihem (yifhem)
underwater *adj* jewwe il-mei
undress *v* niza3 (yinza3)
unemployed *adj* 3aaTil (*f* 3aaTle *pl* 3aaTleen)
unemployment *n* baTaale
unfurnished *adj* ma mu'aththeth (*f* ma mu'aththethe)
unhappy *adj* Hazeen (*f* Hazeene *pl* Hazeeneen)
unhealthy *adj* ma SiHHi (*f* ma siHHiyye)
uniform *n* zei muwaHHad; (*military*) zei 3askari
union *n* niqaabe (niqaabaat)
unionist *n* niqaabi (niqaabiyyeen)
unit *n* wiHde (wiHdaat)
united *adj* muttaHid (*f* muttaHide *pl* muttaHideen)
United Nations *n* il-umem il-muttaHide
United States *n* amreeke, il-wilaayaat il-muttaHide il-amreekiyye
unity *n* ittiHaad
university *n* jaami3a (jaami3aat)
unknown *adj* ma ma3roof (*f* ma ma3roofe), majhool (*f* majhoole)
unsafe *adj* ma ameen (*f* ma ameene)
until *prep* ila an
unusual *adj* istithnaa'i (*f* istithnaa'iyye)
upon *prep* 3ala
upper *adj* a3le
uprising *n* thawre (thawraat)
upset *adj* minzi3ij (*f* minza3je *pl* minza3jeen); ~ **stomach** mi3de
    mkharbuTe
upside down *adv* bil-magloobi
upstairs *adv* fog, iT-Taabiq ith-thaani
up-to-date *adj* Hadeeth (*f* Hadeethe)
uranium *n* yooranyom
urban *adj* mitmaddin (*f* mitmaddine)
urgent *adj* 3aajil (*f* 3aajle)
urine *n* bol
use *v* sta3mal (yista3mil) X; **be used to** mit3awwid *adj* (*f* mit3awwide)
useful *adj* mufeed (*f* mufeede)
usual *adj* 3aadi (*f* 3aadiyye)
usually *adv* 3aadeten

V

vacation *n* 3uTle (3uTel)
vaccination *n* talqeeH (talqeeHaat), taT3eem (taT3eemaat)
vacuum cleaner *n* muknaase kahrabaa'iyye (mekaanis kahrabaa'iyye)
valid *adj* waarid (waarde)
valley *n* waadi (widyaan)
value *n* qeeme
valve *n* Sammaam (Sammaamaat)
vapor *n* bukhaar
various *adj* mitnawwi3 (*f* mitnawwi3a)
vase *n* mezheriyye (mezheriyyaat)
vast *adj* DHakhum (*f* DHakhme), waasi3 (*f* waas3a)
vegetables *n* khuDHrewaat, mkhaDHDHar *coll*
vegetarian *n* nabaati (nabaatiyyeen)
vehicle *n* weseelet naqil (wesaa'il naqil)
veil *n* Hjaab (Hjaabaat)
vein *n* wareed (awride)
ventilator *n* saaHibe (saaHibaat)
verdict *n* Hukum (aHkaam)
very *adv* kullish
veterinarian *n* Tabeeb beiTeri (*pl* aTibbaa' beiTeriyyeen)
veto *n* Haqq il-veeto, in-naqiDH
via *prep* 3an Tareeq, b-waasTet
victim *n* DHaHiyye (DHaHaaya)
victory *n* neSir, intiSaar (intiSaaraat)
video *n* vidyo (vidyowaat); ~tape shareeT il-vidyo; ~ recorder musejjil vidyowaat
view *n* manDHar (manaaDHir)
village *n* qarye (qura)
vinegar *n* khall
violation *n* intihaak (intihaakaat)
violence *n* 3unf, qeswe
virgin *n* 3adhraa'
virus *n* vairos (vairosaat)
visa *n* veeze (veezaat); entry ~ ta'sheeret dukhool (ta'sheeraat dukhool); tourist ~ ta'sheere siyaaHiyye
vision *n* (eyesight) naDHer
visit 1. *n* ziyaare (ziyaaraat) 2. *v* zaar (yzoor)
visiting *m* zaa'ir
visitor *n* DHief (*pl* DHyoof), zaa'ir (*pl* zuwwaar)
voice *n* Sot (aSwaat)
voltage *n* voltiyye

volume *n* (*book*) mujelled (mujelledaat); (*sound*) Sot
voluntary *adj* ikhtiyaari (*f* ikhtiyaariyye), Taw3i (Taw3iyye)
volunteer *n* miTTawwi3 (*f* miTTaw3a)
vomit *v* zaa3 (yzoo3), tqeyye' (yitqeyye') V
vote 1. *n* taSweet 2. *v* Sawwat (ySawwit) II

W

waist *n* kheSir
wait *v* intiDHer (yintiDHir) VIII
waiter *n* boi (boyaat)
waitress *n* gaarsone (gaarsonaat)
walk *v* mishe (yimshi); **go for a ~** tmeshshe (yitmeshshe)
wall *n* HaayiT (HeeTaan)
wallet *n* juzdaan (jazaadeen)
walnut(s) *n* joz *coll*
want *v* raad (yreed)
war *n* Harub (Huroob); **~ crime** jareemet Harub (jaraayim Harub);
          ~ criminal mujrim Harub (mujrimeen Harub)
warden *n* (*prison*) aamir (umeraa')
warehouse *n* mustawda3 (mustawda3aat)
warm 1. *adj* daafi (*f* daafye) 2. *v* deffe (ydeffi) II
warn *v* Hadhdher (yHadhdhir) II
warning *n* taH-dheer (taH-dheeraat)
wash *v* ghisel (yighsil)
washing machine *n* ghassaale kahrabaa'iyye
waste *n* (*squandering*) tabdheer; (*garbage*) zibil
watch 1. *n* saa3a (sa3aat) 2. *v* raaqab (yraaqib) III
water *n* mei; **~ shortage** azmet mei; **~ well** beer (aabaar, byaare)
watermelon *n* reggi *coll*
wave *n* mawje (amwaaj)
wax *n* shami3
way *n* Tareeq (*pl* Turuq)
we *pron* iHne
weak *adj* (*powerless*) DHa3eef (*f* DHa3eefe *pl* DH3aaf); (*light*) khafeef
weapon *n* silaaH (asliHa)
wear *v* libes (yilbes)
weather *n* jaw; **~ forecast** Haalet ij-jawwiyye
wedding *n* 3iris (a3raas); **~ ring** Halqe
Wednesday *n* il-arbi3aa'
week *n* isboo3 (asaabee3)
weekend *n* nihaayet il-isboo3
weekly *adj* isboo3i (*f* isboo3iyye)

weight *n* wezin
welcome *n* ahlan, ahlan wa sahlan; **you're ~** *m* ahlan beek (*see also Unit 4*);
    mamnoon (*response to* shukran **"thank you"**)
well 1. *adv* zien 2. *n* beer (aabaar, byaare)
well-known *adj* ma3roof (*f* ma3roofe *pl* ma3roofeen); mash-hoor
    (*f* mash-hoore *pl* mash-hooreen)
west *n* gharb
western *adj* gharbi (*f* gharbiyye)
wet *adj* mbellel (*f* mbellile)
what *pron* shinoo; **from ~** min esh
wheat *n* HunTe
wheel *n* cherikh (chrookh)
wheelchair *n* kursi mitHarrik (karaasi mitHarrike)
when *adv* shwekit
where *adv* wien; **from ~** mmien
which *pron* yaahoo; *interr* yaa
white *adj* abyeDH (*f* bieDHe)
who *pron*, *interr* minu
whole *adj* kaamil (*f* kaamle); **~ milk** Haleeb kaamil id-desem: **~ wheat**
    TiHeen asmer
why *adv* liesh
wide *adj* 3areeDH (*f* 3areeDHe)
widespread shaayi3 (*f* shaay3a) *adj*
widow *n* armale (araamil)
widower *n* armal (araamil)
wife *n* zawje (zawjaat), mere (niswaan)
wild *adj* (*animals and plants*) barri (*f* barriyye)
will *n* (*testament*) waSiyye (waSiyyaat)
win *v* rubaH (yirbaH)
wind *n* hawe
window *n* shibbaach (shabaabeech)
wine *n* khamur (khimoor)
wing *n* jnaaH (ajniHa, jinHaan)
winter *n* shite
wipe *v* misaH (yimsaH)
wire *n* silk (aslaak), waayer (waayeraat)
wireless *adj* la-silki (*f* la-silkiyye)
wish 1. *n* umniye (umniyaat) 2. *v* tmenne (yitmenne) V
with *prep* wiyye
withdraw *v* traaja3 (yitraaja3) VI, insiHab (yinsiHib) VII
withdrawal *n* taraaju3, insiHaab
within *prep* (*time*) khilaal
without *prep* bidoon
witness *n* shaahid (shihood)

woman *n* mere, mreyye (mreyyaat, niswaan, nisaa')
wonder *n* i3joobe (3ajaayib), falle mal alle
wood *n* khesheb
wooden *adj* kheshebi (*f* kheshebiyye)
wool *n* Soof
word *n* kelime (kelimaat)
work 1. *n* shughul 2. *v* shtighel (yishtughul) VIII
worker *n* 3aamil (3ummaal)
workshop *n* wershe (wershaat)
world *n* 3aalem; dinye
worldwide *adv* bil-3aalem kulle
worried *adj* qaliq (*f* qalqe *pl* qalqeen)
worry *v* qileq (yiqleq)
worse *adj* aswa', angas min
wounded *adj* majrooH (*f* majrooHa *pl* majrooHeen)
wrap *v* leff (yliff)
wrist *n* rusugh
write *v* kiteb (yiktib)
writer *n* kaatib (*f* kaatibe *pl* kuttaab)
wrong *adj* (*mistaken*) ghalTaan (*f* ghalTaane); (*inappropriate*) ghalaT

X

X-ray *n* ashi33a; **take an ~** *v* akhadh ashi33a (yaakhudh ashi33a)

Y

yard *n* (*house*) Hosh (Hwaash) 2. (*measurement*) yaarde (yaardaat)
year *n* sene (senewaat); **New Year** raas is-sene
yellow *adj* aSfar (*f* Safre)
yes *adv* ee, beli, (*formal*) na3am
yesterday *adv* il-baarHa; **day before ~** awwel il-baarHa
yet *adv* ba3ad
yogurt *n* liben; **~ drink** shineene
you *pron* (*informal*) *m* inte, *f* inti, *pl* intu; (*formal*) *m* HaDHirtek
        f HaDHirtich
young *adj* zgheyyir (*f* zgheire *pl* zghaar); **~ man** shaabb, **~ woman** shaabbe
younger than *adj* azghar min
yourself *pron* nefsek *m*, nefsich *f*
yourselves *pron* nefiskum
youth *n* shabaab

Z

zebra crossing *n* 3uboor il-mushaat
zero *n* Sifir
zip code *n* ramz bareedi
zone *n* qaTTaa3 (qaTTaa3aat)
zoo *n* Hadeeqet Haiwaanaat

BEGINNER'S IRAQI ARABIC WITH 2 AUDIO CDS AUDIO PROGRAM

DISC ONE

Unit 1: Pronunciation

1. Consonants with exact equivalents in English
2. Consonants with no exact equivalents in English
3. Short vowels
4. Long vowels
5. Vowel clusters (diphthongs)
6. Vocalization
7. Words with two short vowels
8. Words with a long and short vowel
9. Words with double consonants
10. Syllable separation
11. Drill 1.1
12. Drill 1.2
13. Drill 1.3
14. Drill 1.4
15. Drill 1.5
16. Drill 1.6
17. Drill 1.7
18. Drill 1.8
19. Drill 1.9
20. Drill 1.10
21. Drill 1.11
22. Drill 1.12

Unit 2

Unit 3

Unit 4

Unit 5

51. Dialogue 1 Vocabulary
52. Dialogue 1
53. Dialogue 1 for repetition
54. Dialogue 2 Vocabulary
55. Dialogue 2
56. Dialogue 2 for repetition
57. Useful vocabulary
58. More numbers

Unit 6

59. Dialogue 1 Vocabulary
60. Dialogue 1
61. Dialogue 1 for repetition
62. Dialogue 2 Vocabulary
63. Dialogue 2
64. Dialogue 2 for repetition
65. Useful Vocabulary

Unit 7

66. Dialogue 1 Vocabulary
67. Dialogue 1
68. Dialogue 1 for repetition
69. Dialogue 2 Vocabulary
70. Dialogue 2
71. Dialogue 2 for repetition
72. Useful Vocabulary

DISC TWO

Unit 8

1. Dialogue 1 Vocabulary
2. Dialogue 1
3. Dialogue 1 for repetition
4. Dialogue 2 Vocabulary
5. Dialogue 2
6. Dialogue 2 for repetition
7. Useful Vocabulary

Unit 9

8. Dialogue 1 Vocabulary
9. Dialogue 1
10. Dialogue 1 for repetition
11. Dialogue 2 Vocabulary
12. Dialogue 2
13. Dialogue 2 for repetition
14. Months
15. Seasons
16. Days of the Week
17. Times of the Day
18. Useful Vocabulary

Unit 10

19. Dialogue 1 Vocabulary
20. Dialogue 1
21. Dialogue 1 for repetition
22. Dialogue 2 Vocabulary
23. Dialogue 2
24. Dialogue 2 for repetition
25. Useful Vocabulary

Unit 11

26. Dialogue 1 Vocabulary
27. Dialogue 1
28. Dialogue 1 for repetition
29. Dialogue 2 Vocabulary
30. Dialogue 2
31. Dialogue 2 for repetition
32. Useful Vocabulary
33. Numbers over 1,000
34. Numbers 2,000-10,000
35. Numbers 10,000 to 1 million

Unit 12

36. Dialogue 1 Vocabulary
37. Dialogue 1
38. Dialogue 1 for repetition
39. Dialogue 2 Vocabulary
40. Dialogue 2
41. Dialogue 2 for repetition
42. Useful Vocabulary

Other Middle Eastern Interest Titles from Hippocrene Books

HISTORY & CULTURE

The Middle Eastern Kitchen
240 pages · 8 x 10½ · color photographs · ISBN 0-7818-1023-X · $29.95hc · 487

The Arab World: An Illustrated History
312 pages · 5½ x 8½ · ISBN 0-7818-0990-8 · $14.95pb · 465

Mama Nazima's Jewish-Iraqi Cuisine
192 pages · 6 x 9 · photographs · ISBN 0-7818-0881-2 · $24.95hc · 6

LANGUAGE INSTRUCTION GUIDES

Mastering Arabic with 2 Audio CDs
320 pages · 6 x 9 · ISBN 0-7818-1042-6 · $29.95pb · 66

Pocket Guide to Arabic Script
104 pages · 4 x 6 · ISBN 0-7818-1104-X · $6.95pb · 209

Basic Arabic Workbook
352 pages · 8½ x 11 · ISBN 0-7818-1126-0 · $29.95pb· 288

DICTIONARIES & PHRASEBOOKS

Arabic-English/English-Arabic Dictionary & Phrasebook
4,500 entries · 220 pages · 3¾ x 7½ · ISBN 0-7818-0973-8 · $12.95pb · 445

Arabic-English/English-Arabic Compact Dictionary
3,800 entries · 200 pages · 3¼ x 4¾ · ISBN 0-7818-1044-2 · $8.95pb · 651

Arabic-English/English-Arabic Practical Dictionary
18,000 entries · 440 pages · 4½ x 7 · ISBN 0-7818-1045-0 · $22.50pb · 632

Arabic-English/English-Arabic Concise Dictionary
Egyptian and Syrian Dialect
4,500 entries · 325 pages · 4 x 6 · 0-7818-0686-0 · $12.95pb · 775

Arabic-English/English-Arabic Standard Dictionary
30,000 entries · 460 pages · 5¾ x 8½ · 0-7818-0383-7 · $27.95pb · 195

Prices subject to change without prior notice. **To purchase Hippocrene Books** contact your local bookstore, visit www.hippocrenebooks.com, call (718) 454-2366, or write to: HIPPOCRENE BOOKS, 171 Madison Avenue, New York, NY 10016. Please enclose check or money order, adding $5.00 shipping (UPS) for the first book, and $.50 for each additional book.